Teaching for Proficiency, the Organizing Principle

Edited by Theodore V. Higgs

In conjunction with the American Council on the Teaching of Foreign Languages

National Textbook Company, *Lincolnwood, Illinois U.S.A.*

Contents

Foreword v

Introduction Language Teaching and the Quest for the Holy Grail 1
Theodore V. Higgs

1 The ACTFL Proficiency Guidelines: A Historical 11
Perspective
Judith E. Liskin-Gasparro

2 The Proficiency-Oriented Classroom 43
Alice C. Omaggio

3 Curriculum Development at the Foreign Service 85
Institute
Earl W. Stevick

4 Proficiency Testing for the Other Language 113
Modalities
Jerry W Larson and Randall L. Jones

5 Doing the Unthinkable in the Second-Language 139
Classroom: A Process for the Integration of
Language and Culture
Linda M. Crawford-Lange and Dale L. Lange

6 Preservice and Inservice Teacher Training: Focus 179
on Proficiency
Judith A. Muyskens

7 Proficiency Projects in Action 201
Reynaldo Jiménez and Carol J. Murphy

Appendix A The ACTFL Provisional Proficiency Guidelines 219
(Generic)
Appendix B The Interagency Language Roundtable Level 227
Definitions
Index to Persons Cited 228
Index to Topics and Institutions Cited 233

Foreword

This volume of the ACTFL Foreign Language Education Series is about proficiency, in all aspects of the teaching/learning process. We have called proficiency "the organizing principle" because literally everything that students, teachers, and teacher trainers know and understand about active, spontaneous *use* of language and productive cultural interaction can be subsumed under the proficiency movement's watchwords of *function, content,* and *accuracy.* These terms recur throughout the volume, as the many aspects of language teaching and learning are examined and reinterpreted into a single, unified approach.

Perhaps the most far-reaching position taken in the volume is in Chapter 5, where the authors argue that, "the integration of language and culture is even a more powerful organizing principle for foreign-language education than is language proficiency. . . ." The desirability of and need for such an integration has long been one of the profession's platitudes, but not until now has a specific and exemplified schema for its realization been proposed. The problem itself is extremely complex, and for this reason the chapter merits a thorough and patient reading. The payoff is more than worth the effort.

The Foreword is the place for acknowledging others' contributions to the finished product. First thanks, then, go to the authors themselves, who were often more faithful in meeting deadlines than was their editor. Thanks also to the Advisory Committee—Charles Hancock, Charles James, Dale Lange, Judith Liskin-Gasparro, Alice Omaggio, Joseph Tursi, and Barbara Wing—for their guidance, and to Ed Scebold for absolutely everything. Finally, special thanks to Bob Detweiler and Ernesto Barrera of San Diego State, without whose understanding and support the editor could never have completed the project.

Introduction

Language Teaching and the Quest for the Holy Grail

Theodore V. Higgs
San Diego State University

A Perspective on Methodology

Western cultures have shared a fantasy that the unknowable can be known, the uncontrollable controlled, if only we can come to possess the key. The ancient Hebrews depended on the Urim and Thummim to divine the will of God and thereby know the unknowable. Medieval alchemists were convinced that to control the uncontrollable, they needed only to find the philosophers' stone that would change base metals into gold. Who knows how many good and gentle knights came to grief in their search for the Holy Grail, which would have made them pure and, hence, privy to the Secrets of the Universe?

For our generation, the analog of these quests is our desperately wistful search for the "key" to teaching foreign languages. We have been motivated, I believe, by two compelling forces: the desire to welcome our students into the multicultural/multilingual world that we as language teachers inhabit, and the conviction that there is a right way to accomplish this. By using "the right stuff in the right way," we are certain, our students not only will learn foreign languages but also will enjoy the process.

We have sought our own Holy Grail in a variety of areas, principally in theories of language and/or learning, and we have then developed or

Theodore V. Higgs (Ph.D., Georgetown University) is Associate Professor of Hispanic Linguistics at San Diego State University, where he teaches Spanish and linguistics, coordinates lower-division Spanish courses, and trains the graduate teaching assistants. He has received training in oral proficiency testing from ACTFL, ETS, and Interagency Language Roundtable (ILR) workshops at Houston, The Defense Language Institute, and Miami, and he has presented familiarization and intensive workshops on oral proficiency testing in California, Texas, and New York. His publications have appeared in numerous professional journals and proceedings, and in the ACTFL Foreign Language Education Series, for which he served as editor of Volume 13. He is a member of AAAL, AATSP, and ACTFL.

1

had imposed on us methodologies presumably derived from these. The one observation that to me seems true for all of the theories and their accompanying methodologies is that each has identified some single aspect of language or of language learning and has assumed either explicitly or implicitly that all of human language or language learning can be accounted for by that one aspect. Let us look briefly at just two instances of this.

As we will see in more detail in Chapter 1, the grammar-translation method dominated foreign-language instruction in the United States for more than a century. It was based on a rationalist/universalist linguistic theory, fully amenable to the premise that all natural languages were lexical analogs of each other. Its methodology assumed the validity of mental exercise and its transferability into other cognitive areas. It was ultimately abandoned on practical grounds, *not* because we discovered that it is bad or counterproductive to know the grammar of a language and to be able to translate into and out of it, but because other needs intuitively associated with knowing a language remained conspicuously unsatisfied. The method promised grammar and translation. It delivered grammar and translation.

Foreign-language teaching in postwar America faced a triple threat: the marriage of a linguistic theory (structuralism) to a learning theory (behaviorism), and the issue of this union, the audiolingual method. At last all the questions were answered. Structuralist linguistics showed us that "A language is a complex system of *habits*" (Hockett, 3, p. 137). We understood its lexicon to be a collection or arbitrary and conventional items; its grammar to be a statement of the permissible arrangements into which these items fit. Carroll (1) once defined a sentence as ". . .one or more form classes arranged in any of certain sequence patterns found in a given language" (p. 37). Speech and language were viewed as virtually synonymous, although "the relationship between writing and language [was] close" (Hockett, 3, p. 4). Behaviorism viewed learning as systems of habits acquired and strengthened through repetition and positive reinforcement. The audiolingual method was inevitable: we knew what language was; we knew how it was learned. How to teach it could not have been more obvious. And it didn't work. *Not* because speech is not the primary manifestation of language or because students could not master the patterns of the new language, but because, again, after mastering them, students could not *use* the language as they had expected to. The method promised habits. It delivered habits.

We may never know again as much as we knew during the audiolingual period. No other methodology has since enjoyed such near universal acceptance; no other theories of language or learning have successfully replaced structuralism or behaviorism in the sense of holding the same unchallenged sway. Later models have expanded our understanding and enabled us to ask better questions about language and learning, but no "new paradigm" has emerged to unite us in our approach to understanding our universe.

In linguistics, structuralism gave way to the "Standard Theory" and then to the "Extended Standard Theory," while case grammar, generative semantics, and other models competed for our affections, with none recommending itself as a basis for a new pedagogical grammar. To the extent that linguistic theories have addressed language acquisition, they have done so with black boxes that accept natural language as input and produce grammars as output, but through the mediation of unknown processes.

In learning theory, cognitive psychology has largely supplanted behaviorism, but the implications for language learning remain unclear. A major controversy involves accounting for the decline in second-language learning/acquisition potential associated with puberty. Arguing from the cognitivist position, for example, Krashen (4) hypothesized that this decline may be due to the onset of "formal operations," the highest stage in the Piagetian developmental model. Once that stage is reached natural acquisition may be impossible. In his later writings, however, Krashen (5) leads us to infer that under stable environmental conditions, adult L2 acquisition *is* possible, that it differs little if at all from child L1 acquisition, and that indeed *only* acquisition, i.e., not learning, can account for spontaneous and accurate use of L2.

Schumann (6), on the other hand, suggests that the major block to adult L2 learning is affective rather than cognitive, that it is ". . . only social and psychological development that creates psychological distance between the learner and the speakers of the target language." The major inhibiting affective factors are psychological and social distance, and ego permeability. When these distancing factors are present, neither learning nor acquisition is likely. However, "the affective argument assumes that when the learner has emphatic capacity, and motivation and attitudes which are favorable both to the target language community and to language learning itself, the psychological distance between the learner and the TL group will be minimal and the learner's cognitive processes will automatically function to produce language acquisition" (p. 108). From these two positions we conclude that cognitive development either inhibits or enhances language learning.

Intimately related to the above issues is the radical dichotomy of language learning versus language acquisition (discussed much more fully in Chapter 2). Granting that acquisition is the goal of instruction, the mere existence of this dichotomy places the profession in a methodological dilemma, for no "one-solution mentality" could possibly accommodate the mutually exclusive methodologies implied by these two competing positions: students either should learn *about* the target language in order to facilitate their spontaneous and accurate use of it, or they should not.

Another aspect of learning theory that complicates the picture is the professional literature about identifying and teaching to the preferred learning styles of our students. Little if any of this literature seriously considers the preferred teaching style of instructors. In general, teachers are more effective when they are confident about their own abilities and feel free to capitalize on their perceived strengths while minimizing their weaknesses. A native-speaking instructor of the target language usually feels more comfortable giving copious examples of the language, spontaneously creating them in response to a given situation. Nonnatives, however, usually feel more secure explaining material already presented in text materials. The affective environment in the classroom may well be more influenced by a teacher's feeling of confidence than by externally imposed considerations of methodology.

The theoretical heterogeneity in linguistic and learning theories has resulted in a profusion of postaudiolingual "methods" or "approaches": cognitive code learning, the Natural Approach, Silent Way, Suggestopedia, Total Physical Response, counseling-learning, the input hypothesis, to name a representative sample. Each claims to be the right way, yet each is distinct from the others. So much is on the methodological menu that our professional vocabulary now includes "the eclectic method." Krashen has often called the latter term "an intellectual obscenity," perhaps thereby perpetuating "Holy Grailism" by implicitly supporting the notion that there must be one single method that is right under all circumstances at all instructional levels. We will suggest below that "the eclectic method" may just be an ill-named, inchoate recognition of an underlying reality in foreign-language teaching.

Clearly, the jury is still out on the competing methodologies that have emerged in the postaudiolingual period. But experience suggests that to the extent that they fixate on one aspect of "language knowing," they, too, will have to be adapted, integrated with others, or abandoned.

Proficiency: The Organizing Principle

The fallacy that there is one right way to teach languages, that the right key will unlock the Secrets of the Universe, is revealed when "proficiency as the organizing principle" is understood conceptually. Higgs and Clifford (2) point out that a student cannot simply be declared "proficient" or "competent." He is proficient at something; competent to use the language to some purpose. In the same sense, a "method" cannot be declared "right" or "best." It must be right for something; the best way to accomplish some set of tasks. "Single method-ism" would be possible only if acquiring native or near-native proficiency in a foreign language involved learning a single type of skill. Insights gained over more than thirty years of proficiency testing show that such is not the case.

The cornerstone of the proficiency movement, I believe, is the "Functional Trisection" (see page 36 in this volume). Here we see clearly the necessary interrelationship of function, content, and accuracy, and are able to appreciate the different kinds of skills that contribute to proficiency ratings at different levels. The three factors of function, content, and accuracy are not hierarchically arranged: usually insufficiencies in any of the three areas keep a candidate from the next higher rating.

If we accept the premise of Chapter 1, that the ACTFL proficiency guidelines are a "stepladder for learning" representing "a graduated sequence of steps that can be used to structure a foreign-language program," we must recognize that the proficiency movement is not promoting a method in the "one-solution mentality" sense. Every new level in the ACTFL or ILR level definitions represents a new constellation or interrelationship of the factors of content, function, and accuracy. In addition, the relative contribution of specific language subskills—pronunciation, vocabulary, grammar, fluency, and sociolinguistic appropriateness—changes from level to level. (See Higgs and Clifford 2, pp. 68ff for a description of the relative contribution model.) When the relative contributions of the subskills are graphed, they peak at different levels. For example, sociocultural variables, which play a minimal role at the low end of the rating scale, are crucial to attaining an ILR rating of 4. The peak of the sociolinguistic curve, then, is around the ILR 4 level. (See Figure 1 on the next page.)

The relative contribution model has serious implications for any discussion of methodology. The Novice Level (ILR 0), for example, implicitly recognizes "enumeration of memorized material" as the primary function that can be expressed. Content is concerned with common, isolable semantic groups of lexical items, such as basic objects, weekdays, months, meals, colors, articles of clothing, family members, and greetings. Accuracy is limited to intelligibility. Not surprisingly, at the Novice Level, the vocabulary and pronunciation curves of the relative contribution model are near their peak. If this level is the first step up the proficiency ladder, debate over the merits and liabilities of the grammatical versus the functional/notional syllabus are moot. What is needed is a lexical syllabus. Nothing else could reasonably be asked to pick up the students where they are and move them onward. This does not imply that foreign-language materials and methods should be reconceptualized uniquely in terms of a lexical syllabus. But it does imply that at the most elementary level the lexicon must be the focus of instruction. The methodology must reflect this.

At the Intermediate Level (ILR 1), relationships shift. The student can now create with the language. He can ask and answer basic, concrete questions in areas of immediate personal need. He makes many errors in both pronunciation and grammar but is intelligible to a native speaker of the target language who is accustomed to dealing with nonnatives. This means that the interlocutor must contribute a great deal to a conversation. He must be a virtuoso listener and must be able to use "foreigner talk"

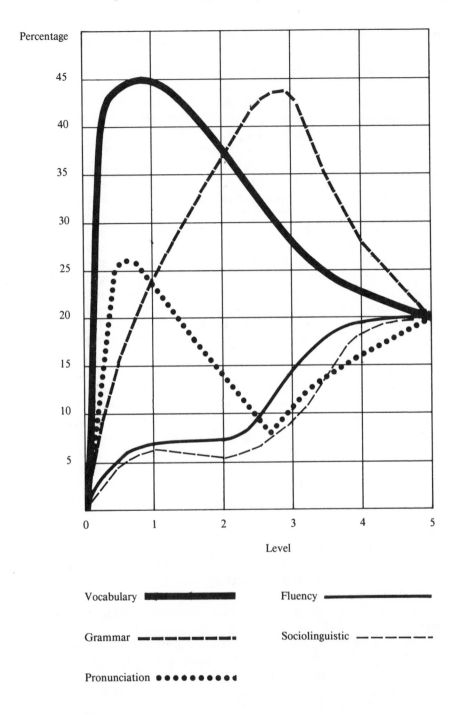

Figure 1. Hypothesized Relative Contribution Model

successfully and appropriately. In classrooms at this level, any of the "input methods" (see, for example, Krashen 5, especially pp. 20–30 and 137–46) is appropriate as the primary methodological focus. Vocabulary and pronunciation curves are still at or very near their peaks and thus demand major instructional attention. Major insights from the literature on functional/notional syllabuses also become applicable at this stage. Proficiency theory predicts that at this level, the grammar curve, though still well below its peak, is ascending sharply, and although a grammatical syllabus as such is contraindicated, even at this level grammatical accuracy is ignored only at great peril.

The Advanced Plus/Superior (ILR 2+/3) borderline finds the grammar curve at its peak. This means that all the basic grammatical structures of the target language must be under control for the candidate to manifest successfully the linguistic functions and content associated with this level: hypothesizing, supporting opinions, dealing with abstractions. Since the grammar curve nears its peak at the 2+ level, proficiency theory predicts that a grammatical syllabus is not only defensible, it is indispensable.

It is not popular these days to stress the need for grammatical accuracy in foreign-language classes. But it is vital to recognize that once a fairly elementary level is surpassed, the grammar itself communicates considerable meaning. In English, it makes a great deal of difference to say, "If you and I are friends, we can discuss this openly" when you mean "If you and I were friends, we could discuss this openly." In Spanish, *cuando nieva* (when it snows) does not mean *cuando nieve* (when it snows). The lexicon alone will not provide for these communicative needs. It is for this reason that attention to grammatical accuracy is an important motivating factor throughout the instructional process. Granted, when one is forced to function at the lexical level, grammatical niceties are a luxury and are perhaps accounted for in the lexico-situational context. While the student who aspires to nothing beyond Intermediate- or Advanced-Level communication will not be held back for having accuracy encouraged from the beginning, it is scarcely fair to lead the serious students along, encouraging them to talk like Tarzan and then saying that future progress is unlikely if not impossible until they get their grammatical act together. Postponing linguistic accuracy is an approach that promises a terminal profile, as defined in Higgs and Clifford (2).

It is perhaps not surprising that a rating of Advanced Plus (ILR 2+) rather than Superior (ILR 3) represents a kind of instructional ceiling. The social and linguistic skills necessary to function at the latter level require that the language be lived, as well as learned. It is no longer sufficient to "survive," to "make oneself understood." At the Superior Level, the nonnative can function socially and professionally in the target language. Krashen's (5) observation that the goal of classroom instruction is to prepare the student to comprehend the language in the outside world is certainly valid.

Summary

This chapter, in addition to serving as an introduction to the rest of the volume, has attempted to put into focus the oft-repeated statement that the proficiency movement is not another methodological bandwagon for the profession to jump on.

Method is a very powerful word. Superficially a method is a statement about how to teach. But underlying such a statement is a series of epistemological propositions concerning what language is, what parts of it should be taught, and how human beings can learn it.

We have tried to show that most "methods" fail because they are self-limiting. They identify an interesting and largely valid aspect of "language knowing" and a set of procedures intended to maximize successful acquisition of that aspect. They typically fail to recognize the multitude of disparate skills and skill types involved in mastering a second language. The method that best fosters one may not successfully have an impact on others.

This brief discussion, while not treating pedagogical techniques at all, has suggested that different approaches may be appropriate at different levels of instruction, and that at all levels, the "end goal" of instruction may crucially determine our focus and our pedagogy. We have hypothesized that the "relative contribution model" is an interesting theoretical orientation for identifying such approaches. At every level of instruction virtually all aspects of meaningful language use in context are present to some degree. The association of a particular approach with a particular level of instruction simply identifies the major pedagogical focus for that time. A lexical syllabus does not mean that vocabulary is taught to the complete exclusion of other skill areas. A functional/notional syllabus depends on pronunciation, vocabulary, morphology, and syntax. A grammatical syllabus presents communicative functions in believable, relevant contexts.

Each of these approaches defines the *focus* not the *limits,* of instruction. If each focus is to be called a method, then methodological eclecticism, far from being an intellectual obscenity, becomes a logical imperative.

In order to build a house, a full toolbox is needed. Builders do not argue among themselves over whether a screwdriver is a better, more valuable tool than a hammer or a saw. Each tool is put to its best use. A proficiency orientation in foreign-language teaching helps us fill our toolbox. It is a "key" to success because it broadens our perspectives. It encourages us to appreciate that many very different kinds of skills are needed to master another language and to select from a variety of approaches the one best suited to our students' immediate and long-range needs.

References, Language Teaching and the Quest for the Holy Grail

1. Carroll, John B. *The Study of Language.* Cambridge, MA: Harvard University Press, 1966.
2. Higgs, Theodore V., and Ray Clifford. "The Push Toward Communication," pp. 57–79 in Theodore V. Higgs, ed., *Curriculum, Competence, and the Foreign Language Teacher.* The ACTFL Foreign Language Education Series, vol. 13. Lincolnwood, IL: National Textbook Co., 1982.
3. Hockett, Charles F. *A Course in Modern Linguistics.* New York: The Macmillan Company, 1958.
4. Krashen, Stephen D. "The Critical Period for Language Acquisition and Its Possible Bases," pp. 211–24 in Doris R. Aaronson and Robert W. Rieber, eds., *Developmental Psycholinguistics and Communication Disorders.* New York: The New York Academy of Sciences, 1975.
5. _____. *Principles and Practice in Second Language Acquisition.* New York: Pergamon Press, 1982.
6. Schumann, John H. *The Pidginization Process.* Rowley, MA: Newbury House, 1978.

The ACTFL Proficiency Guidelines: A Historical Perspective

Judith E. Liskin-Gasparro
Educational Testing Service

Introduction

In November 1982, ACTFL published the *ACTFL Provisional Proficiency Guidelines,* a series of descriptions of proficiency levels for speaking, listening, reading, writing, and culture in a foreign language. These guidelines represent a graduated sequence of steps that can be used to structure a foreign-language program. What exactly are they? Where did they come from? Why were they written? What are their implications for teaching and learning a second language? This chapter will deal with the *what, where from,* and *why* of these guidelines in order to give the reader a sense of the background of the contemporary interest in proficiency as the organizing principle of foreign-language study.

Guidelines: A Stepladder for Learning

The ACTFL guidelines are the result of a project funded by the International Research and Studies Program of the U.S. Department of Education entitled "A Design for Measuring and Communicating Foreign Language Proficiency." They were developed in direct response to a recommendation of the President's Commission on Foreign Language and International Studies (24) to establish "language proficiency achievement goals for the end of each year of study at all levels, with special attention

Judith E. Liskin-Gasparro (ABD, Princeton University) is an Examiner in Test Development for the College Board Program of the Educational Testing Service. She has written several manuals on oral proficiency testing and on organizing training workshops. She is coeditor of *Measuring Spoken Language Proficiency (1983)* and is a member of the ACTFL Advisory Committee.

to speaking proficiency." The guidelines consist of both generic and language-specific descriptions of proficiency that range from the most minimal acquaintance with the language to adult professional-level skill. These graduated descriptions of proficiency have been written for French, German, and Spanish. Plans are under way to write comparable guidelines for the other Western European languages, as well as for four less commonly taught languages of critical national importance—Arabic, Chinese, Japanese, and Russian. The generic guidelines are found in Appendix A of this volume. The full set of language-specific guidelines is available at nominal cost from the ACTFL Materials Center.

It has been acknowledged that the language-teaching profession lacks a generally accepted sequence of learning objectives. The pragmatic atmosphere of the 1970s, the push for accountability, and the desire to establish measurable objectives have reemphasized the need for an organizing principle that would guide instruction. Omaggio (18) has recently observed that the history of foreign-language education is replete with battles over methodology, over the "right way" to teach a language. The entry of the discussions about language proficiency and the development of the ACTFL guidelines are a signal that, as Omaggio says, "we may be realizing that the controversy has been raging on the wrong battlefield. Instead of searching for one definitive approach to language teaching—a search that has consistently ended in frustration and a sense of failure—we should be identifying some 'organizing principle' by which various other methods, approaches, materials, and curricula might begin to make collective sense." The organizing principle that is reflected in the ACTFL guidelines is *language proficiency*: the ability to function effectively in the language in real-life contexts.

In an earlier, more innocent era, one could accept the illusion that language study was a classroom activity with little or no application in the outside world. One could create a closed system of curriculum, textbook, and tests. Success could be efficiently gauged in terms of how well the students learned the material they were taught, i.e., by their level of achievement. The question of probable success or failure with the language outside the classroom was seldom asked. The only accountability was internal: whether the students measured up to the expectations of the teacher.

The foreign-language profession has, at various points in our country's history, been jolted into action by national emergencies. Events such as two world wars, the launching of *Sputnik 1,* the Vietnam War, and the current crisis in the automobile industry have forcefully reminded the nation of the critical importance that foreign-language skills and understanding of other cultures play in questions of diplomacy, defense, and commerce.

It is in this context that the guidelines have been developed. Questions that have always troubled the foreign-language profession are being asked more insistently these days, not only from within (for we have always been an introspective and self-analytical group) but also from without: What should a student be able to do with the language after one, two, or four semesters of study? What goals are realistically attainable? How much knowledge of culture can we expect of students in a typical two-year high school sequence? Should some skills be emphasized more than others? How does the college language department know how an entering student can function in the language? What can a company know about the language skills of a candidate for a position called "bilingual secretary," and how "bilingual" does the company really want or need this secretary to be? The guidelines promise to be a "common yardstick" for the foreign-language profession that will allow us to organize much needed proficiency-based curricula, materials, evaluation instruments, and articulation plans around well-defined levels of language skill.

History of the Guidelines: The Early Antecedents

It has often been said that there are no new ideas; everything that is now being thought or planned or developed is not original but is a different way of stating an old truth. The guidelines have their most recent antecedents in the President's Commission report, in the various government agencies' efforts to teach and test functional language ability, and in the work in communicative syllabuses that has occupied our European colleagues for most of the last decade. From this viewpoint the guidelines are indeed an extension of already existing ideas. From a broader perspective, however, they have grown out of centuries of teaching, thinking, and theorizing about language, and they must be placed in this context as well.

Fifty centuries of language proficiency

The quest for proficiency, in the sense of mastery of a subject or the attainment of a usable level of skill, has always been with us. Titone (26), who traces foreign-language teaching back to 3000 B.C., recognizes that "the necessity to communicate with foreign peoples . . . is as old as the human race, or at least the Tower of Babel!" (p. 4). Indeed, archeologists have found bilingual dictionaries dating from the third millennium B.C.

Whether foreign languages were learned by conquering or conquered peoples or, as in Renaissance Europe, by young men as part of their general education, the goal of instruction seems largely to have been *practical communicative ability.* Titone (26) reports that textbooks in use until the beginning of the nineteenth century were written mostly in the target language and that ideas about foreign-language teaching from the Renaissance into the eighteenth century would seem surprisingly modern to today's foreign-language educators concerned with teaching for language proficiency.

A seventeenth-century proponent of an early version of what we might term the direct method was the Czech educator Jan Amos Komensky (1592–1670). His methods featured prominently the use of sensory experience to develop intuition, and a large number of examples to help students make the inductive leap from the concrete language to the abstract rules of grammar. While contemporary foreign languages were taught during this period by contact and conversation with native speakers and were synthesized into more complex forms through practice, new directions were being undertaken in the teaching of Latin. In the Middle Ages when Latin was commonly spoken and written in Europe for any kind of formal communication, it was taught in the schools as a first language, and all educated people were naturally bilingual. In the sixteenth and seventeenth centuries, when Latin came to be studied only as a written language, new methods were developed to teach it. The memory of Latin as a living, spoken language was still recent; what was lacking were native speakers who could teach students by the direct, conversational approach.

The Englishman Roger Ascham (1515–1568) and the German Wolfgang Ratke (1571–1635) both organized Latin language instruction around a written text. The teacher's first task was to translate the text for the student, word by word, until the student could translate accurately from and into Latin. Rules of grammar, deduced from examples in the Latin text, were then taught, but always in the context of the students' previous experience with the text.

John Locke, writing in the second half of the seventeenth century, advocated the translation method of teaching Latin and rejected the practice of teaching grammar rules in order to facilitate accurate and fluent usage. Grammar was to be taught as a cognitive system to those who already knew the language. In *Some Thoughts Concerning Education* (1693), Locke anticipated the ACTFL guidelines' concern with accuracy when he wrote,

> For Languages are only to be learned by rote; and a Man who does not speak *English* or *Latin* perfectly by rote, so that having thought of the thing he would speak of, his Tongue of Course, without Thought of Rule or Grammar, falls into the proper Expression and Idiom of that Language, does not speak it well, nor is Master of it. [Quoted by Titone, 26, p. 16]

By the nineteenth century, Latin teaching had become extremely grammar oriented. The study of the classics had become a kind of "mental gymnastics," intended to produce "an excellent mental discipline, a fortitude of spirit and a broad humane understanding of life" (Mallinson, 16, p. 8). Herron (10) notes that this view of Latin study reflected a general theory of education prominent during that period in which it was believed that certain academic exercises (connected with the study of Greek, Latin, and mathematics) could serve to develop mental faculties, such as perception, imagination, memory, reason, feeling, and will. When the modern foreign languages began to achieve greater prominence in the curriculum, this same justification for study was applied to them as well.

The grammar-translation method, which dominated foreign-language education in the United States for over a century, began in Europe in the late eighteenth century and flourished in the nineteenth. Just as the direct methods of the Renaissance through the eighteenth century had aimed to teach students mastery of the written and spoken language, so too the grammar-translation method was born of goals that had "mastery" or proficiency at their base. The best-known early grammar-translation textbooks were probably those of Ollendorf (17), which were first published in the 1840s, and later those of Plötz (20). Kelly (12) describes the standard format of this type of text: "a statement of the rule, followed by a vocabulary list and translation exercises. . . . [M]ore importance was accorded to exceptions than would have been considered justified during the Renaissance" (p. 52).

Under the grammar-translation system, mental discipline was most important; therefore, students were trained to analyze structures and memorize forms and vocabulary lists. Since the sequence of instruction was structurally rather than textually or communicatively based, no effort was made to relate the instructional material to the students' own needs. Instead, students memorized and translated from one language into the other series of discrete sentences that illustrated particular rules of grammar and their exceptions. As Kelly (12) puts it, "language skill was equated with ability to conjugate and decline" (p. 53).

Arguments over methodology in the nineteenth century seem to have been as heated as they are today, and there is considerable evidence of strong reaction against the grammar-translation approach. For example, Kelly (12) quotes Rouse, who wrote acerbically in 1925:

> I will only add finally, that the current method . . . is the offspring of German scholarship, which seeks to know everything about something rather than the thing itself. . . . [P. 53]

Writing in a similar vein, Bahlsen, quoted by Titone (26), reflected in 1905 on his own training in French under Plötz:

> Committing words to memory, translating sentences, drilling irregular verbs, later memorizing, repeating, and applying grammatical rules with their exceptions. . . . [It was] a barren waste of insipid sentence translations. [P. 28]

Although the grammar-translation method prevailed until well into the twentieth century, methodological reform was also in evidence. Several varieties of a kind of "natural method," later termed the "direct method," attempted to bring the focus of language teaching back to the living language itself.

The reforms in language teaching at the end of the nineteenth century were motivated, according to Titone (26), by both economic and scientific considerations. Colonialism and expanded international commerce gave functional foreign-language skills a practical importance that had been lacking for centuries. The new science of descriptive linguistics focused on bringing the spoken language to a place of prominence. Scientific methods of language teaching emphasized mastering the sound system, integrating the study of grammar in stages appropriate in complexity to the student's overall mastery of the language, and gradual sequencing of material.

That there was considerable confusion and lack of consensus on the question of foreign-language methodology in the United States at the end of the nineteenth century is indicated by the appointment of the Committee of Twelve in 1896 by the National Education Association. The mission of this committee was to investigate the place of modern languages in secondary education and to make recommendations in the areas of methodology and teacher training, as well as on some other questions concerning the teaching of modern languages in secondary and postsecondary institutions. A survey was conducted, and a report issued in 1899 confirmed the lack of consensus in methodology within the teaching profession. The report recommended a balanced approach of the phonetic method, some study of grammar, reading-translation of graded texts, oral practice in the language, and written composition. These components were sequenced according to the length of the program, the age of the pupils at the time they began language study, and the goals of instruction.

Foreign-language instruction in the twentieth century

In the early years of the twentieth century, a majority of high school students in the United States studied foreign languages in a "normal" four-year sequence. But the post-World War I xenophobia that predominated in the 1920s reduced enrollments and caused most schools to limit themselves to a two-year sequence of study. This in turn limited the level of proficiency that students could realistically be expected to attain. In addition, communicative skills were shunned, due to the extreme isolationist philosophy of the decade. The Coleman Report, published in 1929 as part of the Modern Foreign Language Study commissioned by the Carnegie Corporation, reflected the ethos of the times by recommending that only reading be taught, since that was the only goal attainable in a two-year sequence of study.

Rivers (21) points out that the Coleman Report appeared at a time when foreign-language professionals in the United States and abroad were reassessing their goals and methods, and it therefore had considerable impact. It took firm hold in the United States, in spite of the fact that its premises and methods were somewhat questionable (Titone, 26). The goal of the reading method was to produce proficient readers of authentic foreign-language texts who could comprehend directly, without recourse to a dictionary or a translation. The method inspired the production of graded readers geared to the various levels of language study. Since most students studied a language for only two years, they never had the opportunity to progress to ungraded materials (Rivers, 21). Thus, even the limited goal of achieving proficiency in reading was not realized. In addition, the exclusive emphasis on reading resulted in a nation of foreign-language students who could read only limited material and speak and understand the language not at all.

Intensive Language Instruction: Herald of Change _____

The linguistic isolationism so characteristic of the 1920s and 1930s ended with this country's involvement in World War II. It was realized early on that having military experts trained in foreign languages was vital to the national security. In fact, the roots of both the audiolingual movement and the current government language-teaching programs go back before World War II to an intensive language instruction project developed by the American Council of Learned Societies (ACLS) and supported by the Rockefeller Foundation. The project focused on the uncommonly taught languages of potential military and diplomatic importance in a systematic effort to bring the insights of linguistics to the field of language teaching (Thompson, 25).

Soon after its inception, the ACLS Intensive Language Program was offering courses in twenty-six languages at eighteen universities. Based on principles of language acquisition, the program included (1) an under-standing of language as a set of habits and (2) a belief that the spoken form of the language should be presented to the students well before the written form, in imitation of the way in which children acquire their first language. The program maintained a low teacher-student ratio and included long hours of drill and oral practice. The immediate need of the military for trained personnel who could communicate with native speakers of other languages made the Intensive Language Program an invaluable resource, and project personnel soon began providing support for new language programs in the government that were being constructed on the same model. Of these, the Army Specialized Training Program (ASTP), the Education Branch of the Special Services Division (also known as the Army Language Section), and the Foreign Language and Area Programs of the Provost Marshall General's Office, Department of the Army, drew most notably on the resources and experience of the ACLS program. The

ACLS method depended on the coordinated teaching efforts of linguistic experts, who explained the structure of the language, and native informants, who practiced with the students extensive drills and conversation based on graded materials. As Thompson (25) and Rivers (21) point out, the philosophy of language teaching on which this system was based became, more than a decade later, the cornerstone of the audiolingual method.

ACLS and government language teaching

After the war and the closing of the military language programs, the ACLS continued its involvement in foreign-language instruction by forming the Committee on the Language Program (Thompson, 25). Among other endeavors, the committee facilitated the publication of self-study guides in twenty-two languages that had been produced during the war by the Education Branch of the Special Services Division of the Army. Each program consisted of graded text materials and two phonograph records that comprised the equivalent of approximately a year-long course. The collaboration of linguistic scientists in the language-learning projects of that time is apparent in the list of authors of these materials. Thompson (25) remarks that "the authors of these manuals read like a *Who's Who* of American linguists (Bloomfield, Block, Dyen, Hockett, Hodge, Moulton, and Sebeok, to name a few)" (p. 281).

The goals and methods of wartime foreign-language study were continued after World War II at the Foreign Service Institute's (FSI) School of Languages and Linguistics. Its mission was and is today to teach Foreign Service personnel languages that they will need in their work abroad. Carroll (5) wrote that the programs were based on linguistic analysis to an even greater degree than in the Intensive Language Program model on which they were based.

> As might be expected, aural-oral skills are emphasized, since the primary objective is to give the student a speaking knowledge of the language being taught. Instruction in the written language plays a secondary role. The program could be characterized as carrying the Intensive Language Program to its logical extreme. What differentiates this instruction from the wartime methods is its even greater emphasis on linguistic analysis. [P. 182]

The designers of the language programs at the FSI were soon faced with the need to measure their results. This effort began in 1952 when, under the National Mobilization and Manpower Act, the Civil Service Commission undertook the creation of a register of government employees with skills, background, and experience in foreign languages and cultures. The register would categorize degrees of foreign-language ability so that individuals could be classified. Sollenberger (23) reports that the project was sidetracked for a number of bureaucratic reasons, but not until preliminary skill-level descriptions had been defined for reading and speaking.

In 1955 the Foreign Service Institute ordered a survey of foreign-language skills. A self-appraisal survey carried out in 1956 revealed that "less than half of the 4,041 regular, reserve, and staff officers surveyed had a [useful] proficiency in French, German, or Spanish." "Useful" was defined as "sufficient control of the structure of a language, and adequate vocabulary, to handle routine representation requirements and professional discussions within one or more special fields, and—with the exception of languages such as Chinese, Japanese, Arabic, etc.—the ability to read nontechnical news or technical writing in a special field" (Sollenberger, 23, p. 5).

Sollenberger (23) further reports that these findings led to the announcement of a language policy for the Foreign Language Service in November of 1956 that was based on the premise that foreign-language skills are vital in the conduct of foreign affairs. It committed the Foreign Service Institute to test its officers and to verify whether they had achieved a "useful" level of skill, as defined above.

This mandate thrust the FSI into virgin territory in the field of evaluation. As Wilds (30), who was deeply involved in the development of the oral interview, understatedly says, "Both the scope and restrictions of the testing situation provided problems previously unknown in language testing" (p. 29). The procedure that was developed was a face-to-face interview test, tailored to each candidate's interests, experience, and ability in the language. The rating scale used built on the original 1952 descriptions and expanded them to include both functional and linguistic components.

In the next decade, use of the rating scale spread to other government agencies, such as the Defense Language Institute (DLI), the Language School of the Central Intelligence Agency, and ACTION/Peace Corps. Representatives of the user agencies met in 1968 to standardize the level definitions. The latter, now termed the ILR (Interagency Language Roundtable) definitions, are found in this volume as Appendix B.

Academic Language Programs after World War II _____

The ACLS Intensive Language Program influenced language teaching in schools and colleges, as well as in the government. Impressed by the results attained by the "Army Method," institutions such as the University of Michigan continued after the war to experiment with language teaching based on new ideas of linguistic analysis to teach structure and on oral practice to form verbal habits. The development of the tape recorder in the 1950s allowed the substitution of recorded native speech for the native informants that the ACLS system had used in the Armed Forces language program.

The launching of *Sputnik 1* in 1957 brought national attention to the language-teaching profession. The minority of professionals, working toward aural-oral language-teaching reform based on the ACLS experience, quickly swelled to a majority, as external agencies made large sums of money available to education "in the national interest." The National Defense Education Act (NDEA) of 1957 included foreign languages as one of its targeted areas. With the incentive of financial support, school boards were urged to increase enrollments in foreign languages, push for longer sequences, and buy state-of-the-art instructional equipment and materials. Summer and even year-long inservice institutes were created to upgrade teachers' skills and instruct them in new ways of teaching foreign languages.

NDEA funds also provided for the development of new instructional materials. These were commercially printed and distributed and came to be known as "audiolingual materials." The term *audiolingual* had been coined by Nelson Brooks (2) and appeared in print for the first time in 1958. Brooks used the term to refer to verbal language in a general sense, or, as he described it, "language in the air [as opposed to] language on paper" (p. 236). He states that he had searched for a term that would be clearer to the ear than the homophonous "aural-oral." In spite of its modest origins, the term *audiolingual* quickly came to encompass not just a set of materials intended to teach students to speak and comprehend the spoken language, but an entire methodology. Brooks considers this use a misapplication of the term which caused significant harm.

> So the official name became "Audiolingual Materials" with the four words Listening, Speaking, Reading, and Writing prominently printed close beside. However, . . . many people see method in everything, and the quite inaccurate and indeed misleading and harmful term "audiolingual method" came into use. This was, quite simply, too bad. Method is far too valuable a word to be used so carelessly and incorrectly. In the very nature of our language programs, audiolingual could never become a method, for who proposes to do without printing altogether? [Pp. 236–37]

Lack of logic notwithstanding, the audiolingual materials became identified with a method of teaching that was attempted in the United States in the 1960s. Much has been said and written about the theory and practices associated with it and about the success or failure of language teaching of that period. Looking back from a contemporary vantage point, three features of the audiolingual movement stand out: (1) the revolutionary nature of the reforms, (2) the embrace of audiolingualism as the "final answer" to the problem of teaching language, and (3) a general aura of optimism and enthusiasm, which is reflected in the professional literature of the decade.

The language-teaching profession underwent a swift alteration. The influx of NDEA funds accounted for much of this, as did the involvement of all sectors of the educational establishment in the change process: school boards, teachers, teacher trainers, students preparing to become foreign-language teachers, and the learners themselves. Grittner (8) reports that the number of language labs in secondary schools rose from about 60 in 1957 to 6,000 five years later, and the number of high school students enrolled in modern foreign-language courses jumped from 16.5 to 27.7 percent between 1958 and 1968.

The "one-solution mentality" of the 1960s is reflected most dramatically in the proliferation of methods and approaches that developed in reaction to it in the 1970s: cognitive methodology, the confluent approach, Total Physical Response, Suggestopedia, the Natural Approach, individualized instruction, the counseling-learning model, the Silent Way, and finally, the eclectic method, which embraced none exclusively yet all generally of the above. New approaches in the 1970s focused on differences among students and differences among teachers, in part as a reaction to the rigidity of techniques of repetition, memorization, and drill that had characterized language teaching a decade before.

The optimism and forward-looking atmosphere of the 1960s could be seen in the expansion of expectations and activities. The NDEA institutes stimulated work that had already been under way in the area of teacher competency, and resulted in the publication in 1966 of *Guidelines for Teacher Education Programs in Modern Foreign Languages,* a document that assessed the status of teacher education programs, made a case for new directions, and presented a comprehensive framework within which new programs could be developed (Paquette, 19).

One of the crucial areas to examine in light of the ACTFL guidelines involves minimal competencies that the foreign-language teacher should have. The MLA guidelines addressed this need and covered seven areas: (1) aural understanding, (2) speaking, (3) reading, (4) writing, (5) language analysis, (6) culture, and (7) professional preparation. A battery of tests, the MLA Foreign Language Proficiency Tests for Teachers and Advanced Students, was developed to measure competence in these seven areas. The debates of the late 1960s and early 1970s over the adequacy of the tests, the use to which scores should be put, the need for a criterion-referenced rather than a norm-referenced test are not unlike the questions that are certain to arise with respect to the ACTFL guidelines, published more than 15 years later. The experience of applying the teacher-education guidelines and the MLA Proficiency Tests to foreign-language education programs is discussed in detail by Valette (28) and Lange (13). It is clear that these earlier efforts set the stage for guidelines that would be proficiency oriented and would start from the very lowest levels of language learning.

Oral Proficiency Testing Moves Outside the Government

Foreign-language training in academe and the government moved in substantially different directions from the post-World War II years until well into the 1970s. The ACTFL guidelines, based on the government's work with language, particularly oral language proficiency assessment, reflect a convergence of the governmental and academic educational sectors. This rapprochement is due in large part to the private sector's acquaintance with the ILR oral proficiency interview and rating scale at the end of the 1960s in connection with its use in the Peace Corps. In the late 1960s the Peace Corps was teaching languages to thousands of trainees in the United States and abroad. At first, the FSI tested trainees and volunteers, typically at the beginning, the midpoint, and the end of their training, and again after one and/or two years in the field. When the task strained government resources, Educational Testing Service (ETS) was asked to assume the language-testing activities. ETS staff members were trained by the FSI, and later these staff members trained Peace Corps Training Center staff to conduct and rate interviews. The Peace Corps project was the first large-scale interview testing activity not operated directly by a government agency.

Perhaps the principal application of the oral interview procedure outside the government during the 1970s was as a certification instrument in bilingual education. As of this writing, the oral interview is used for this purpose in California, Florida, Illinois, New Jersey, and Texas. Details of programs, administration, and the minimum standard for certification vary from state to state, but the requirement that teacher candidates, or in some states inservice teachers as well, demonstrate their ability to speak the languages of instruction is a constant. New Jersey, for example, set bilingual certification standards based on the results of a study conducted by ETS (Livingston, 15). The goal of that program, as for those of other states, was to provide assurance that the teacher could "function effectively" in the classroom. Brown (3) described this level of language proficiency as follows.

> The ability to function effectively would be manifested by such things as (1) the ability to comprehend completely the "talk" of children and parents, both English speaking and Spanish speaking; (2) the ability to communicate in both English and Spanish with children and parents on school-related and other topics; and (3) the ability to present subject matter in the classroom, carry on classroom discussion, ask and answer questions, and explain concepts in both English and Spanish. [P. 68]

ETS developed the certification program for New Jersey. Ongoing management was turned over to the state in 1979, and it has since been institutionalized in the colleges that offer degree programs in both bilingual and ESL teacher education. In addition to the certification of bilingual and ESL teachers, the oral interview found other nongovernmental applications during the 1970s, among them the Experiment in International Living, the Missionary Training Center (formerly the Language Training Mission) of the Church of Jesus Christ of Latter-Day Saints at Brigham Young University, and the New Brunswick (Canada) Education Department.

The FSI Testing Kit Workshops

The expansion of the oral proficiency interview outside the government might well have remained within the modest confines described above had it not been for the efforts of James R. Frith, now Dean Emeritus of the School of Language Studies of the Foreign Service Institute. In 1979, the FSI held the first of a series of three "Testing Kit Workshops," to which ten college and university professors of Spanish and French were invited (Frith, 7). The goals of the initial workshop project were (1) to determine to what degree the French/Spanish Testing Kit, a brochure on the principles and techniques of oral proficiency assessment accompanied by eight cassette tape recordings of demonstration interview tests, could function as a stand-alone document to train oral proficiency testers; (2) to find out whether the language-teaching profession could find useful academic applications for the FSI system of evaluating foreign-language speaking proficiency; and (3) to decide if further collaboration between FSI and academe should be pursued.

The project design included four phases. Phase 1 was the workshop itself at FSI, which included a theoretical introduction to oral proficiency testing, observation and discussion of videotaped and live interview tests, and some opportunity for the participants to conduct their own practice interviews. The FSI team-testing model was followed, in which an interviewer poses the questions and engages the examinee in conversation, while an examiner observes the interview and evaluates the examinee's performance. In the FSI and other governmental agencies, the interviewer is always a native speaker of the language of the test.

After the workshops, the participants undertook phase 2 of the project: rating a set of twelve to sixteen taped interviews (*not* the same tapes that had been included with the kit). Participants consulted by telephone with FSI testers about each tape, discussing their ratings and rationale. The inter-rater agreement between the college- and university-professor ratings and the official FSI ratings was high: 84 percent on the first eight tapes, and 96 percent for those after the first eight.

As a control, the FSI had arranged for eight additional professors, largely from the same institutions, to rate the same set of tapes after studying the testing kit materials, but without benefit of formal training. The inter-rater agreement of this latter group with the FSI rating was remarkably similar: 84 percent on the first eight tapes, and 94 percent on the remainder. The conclusion after phase 2 of the project was that the testing kit alone, without the FSI workshop experience, served adequately to train college professors to evaluate oral proficiency interviews. The "telephone training" proved to be very valuable to both groups of participants in improving their rating skills.

Phase 3 of the project addressed elicitation technique. During this phase the participants interviewed their students, taped the interviews, and sent the tapes to FSI for evaluation. The judgment of the FSI evaluators was that the participants needed considerably more training in elicitation technique and that a revision of the testing kit would have to include more material in this area.

The last phase of the project was a second workshop at FSI intended to provide additional training in interviewing skills and to seek from the participants their advice about revising the Testing Kit. This first project proved to be so well received that funding was secured for additional ones.

The various groups of workshop participants found numerous applications for the oral interview at their institutions. As reported by Young (31), one of the possible applications, "establish[ing] a reasonable oral proficiency level (perhaps S-1) for the fulfillment of the language requirement ... a stunning example of the improvement in articulation that widely accepted standards would generate," (p. 67) has in fact been realized by some language departments at the University of Pennsylvania (Freed, 6). Other possibilities are treated in more detail in Chapter 7 of this volume.

The experience of college professors with the oral interview and rating scale revealed limitations of the scale for use outside the government that were to feature prominently in subsequent work. Frith (7) reported the FSI evaluators' concern that nonnative speakers could not interview very high-level candidates, and a goodly portion of the followup workshop with the first group of Testing Kit participants focused on testing at the higher levels. It was clear that college professors, most of whom are not native speakers of the language they teach, would not be able to interview or evaluate candidates at Levels 4 and 4+ as fully and definitively as they would candidates at Levels 0+ through 3. In addition, Young (31) mentions some concern that the 0–5 rating scale cannot make distinctions as fine as can course grades.

Some of these same concerns emerged from the testing and training that ETS had undertaken in connection with ACTION/Peace Corps a decade earlier. Some of the Peace Corps trainees were adults, but many were young people just out of college. The experience of administering oral interviews to these young people gave rise to reflections on the rating scale and its appropriateness for measuring the speaking ability of high school and college students.

The ACTFL Guidelines: The Immediate Antecedents _____

To the uninitiated, one surprising characteristic of the rating scale is that it is not linear. Instead, the level descriptions correspond to various degrees of real-life "usable" language proficiency, ranging from 0 at the bottom (no functional proficiency) to 5 at the top (native, or bilingual proficiency). The descriptions in between are as follows:

Level 1   elementary (survival-level) proficiency
Level 2   limited working proficiency
Level 3   professional working proficiency
Level 4   full professional proficiency, or representational proficiency

If one were to represent the scale graphically, it would look something like the drawing in Figure 1.

It is clear from this depiction that relatively little language is needed to go from Level 0 to Level 1, relatively more from Level 1 to Level 2, and so on. The most difficult leap is from Level 4 to Level 5. No matter how long one studies the language or lives in a place where it is spoken, it is most unusual to reach Level 5, i.e., to be taken for an educated native speaker of the language.

The Carroll study

John Carroll (5) reported the results of a battery of language tests administered to college majors of French, German, Russian, and Spanish in the second semester of their senior year. In the oral interview, the typical rating was 2 or 2+. (In the FSI/ILR testing system, a plus is awarded for performance that substantially exceed the requirements of the base level but does not represent consistent functioning at the next higher level.) These students were *majors* who had concentrated on the study of the language and its literature for their four undergraduate years, who might have studied the language in high school as well, and who might even have spent some time studying abroad. Even so, very few reached Level 3, "professional working proficiency." The goal of government language schools is to train professional personnel to achieve a useful level of language proficiency, and thus, the levels below 3 are seen largely as way stations in the training process. Since the most proficient of the nation's college students apparently reach only Level 2/2+, clearly any use of the rating scale and the interview in secondary schools and colleges must focus on levels below 2.

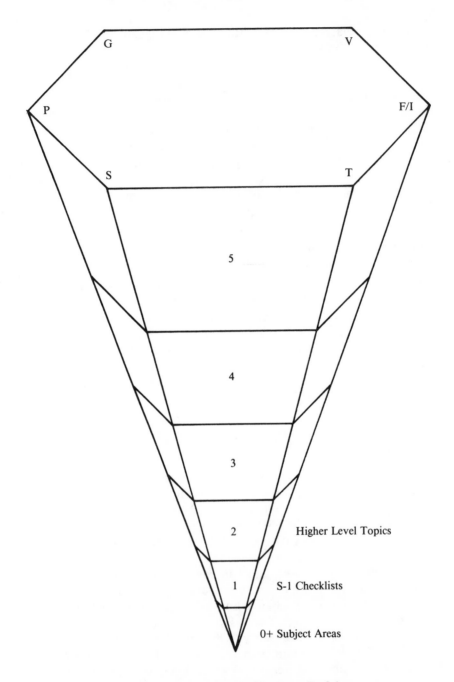

Figure 1. Inverted Pyramid of Language Proficiency

Reprinted with permission from the *Manual for LS Oral Interview Workshops (June 1980).*

The ETS study

Even within these relatively narrow ranges at the low end of the scale, the definition at each level reflects a wide variety of possible performances. The intuitive perception of the ETS staff who had worked with Peace Corps volunteers was that the scale was not sensitive enough to register substantial differences in performance, such as those that would take place during one semester or one year of study. A student might well start a course with Level 1 proficiency, improve considerably, and finish the course still at Level 1. This untested perception was affirmed by an informal study carried out at ETS in 1979. ETS staff members conducted oral proficiency interviews with approximately thirty first- and second-year high school Spanish students. Although the students varied considerably in their ability to communicate orally, none of them reached Level 1. Some of them were rated 0+ but most would have rated a 0 on the ILR scale. The hypothesis was confirmed that the low end of the scale did not effectively discriminate among students whom teachers would judge to be significantly different in oral ability.

One major outcome of both this informal ETS study and the FSI Testing Kit Workshops was consensus on the need to expand the low end of the ILR scale to make it more applicable to students in traditional academic environments. The ILR scale provides for five ranges of proficiency between Levels 0 and 2: 0, 0+, 1, 1+, and 2. There had to be more definable benchmarks between Levels 0 and 2 for academic use so that students' progress could be more readily registered.

The ETS Common Yardstick Project

At about the same time, ETS was approaching the question of an academically oriented speaking scale from another perspective. As early as 1970, Protase Woodford coined the term "Common Yardstick," which was later applied to a project jointly undertaken by the English Speaking Union of Great Britain, the British Council, ETS, the Deutscher Volkshochschul Verband, representatives of the United States government, and various business and academic groups which met to develop or adapt a series of descriptors of language ability. Several groups presented draft scales for consideration by the group. After two meetings in Great Britain and the United States, a grant to ETS from the U.S. Office of Education provided for further refinement of the Common Yardstick scales.

The outcome of the project was the development of additional, intralevel descriptions for Levels 0 and 1 of the ILR rating scale. In addition, the decision was made to rename the levels, since the denominations 0, 1, 2, etc., tended to give the impression that the proficiency levels were equivalent to the academic understanding of "level" as "year of study."

A side-by-side comparison of the ILR and ACTFL scales shows the expansion of the discretely describable levels of proficiency at the bottom of the scale, and the corresponding decision to combine levels of proficiency at the top. (See Figure 2.)

ILR	ACTFL/ETS (Academic)
0	0 (no ability whatsoever) Novice Low Novice Mid
0+	Novice High
1	Intermediate Low Intermediate Mid
1+	Intermediate High
2	Advanced
2+	Advanced Plus
3 3+ 4 4+ 5	Superior

Figure 2. The ILR and ACTFL Scales

The project also produced verbal descriptions for the newly created proficiency levels, which were subsequently validated in a study undertaken jointly by ETS, ACTFL, and the CIA Language School. The expanded lower end of the speaking scale was developed at a fortuitous moment, because ACTFL was just beginning to work on the Proficiency Guidelines Project. These operationally validated descriptions were used as the cornerstone of the generic guidelines.

The MLA-ACLS Language Task Forces Project

Slightly earlier in time, when the financial support of the Rockefeller Foundation and the National Endowment for the Humanities, the Modern Language Association and the American Council of Learned Societies convened the MLA-ACLS Language Task Forces Project. The latter included task forces on Institutional Language Policy, the Commonly Taught Languages, the Less Commonly Taught Languages, Public Awareness, and Government Relations. Recommendations from each task force were produced during the academic year 1977–78 and were available for the first meeting of the President's Commission on Foreign Language and

International Studies in October 1978. Both the Task Force on Institutional Language Policy and the Task Force on the Commonly Taught Languages recommended the establishment of nationally recognized proficiency standards for foreign-language study. Their effect on the philosophy underlying the ACTFL Language Proficiency Guidelines was such that they should be printed in full. The report of the Task Force on Institutional Language Policy reads:

> Recommendation 10. Institutions and, where appropriate, state educational systems should be encouraged by the Modern Language Association to adopt *nationally recognized performance or proficiency standards,* and make such standards known widely to students and faculty.

> Recommendation 12. The Modern Language Association and the American Council on the Teaching of Foreign Languages should secure funding for the *revision and redevelopment of tests for the measurement of proficiencies in the four language skills in all the most commonly taught and wide-use languages.* Such tests should be developed by committees consisting of both secondary school and college teachers.

The explanation for the latter recommendation lists some possible uses for such examinations:

> The proficiency tests should be used for (a) state high school diplomas, (b) special-proficiency certification and teacher certification, (c) college entrance, and (d) college graduation. Schools and colleges should provide graduates who have studied a foreign language with a certificate detailing their proficiency in the four language skills as measured by the proposed scale. [Brod, 1, p. 11]

The first recommendation of the report of the Task Force on the Commonly Taught Languages reads as follows:

> The Modern Language Association and the American Council on the Teaching of Foreign Languages, in association with other professional groups and testing organizations, should develop an *outline of realistic proficiency goals by stages of achievement.*

The report further explains that:

> The purpose of this recommendation is to develop a set of standards whereby achieved proficiency can be demonstrated in ways that are universally accepted and understood, similar perhaps to those used

by the Foreign Service Institute. It is assumed that courses offered at the various levels . . . will require different lengths of time to reach the established goals. [Brod, 1, p. 29]

The President's Commission on Foreign Language and International Studies

On April 21, 1978, the President's Commission on Foreign Language and International Studies (24) joined the general climate of planning for positive change. The commission was charged with four tasks: (1) to recommend how public attention should be directed to the importance of foreign-language and international studies, (2) to assess the need in the United States for foreign-language and area specialists and the job market for such specialists, (3) to recommend what foreign-language and international education programs are appropriate at different levels, and (4) to specify legislative changes needed to implement the commission's recommendations (Burn, 4).

The foreign-language profession will for a long time owe special thanks to Representative Paul Simon of Illinois for bringing to national attention his concern that foreign-language and area studies in the United States were not being pursued to an extent consistent with the Helsinki Accords. Under these Accords, the United States had agreed to "encourage the study of foreign languages and civilizations" in order to increase cross-cultural understanding. According to Burn (4), Simon's efforts coincided with a concern of the State Department and the National Security Council for the nation's capability in foreign areas and training and research. This coalescence of concerns from several sources resulted in the appointment of the commission and in the focusing by the foreign-language profession as a whole on the areas which the commission had been mandated to address.

After a year of study, public hearings, and meetings, the commission presented its report to President Carter on October 15, 1979. Among its recommendations was one that addressed directly the issue of language proficiency. In the Foreign Languages section, the commission included as one of its principal recommendations the establishment of "a National Criteria and Assessment Program, funded by NIE [to] develop foreign language proficiency tests, and report on, monitor, and assess foreign language teaching in the U.S." (24, p. 15). The functions of the proposed National Criteria and Assessment Program are spelled out in the body of the report. The program would "establish language proficiency achievement goals for the end of each year of study, with special attention to speaking proficiency," and would, in addition, develop tests to "assess the proficiency of both students and teachers in existing as well as new or experimental foreign language programs" (24, p. 38). The report goes on to cite the FSI Testing Kit Workshops as a valuable effort to bring techniques of language proficiency assessment to the academic sector that should serve as a base for continued work in this area.

The MLA-ACLS Language Task Forces' Reports and the President's Commission Report, with their recommendations that the profession establish proficiency-based course goals and construct proficiency tests to measure these outcomes, combined with the recommendation of the ETS Common Yardstick Project on the expansion of the lower end of the government oral proficiency scale and the enthusiastic reaction of the participants at the FSI Testing Kit Workshops set the stage for the appearance of the ACTFL Provisional Proficiency Guidelines in 1982.

Elements of a Proficiency-Oriented Program

A proficiency-oriented program is one that trains students to use the language outside the classroom, independently of the materials and activities of the course. The grammatically oriented text, the legacy of Ollendorf and Plötz, has conditioned language teachers to make the *structure* of the language, rather than proficiency in the *use* of the language, the focus of a course of study. Most major textbooks currently in use are organized around a structural or grammatical syllabus. A glance at their contents reveals that they are all organized around grammatical topics, with only minor differences in sequencing. The grammatical syllabus assumes that all students must learn the same representative corpus of the language over the same period of time. Operationally, this leads to a "coverage approach," in which progress is measured in "chapters covered." Warriner (29) discusses the disadvantages to this type of curriculum in her background paper on methodology for the President's Commission.

The functional/notional syllabus

An alternative, the functional/notional syllabus, has been developed and used successfully by the Council of Europe. Such a syllabus organizes the material not by grammatical topics and vocabulary but by the uses to which language can be put. A functional/notional syllabus will include much of the same content as the grammatical syllabus, while organizing it differently. For example, a traditional textbook treats topics such as present tense endings for regular verbs, the formation of adjectives of comparison, or noun-adjective agreement; a functional/notional textbook deals with topics such as asking questions, making suggestions, or expressing disagreement. Teaching grammatical forms at a fixed pace can give the false impression that knowing the forms is equivalent to knowing how, when, and where to use them. The functional/notional syllabus places the forms in contexts in which they can be readily and meaningfully employed.

The grammatical syllabus is inherently analytical; it abstracts one aspect of the language from its many contexts and lays it out for study. The functional/notional syllabus is synthetic; it selects particular linguistic functions in real-life contexts for study. Although compiling an exhaustive list of linguistic functions probably is impossible, and even though the selection of certain functions for particular courses and the sequencing of materials are still in their formative stages, one can see major differences in the two approaches in pedagogy and especially in evaluation.

Valdman (27) counterposes the linear approach of the grammatical syllabus with the cyclical progression suggested by the functional/notional or other communicatively oriented syllabus. In the former, progression is necessarily linear. The structural items are presented in contrived, artificial settings. This results in a heavy grammatical load, difficulty in distinguishing between linguistic features targeted for receptive control versus productive mastery, lack of definition of different levels of mastery, and the absence of authentic texts.

As an alternative to this linear coverage, Valdman (27) recommends a cyclical syllabus. This approach "requires a precise definition of mastery levels at each phase of the instructional program: which features will be targeted for recognition, which for limited productive control . . ., which for use in communicative activities" (p. 19). Integral to this approach is the breaking down of the traditional grammatical paradigms, teaching the various parts separately, and expecting different kinds and degrees of mastery of them at any given time. The cyclical approach involves teaching some features of the paradigm for active mastery and others for comprehension only. The next time through, students get additional practice in the items already studied, work on active use of the items presented passively before, and then study additional features for passive recognition. This allows students to focus on fewer features at a time, to review systematically, and to treat reception and production differently. The cyclical approach works for functions as well as for structures.

Evaluation is a second area that would be treated very differently under a grammatical versus a functional/notional syllabus. A major testing problem with a grammatical syllabus is that it is far easier to list the goals than to describe the desired degree of mastery. A typical Level I high school syllabus lists the following under a heading of "Basic Instructional Objectives" for French, Spanish, and Italian:

1. Regular and irregular verbs—present tense, commands
2. Grammar usage—appropriate idioms and basic grammar
3. Expressions of language: numbers, dates, times, seasons, weather, pronouns, adjectives, cooking, family, sports, classroom, colors, nationalities.

Objectives like these present difficulties for testing. Let us look for an example to one goal for Spanish: "Present tense of regular verbs." We will assume that the Spanish I teacher has used a variety of grammatical explanations, choral repetition, pattern drills, fill-in-the blanks worksheets, and oral exercises to teach and reinforce the use of regular verbs in the present tense.

One of the ground rules in evaluation is that the test should not contain any surprises; it should be a microcosm of the activities and subject matter of the course. One logical way to test mastery of the subject matter of the course described above would be to present students with a series of statements in Spanish with blanks where the verbs belong. The students would fill in the blanks with the correct form of the verb. Another possibility, suggested by Grittner (8), would be to present a series of drawings of activities. Students would then state orally in a complete sentence the activity illustrated in each drawing.

In the first exercise, the teacher would learn whether students knew the verb endings and could match them to a given subject. On this basis would one know that the student had "mastered" the regular verbs in the present tense? The "basic instructional objective" leaves many questions unanswered: Which verbs? How many? Mastery to what degree and to what purpose? There may be little or no carry-over from filling in a blank to evoking and using the same form of the same verb in a less structured situation, such as a composition or a conversation. Students could fill in the blanks of all the sentences on the test, and thus would demonstrate in a discrete-point fashion that they have "mastered the present tense of regular verbs." Yet we have no idea whether or how well they could make themselves understood to native speakers of the language.

A more communicatively oriented test of "regular verbs in the present tense," although no less problematic, is the second exercise described above. One possible format might be to present a picture of a boy talking on the phone. The student who has studied well and remembers lines from the pattern drills may respond correctly, *El muchacho habla por teléfono* (the boy is talking on the phone). What does the teacher do with the student who responds, *Juan **hablo** en teléfono con su amigo Jorge que **es** en el hospital porque **es** enfermo* (John is talking on the phone with his friend George who is in the hospital because he is sick [boldface italic portions represent errors])? This second student perhaps has not "mastered" the objective but certainly has understood that a language is learned to fulfill certain needs or functions, in this case the recounting of an event.

How does the teacher grade these two students? Does the first get a perfect score, and the second a lower one? Should the errors other than the incorrect present tense verb ending "not count," since the test is aimed at a single objective? Or should the second student be rewarded for "creating" with language to express his own thoughts?

One of the disadvantages of behavioral objectives based on a grammatical syllabus is that they encourage a discrete-point "achievement-type" orientation to teaching, testing, and learning. We need to look beyond structured manipulation of bits and pieces of language to the larger goals of language use. Grittner (8) expresses it in this way:

> [If] language use is creative and idiosyncratic, students should be taught to apply to unanticipated situations functional principles that they perceive to be relevant rather than being expected to meet arbitrarily stated objectives based on someone else's formulations of reality. This means, in effect, that such things as grammatical forms, syntactical patterns, and vocabulary items should not be treated as specific, behavioralizable learning "outputs" but rather as tools for receiving and communicating thoughts and feelings. [P. 118]

What kind of evaluation instrument would be appropriate in a proficiency-oriented course? A first-year high school Spanish course designed from this perspective might well have the following as one of its objectives: "Able to ask for directions and other information with sufficient structural and phonological accuracy to be intelligible to a native speaker used to dealing with foreigners." Linguistic *functions*—asking for information and asking for directions—are defined; the *content*—simple facts about a place or a person—while not spelled out, is implied; and the *accuracy* is defined as intelligibility to a sympathetic and linguistically supportive native speaker.

The statement of the objective, including the elements of *function, content,* and *accuracy,* points to a global testing mode. It will be difficult if not impossible to draw up an answer key for such a test, since what is to be elicited from the student is not a preset list of answers but rather variable answers that achieve the purpose of giving or getting information on a given topic. Teachers might profitably decide to set up the test as a role play, putting themselves in the role of the native speaker. Instructions for a role play might look like this:

A friend calls to invite you to a party. In your conversation, be sure to ask the following:
1. When and where the party will take place
2. Directions to the party
3. If your friend wants you to take something (records, refreshments, etc.)

An exchange student from France is at your school for the year. You invite him to spend Saturday afternoon at your house. In your conversation, ask him:
1. If he can come over in the afternoon and stay for dinner
2. If he'd like to go to the movies
3. If his American "brother" would like to come too

A number of such role plays could be constructed with different details but within the general context of an invitation to a social event. No two students would have the identical test, but each would go through the same testing procedure measuring the same linguistic functions in contexts of equal difficulty and including the same requirements of intelligibility.

The ACTFL Guidelines in the Proficiency-Oriented Program

The ACTFL guidelines attempt to take the functional/notional emphasis on language in context for a particular purpose and apply it to the academic setting in the United States. Their point of departure was the proficiency-based approach of the functional/notional syllabus rather than the structural orientation of the grammatical syllabus.

Writing in 1978, Harlow (9) recognized the promise of proficiency-based curricula.

We all know how important it is to develop behavioral objectives for a program and how difficult and time-consuming they can be to formulate. A program using functional/notional organization would almost eliminate that problem, since each unit would be focused around the grammatical structures, vocabulary items, and their use in a particular linguistic function. The ease of testing becomes evident also if we assume that what we want to teach is what we want to test. [P. 562]

The ACTFL guidelines are a first step in creating proficiency-based curricula that respond to the need of the profession to define what students should be able to *do* with the language at various stages in the learning process.

The guidelines are modeled on the ACTFL oral proficiency rating scale, which is in turn an adaptation of the ILR oral proficiency scale. The descriptions of proficiency at each level include statements about linguistic *functions* that the speaker is able to express, about the topics or *content* that can be discussed, and about the degree of *accuracy* of the communicated message. These have been developed for speaking ability by the CIA Language School and are reproduced in Figure 3.

The literature of the last several years, beginning with specific consideration of the functional/notional syllabus and continuing with more general discussions of communicatively oriented curricula, has focused on the need to broaden our understanding of the term "communicative

Level	Functions	Content	Accuracy
ILR Speaking Level		Topics, subject areas, activities, and jobs addressed.	Acceptability, quality, and accuracy of message conveyed.
5	Functions equivalent to an Educated Native Speaker (ENS).	All subjects.	Performance equivalent to Educated Native Speaker.
4	Able to tailor language to fit audience, counsel, persuade, negotiate, represent a point of view, and interpret for dignitaries.	All topics normally pertinent to professional needs.	Nearly equivalent to ENS. Speech is extensive, precise, appropriate to every occasion with only occasional errors.
3	Can converse in formal and informal situations, resolve problem situations, deal with unfamiliar topics, provide explanations, describe in detail, support opinions, and hypothesize.	Practical, social, professional, and abstract topics, particular interests, and special fields of competence.	Errors never interfere with understanding and rarely disturb the ENS. Only sporadic errors in basic structures.
2	Able to fully participate in casual conversations; can express facts; give instructions; describe, report on, and provide narration about current, past, and future activities.	Concrete topics such as own background, family, and interests, work, travel, and current events.	Understandable to NS *not* used to dealing with foreigners; sometimes miscommunicates.
1	Can create with the language; ask and answer questions, participate in short conversations.	Everyday survival topics and courtesy requirements.	Intelligible to an NS used to dealing with foreigners.
0	No functional ability.	None.	Unintelligible.

Figure 3. Functional Trisection

competence" to include more than simply getting the message across. Higgs and Clifford (11) have written that:

> A student cannot merely be declared competent in communication. The functions that he is competent to express must be specified. The degree of proficiency required to survive as a tourist or a student is not the same as that required to negotiate treaties. One finds that content areas and language functions needed for discussing abstract ideas differ from those used in telling about one's immediate needs or one's latest European vacation. . . . We must tell [our students] not that they are competent to speak German, but that they are competent to meet routine physical and social obligations in an environment where German is spoken. [Pp. 60–61]

In the descriptions of proficiency on speaking, listening, reading, writing, and culture in the ACTFL guidelines, *function, context,* and *accuracy* are all interwoven. Judgments of an individual's proficiency, made by comparing performance with the descriptions, take all three factors into account.

These proficiency descriptions were developed empirically, that is, by observing how second-language learners progress in the functions they can express or comprehend, the topic areas they can deal with, and the accuracy with which they receive or convey a message. The guidelines, then, are descriptive rather than prescriptive, based on experience rather than theory. Omaggio (18) points out that the progressive nature of the guidelines makes them a valuable tool for designing curricula.

> Knowing what competencies lie at the *next* level will help us sequence materials to conform to natural developmental patterns in adult second-language learners and prepare them for making progress. The descriptions will also allow us to keep in mind the *ultimate* goal(s) learners hope to achieve. Our instructional materials, as well as the design of our courses, should be influenced by those ultimate goals.

Conclusion: Future Directions

What, then, are the next steps? What can we hope for from the guidelines? There are several directions in which the guidelines take us, and ACTFL is already at work on most of them. These next steps fall into the general categories of (1) further work on the guidelines themselves, (2) curriculum and materials development, (3) testing, and (4) teacher training and certification.

Further work on the guidelines

The ACTFL guidelines as published are still provisional. An important next step in their development will consist of close inspection by the profession and suggestions for change. It is anticipated that alterations will have to be made in the wording and format, as well as in the sequencing of some of the functions. We may also find that the finer distinctions at the lower end of the scale that have been so valuable in the speaking descriptions will not be as operationally useful, or perhaps even measurable, in the receptive skills. The culture guidelines, which have no antecedents in government language training programs will clearly need more informal and formal field testing to see if they are meaningful for instructional purposes. Chapter 5 in this volume, in fact, presents a radical new way of defining "culture" and treating it in the classroom. Finally, the generic guidelines will undoubtedly be generalized still further, or an alternative set will be written to meet the requirements of languages more distant from English.

Curriculum and materials development

The guidelines make no statements about how much each course in a sequence should attempt, about methods or materials that might be used, or about the relative emphasis that should be placed on the various skill modalities. All of these decisions rest with curriculum planners, textbook writers, and teachers. The next step is to design curricula, classroom activities, and materials that are designed to move students from one level of the guidelines to the next. The 1983 ACTFL Summer Institute for Secondary-School Teachers, funded by NEH, was the first organized effort to apply the guidelines to curriculum projects. Chapter 2 in this volume deals with classroom activities, while Chapter 3 details some curriculum development projects now under way at the Foreign Service Institute Language School.

Another step, somewhat more distant but no less important, is the development of proficiency-based materials. College teachers of French and Spanish who participated in the ACTFL/ETS oral proficiency testing workshop at Houston in February of 1982 have reported changing their methods, expectations, and to some degree, their materials as a result of insights gained at the workshop. These changes are reported in depth in Chapter 7 of this volume. It is expected that efforts in this area will continue to grow and be shared through the professional literature until a consensus emerges within the profession to support the development of commercially published basal programs.

Testing

The government oral proficiency interview has needed only minor modifications to be usable in high schools and colleges. Although problems still remain, they are logistical rather than theoretical—how to cope with the demands of time and teacher power that the interview requires. Thirty years of use of and research with the interview have demonstrated that it is a valid and reliable procedure for testing second-language oral proficiency. The next step is to develop similar evaluation procedures to measure attainment of proficiency in the other skill modalities and in culture. Chapter 4 in this volume examines some possibilities along these lines.

At the end of 1982, ACTFL received from the Exxon Foundation an unsolicited grant of $50,000 to establish a model regional assessment center. Such a center, in addition to conducting oral proficiency tests for students, teacher candidates, job seekers, or anyone else interested in obtaining an official oral proficiency rating, could also serve as a site for proficiency workshops and research on and development of proficiency testing in the other skill modalities.

A related issue that will soon have to be addressed is the certification of testers. Through the federally funded training projects that have taken place so far under the auspices of ACTFL, the Illinois Foreign Language Teachers' Association, and the University of New Hampshire, a procedure for training oral proficiency testers has emerged. It includes an intensive four- to five-day workshop with a small enough trainer-participant ratio that each trainee has a chance to conduct several supervised interviews and observe some twenty more, and later conduct twenty-five postworkshop interviews. These interviews are usually conducted in two sets. A portion of the first set is rated and critiqued by the trainers. These critiques are then discussed with the trainees before they conduct their second group of interviews.

Once this training system has been formalized, procedures must be developed for certifying proficient testers, and to recertify them periodically to ensure that they have retained their skills. It is anticipated that the proposed regional assessment centers can provide some of these certification and recertification services.

Teacher training and certification

No one has been able to describe completely the characteristics of the effective teacher, and the experience of the Pennsylvania studies (Smith, 22) cautions us not to assume that a high degree of foreign-language skill alone will make for a competent teacher. Nevertheless, the development of language skills is an important priority in teacher-training programs.

The guidelines can be applied to teacher candidates and other adults, and it is hoped that ultimately all persons whose jobs demand a professional level of language will attain a rating of Superior in the relevant skill areas. A research project currently under way at ETS will result in the development of a self-assessment questionnaire, validated against the oral proficiency interview, that can be used to survey the oral proficiency of secondary school teachers of French and Spanish. This will provide valuable baseline data as we begin to focus on proficiency-based teaching of students, including prospective teachers.

As of this writing, ACTFL and the state of Texas are planning a model proficiency-based foreign-language teacher certification program. As in bilingual teacher certification in a number of states, a teacher candidate's linguistic competence would be measured directly by means of proficiency tests, rather than simply be assumed on the basis of years of study or courses passed.

Summary

This is an exciting time in foreign-language education. Interest in our efforts outside the profession is at a high point that has not been enjoyed since the heydey of the NDEA almost twenty-five years ago. Our understanding of how language is acquired has never been greater, and textbooks, for all we may complain about their imperfections, have never been better. The ACTFL guidelines are one of several important tools that can help us as we work to help our students and ourselves attain a greater level of language proficiency.

References, The ACTFL Proficiency Guidelines: A Historical Perspective

1. Brod, Richard I., ed. *Language Study for the 1980s: Reports of the MLA-ACLS Language Task Forces.* New York: The Modern Language Association, 1980.
2. Brooks, Nelson. "The Meaning of Audiolingual." *Modern Language Journal* 59 (1975):234–40.
3. Brown, Richard W. "Oral Proficiency Testing in New Jersey Bilingual and English as a Second Language Teacher Certification," pp. 65–73 in John L. D. Clark, ed., *Direct Testing of Speaking Proficiency: Theory and Application.* Princeton, NJ: Educational Testing Service, 1978.
4. Burn, Barbara B. "The President's Commission on Foreign Language and International Studies: Its Origin and Work." *Modern Language Journal* 64 (1980):7–8.
5. Carroll, John B. "Foreign Language Proficiency Levels Attained by Language Majors Near Graduation from College." *Foreign Language Annals* 1 (1967): 131–51.
6. Freed, Barbara F. "Establishing Proficiency-Based Language Requirements." *ADFL Bulletin* 13 (1982):6–12.

7. Frith, James R. "Testing the FSI Testing Kit." *ADFL Bulletin* 11 (1979): 12–14.
8. Grittner, Frank M. *Teaching Foreign Languages,* 2nd ed. New York: Harper & Row, 1977.
9. Harlow, Linda L. "An Alternative to Structurally Oriented Textbooks." *Foreign Language Annals* 11 (1978):559–63.
10. Herron, Carol. "Who Should Study a Foreign Language: The Myth of Elitism." *Foreign Language Annals* 15 (1982):441–49.
11. Higgs, Theodore V., and Ray Clifford. "The Push Toward Communication," pp. 57–79 in Theodore V. Higgs, ed., *Curriculum, Competence, and the Foreign Language Teacher.* The ACTFL Foreign Language Education Series, vol. 13. Lincolnwood, IL: National Textbook Co., 1982.
12. Kelly, Louis G. *25 Centuries of Language Teaching.* Rowley, MA: Newbury House, 1969.
13. Lange, Dale L. "Methods," pp. 281–310 in Emma Marie Birkmaier, ed., *Foreign Language Education: An Overview.* The ACTFL Foreign Language Education Series, vol. 1. Lincolnwood, IL: National Textbook Co., 1969.
14. Liskin-Gasparro, Judith E. *ETS Oral Proficiency Testing Manual.* Princeton, NJ: Educational Testing Service, 1982.
15. Livingston, Samuel A. "Setting Standards of Speaking Proficiency," pp. 255–70 in John L. D. Clark, ed., *Direct Testing of Speaking Proficiency: Theory and Application.* Princeton, NJ: Educational Testing Service, 1978.
16. Mallinson, Vernon. *Teaching a Modern Language.* London: Heinemann, 1957.
17. Ollendorf, H. G. *New Method of Learning to Read, Write, and Speak the French Language.* New York: 1846.
18. Omaggio, Alice C. "Methodology in Transition: The New Focus on Proficiency." *Modern Language Journal,* in press.
19. Paquette, F. André, comp. "Guidelines for Teacher Education Programs in Modern Foreign Languages—An Exposition." *Modern Language Journal* 50 (1966):323–424.
20. Plötz, K. *Elementarbuch der französischen Sprache.* New York: 1865.
21. Rivers, Wilga M. *Teaching Foreign-Language Skills,* 1st ed. Chicago: University of Chicago Press, 1968.
22. Smith, Philip D., Jr. "The Pennsylvania Foreign Language Research Project: Teacher Proficiency and Class Achievement in Two Modern Foreign Languages." *Foreign Language Annals* 3 (1969):194–297.
23. Sollenberger, Howard E. "Development and Current Use of the FSI Oral Interview Test," pp. 1–12 in John L. D. Clark, ed., *Direct Testing of Speaking Proficiency: Theory and Application.* Princeton, NJ: Educational Testing Service, 1978.
24. *Strength through Wisdom: A Critique of U.S. Capability. A Report to the President from the President's Commission on Foreign Languages and International Studies.* Washington, DC: U.S. Government Printing Office, 1979.
25. Thompson, Richard T. "Modern Foreign Language Teaching in the Uncommonly Taught Languages," pp. 279–310 in Dale L. Lange, ed., *Pluralism in Foreign Language Education.* The ACTFL Foreign Language Education Series, vol. 3. Lincolnwood, IL: National Textbook Co., 1971.
26. Titone, Renzo. *Teaching Foreign Languages: An Historical Sketch.* Washington, DC: Georgetown University Press, 1968.
27. Valdman, Albert. "The Incorporation of the Notion of Communicative Competence in the Design of the Introductory Foreign Language Course Syllabus," pp. 18–23 in Dale L. Lange, ed., *Proceedings of the National Conference on Professional Priorities.* Hastings-on-Hudson, NY: American Council on the Teaching of Foreign Languages, 1981.

28. Valette, Rebecca M. "Testing," pp. 343–74 in Emma Marie Birkmaier, ed., *Foreign Language Education: An Overview.* The ACTFL Foreign Language Education Series, vol. 1. Lincolnwood, IL: National Textbook Co., 1969.
29. Warriner, Helen P. "Foreign Language Teaching in the Schools—1979: Focus on Methodology." *Modern Language Journal* 64 (1980):81–87.
30. Wilds, Claudia P. "The Oral Interview Tests," pp. 29–44 in Randall L. Jones and Bernard Spolsky, eds., *Testing Language Proficiency.* Arlington, VA: Center for Applied Linguistics, 1975.
31. Young, Howard T. "On Using Foreign Service Institute Tests and Standards on Campuses," pp. 64–69 in James R. Frith, ed., *Measuring Spoken Language Proficiency.* Washington, DC: Georgetown University Press, 1980.

2

The Proficiency-Oriented Classroom

Alice C. Omaggio
University of Illinois

Introduction

The question addressed in this chapter is as old as the language-teaching profession itself: How do we help students learning a second language in a classroom setting become proficient in that language? Historically, the responses to this question have been as varied as the talents and creativity of those who have tried to answer it. And still we feel compelled in the present volume to pose the question again, and to answer it again in the light of our understanding of what we are about as a profession.

Like all fundamental questions, this one is not easily answerable. In the past, responses to this question have been widely divergent. Volumes of material have been written in which new theories of language acquisition have been advanced, new "revolutions" started, and a long succession of "innovative" methods and approaches proposed. This proliferation of ideas has resulted in some extremely valuable insights into the learning and teaching process; it has also left many of us feeling somewhat bewildered, once the dust has settled, about how we are to apply our newly acquired knowledge to change what is going on in the classroom.

This chapter is not designed to raise new dust. It does not propose any new theories or methodologies. Rather, it seeks to extract from our rich heritage of resources and practices those elements that seem most sound and to reevaluate them in terms of the organizing principle of proficiency.

Alice C. Omaggio (Ph.D., The Ohio State University) is an Assistant Professor at the University of Illinois at Champaign-Urbana, where she coordinates elementary and intermediate language courses and supervises teaching assistants. She is the author of three college French texts, and her publications have appeared in various professional journals. She is a member of the ACTFL Executive Council and has served as consultant to the ACTFL/ETS Proficiency Projects. She has received both the Stephen A. Freeman Award and the Pimsleur Award for Research in Foreign Language Education.

By using the ACTFL guidelines as the organizing principle for designing classroom instruction, we obtain a powerful focusing mechanism that enables us to make better sense than we ever have before of the kaleidoscope of methods, techniques, and materials our collective efforts have generated over the past few decades. The guidelines also help us state more precisely the *ultimate* goals learners might hope to achieve in the course of instruction, thereby directing more clearly our daily choice of materials and classroom tasks to ensure that those goals eventually can be met.

The proficiency definitions are ideally suited for organizing instruction for several reasons. First, they are experientially rather than theoretically based. They describe how language learners and acquirers typically function across a range of possible levels of competence, rather than prescribe the way any given theorist thinks learners *ought* to function. Because the guidelines represent actual rather than hypothetical language production, teachers can amend their expectations for students' linguistic and communicative development to conform to reality. The descriptions should prove useful in designing language programs, precisely because they outline for each level of competence described (1) communicative *functions* performed, (2) areas of *content* and situations handled with reasonable ease, and (3) the degree of *accuracy* to which representative grammatical features are mastered.

The guidelines are also ideally suited for organizing instruction because they are progressive. Knowing what competencies lie at the next level helps us sequence materials that conform to natural developmental patterns among adult second-language learners and choose activities that enable them to make progress toward the goals identified at the beginning of instruction.

Perhaps the best reason for using the proficiency definitions as an organizing principle for instruction is that they provide us with a means of defining, in a way that can be universally understood, what it means to "know" a language. Once we identify what students have to know in order to function at or beyond a given level of competence, we will have come a long way toward knowing what we have to teach. The next sections deal in more detail with these issues.

What It Is to Know a Language

What do students have to know—in terms of grammar, vocabulary, sociolinguistic appropriateness, kinesics, cultural understanding, and the like—in order to know a language well enough to use it? Traditionally, answers to this question have been somewhat disparate; in recent years, though still the subject of some debate, they have been coalescing to a point where a consensus may be near. Canale and Swain (5) identify four types of competence that should be considered in any definitions of proficiency.

1. *Grammatical competence,* which implies mastery of the linguistic code;
2. *Sociolinguistic competence,* which addresses the extent to which grammatical forms can be used or understood appropriately in various contexts;
3. *Discourse competence,* involving the ability to combine ideas to achieve cohesion in form and cohesion in thought;
4. *Strategic competence,* involving the use of verbal and nonverbal communication strategies to compensate for gaps in the language user's knowledge of the code or for breakdown in communication for other reasons.

Note the resurgence of the importance of grammaticality, minimized somewhat in the 1970s with the rhetoric surrounding the term "communicative competence." More recent definitions of proficiency, like the ACTFL Provisional Proficiency Guidelines, do include accuracy statements. As Higgs and Clifford (21) point out, the crucial question is not *whether* students can communicate, but *what* they can communicate, and *how well.* The *what* refers to the content (context or topic) and the language functions (tasks) that are to be performed in that context. The *how well* relates to the linguistic accuracy and the cultural authenticity with which the task is carried out. How well learners know a language is measured against these three interrelated criteria of *content, function,* and *accuracy*; and a judgment is made that specifies the range of situations and contexts in which they can expect to function comfortably in the target culture or other settings where the language is used. What it is to know a language, then, becomes a relative thing. The proficiency guidelines describe a hierarchy of competencies that enable us to answer the question more extensively and more precisely than we could until now.

With the guidelines as a frame of reference for determining what students can hope to "know," both at the end of a given course as well as ultimately, we can begin to hypothesize what the proficiency-oriented classroom might be like. It is important to recognize, however, that different approaches may lead to different "ultimate" outcomes. As Higgs and Clifford (21) have noted, it is possible to offer two basic "tracks" in beginning and intermediate instructional sequences. If the program goal is limited to helping students function marginally well in the second language, then a "communicative" track could be designed that would focus on the development of vocabulary, stock phrases, and a certain level of fluency, without much concern for grammatical accuracy. A second "linguistic competence" track might be designed for those who hope eventually to use the language in their profession. Higgs and Clifford warn, however, of the danger of such a two-track option.

What is at issue is whether we opt for a program that produces a terminal 2/2+ or for one that produces a 2/2+ capable of going on . . . to become a 3, a 4, or, in rare cases, even a 5. . . . The danger in the two-track approach ... is that a student who completes the "communicative track" and has become genuinely excited about the target language may find it impossible to switch over. Evidence suggests that four semesters of instruction are enough to produce a terminal profile, and the time needed may in fact be even less than that. [Pp. 75–76]

Higgs and Clifford base their conclusions on their hypothesized "relative contribution model" of oral proficiency and on a preliminary analysis of data generated within a government language school population. While their hypotheses must still be subjected to validation studies, this is true of virtually all current hypotheses relating to adult language acquisition. We do not know precisely how or why people develop terminal profiles, nor how adults acquire and/or learn second languages in either formal or informal settings. The language acquisition/learning controversy is still in the hypothesis-testing stage and may remain so for years to come. Although the question of how adults acquire/learn languages cannot be resolved in this chapter, it is important that we recognize major theoretical positions on this issue and take them into account when discussing what might happen in the classroom. A brief sketch of one major theoretical position, as well as some counter positions, is therefore given in the next section.

How Do Adults Become Proficient in a Second Language?

Undoubtedly the most talked-about theoretical model of language acquisition in recent years has been Krashen's Monitor Model, which continues to evolve as new research studies are carried out to verify and/or modify it. Krashen's most recent version of the theory (29) consists of five hypotheses.

The first of these is the *acquisition/learning distinction,* which states that adults have two distinct and independent ways of developing competence in a second language: through acquisition, a subconscious process similar if not identical to the way children develop ability in their first language; and through learning, a conscious process in which the rules of grammar of the second language and their application in production are learned.

The second is the *natural order hypothesis,* which maintains that natural acquisition of grammatical structures (primarily morphemes) proceeds in a predictable order, even across languages.

Third is the *Monitor hypothesis,* which states that *acquisition* is the sole "initiator" of all spontaneous second-language utterances and is responsible for fluency, while *learning,* i.e., conscious knowledge of rules, functions only as an "editor" or "monitor" for the output. The monitor operates only under conditions where there is sufficient time, the focus is on form, and the language user knows the rule being applied.

Fourth is the *input hypothesis,* which maintains that we acquire language only when we are exposed to "comprehensible input," language that contains structures that are "a little beyond" our current level of competence *(i + 1)* but that are comprehensible through context, knowledge of the world, and other extralinguistic cues. According to this hypothesis, acquirers "go for meaning" first, and as a result, acquire structure as well. A third part of this hypothesis states that input need not be deliberately planned to contain $i + 1$; if communication is successful and there is enough of it, $i + 1$ will be provided automatically. A final part of the input hypothesis maintains that speaking fluency cannot be taught directly; rather, it "emerges" naturally over time. Krashen maintains that although early speech is not grammatically accurate, accuracy will develop over time as the acquirer hears and understands more input. (Note that this last assertion is contrary to the position taken by Higgs and Clifford.)

The fifth and final hypothesis posits the existence of an *affective filter.* Krashen argues that comprehensible input can have its effect on acquisition only when affective conditions are optimal: (1) the acquirer is motivated, (2) he or she has self-confidence and a good self-image, and (3) his or her level of anxiety is low. When learners are "put on the defensive" (Stevick, 64), the affective filter is high, and comprehensible input cannot "get in."

Krashen posits certain implications for classroom practice consistent with his theory, some of which are summarized below.

1. The main function of the classroom may be to provide comprehensible input in an environment conducive to a low affective filter (i.e., high motivation, low anxiety).
2. The classroom is most useful for beginners, who cannot easily utilize the informal—i.e., external or natural—environment for input.
3. The requirements for optimal input are that it be (a) comprehensible, (b) interesting/relevant, (c) *not* grammatically sequenced, (d) provided in sufficient quantity to supply $i + 1,$ and (e) delivered in an environment where students are "off the defensive."
4. Error correction should be minimal in the classroom; it is of some limited use when the goal is learning but of no use when the goal is acquisition. Error correction raises the affective filter and, therefore, should not be used in free conversation or when acquisition is likely to take place.
5. Students should never be required to produce speech in the second language unless they are ready to do so. Speaking fluency cannot be taught; it "emerges" naturally in time with enough comprehensible input.

Many of the hypotheses and assertions in Krashen's theory of second-language acquisition have been challenged by various theoreticians and practitioners. McLaughlin's (37) main objection to the Monitor Model is the acquisition/learning distinction and Krashen's central thesis that what one has "learned" is not available for initiating utterances. McLaughlin finds this both counterintuitive and unsupported by evidence. He suggests an alternative distinction that he maintains is "more empirically based" and that "ties into a general theory of human information processing." This is the distinction between "controlled" and "automatic" processing, roughly parallel to "learning" and "acquisition," yet in some ways different. In controlled processing, the individual activates a temporary sequence of nodes in short-term memory to carry out a cognitive task; such a process requires the individual's active attention, even though he or she may not always perceive the process consciously or be able to verbalize it. In this view of cognitive processing, "learning" is defined as the transfer of information from short-term to long-term memory. Because controlled processes regulate the flow of information into the long-term store, they underlie all learning.

In automatic processing, a sequence of nodes almost always becomes activated in response to a particular input configuration, without necessitating active control or attention by the individual. Automatic processes use a relatively permanent set of associative connections in long-term memory, and once learned, these responses are difficult to suppress or alter.

Since automatic processes (parallel to what Krashen calls acquisition) are learned *after* the earlier use of controlled processes (learning, in many instances in Krashen's view), it seems that the central thesis of the Monitor Model should be reversed. That is, in second-language learning, the initial stage would require the use of controlled processes in order to perform accurately, albeit slowly. But as the material becomes more familiar, automatic processes (acquisition) would develop, so that eventually accurate production would demand less attention and allow for faster and more fluent output (37, p. 318).

McLaughlin is suggesting, in other words, that learners can and do use what they learn in order to generate utterances, and that with practice and repeated application of such learning to one's output, the processing of language production and comprehension eventually becomes "automatic" and quite subconscious. He argues that in learning a second language, the individual works on external input to produce a series of interim grammars, which he calls schemata. These schemata develop in the direction of target language norms; though he maintains that they tend to fossilize for the most part before that norm is ever reached (37, pp. 320–21).

McLaughlin hypothesizes that learners use two types of discovery procedures in building schemata: (1) *acquisition heuristics,* which are fairly universal and include processes such as simplification, generalization, imitation of formulaic or prefabricated routines, and avoidance of unknown or complex structures; and (2) *operating procedures,* which are subject to individual variation and include the use of formal rules, the use of repairs and fillers as conversation tactics, rote memorization or deliberate rehearsal of vocabulary, and cognitive strategies such as contextual guessing or looking for recurring patterns, as well as social strategies, such as seeking out opportunities to speak or hear the target language or counting on others for help (37, pp. 321–25).

In his conclusion, McLaughlin states that Krashen's contention that acquisition is central and learning is peripheral does not, in his view, correspond to experience. He maintains instead that "it is better to speak of controlled processes becoming automatic as they are practiced and committed to long-term store" (p. 327) than to assume that learning can never lead to acquisition, as Krashen maintains.

Seliger (58) also challenges aspects of the Monitor Model, particularly regarding the function of conscious grammar rules as mechanisms for controlling the quality of language learners' production. He argues that conscious rules, either those invented by the learner or those provided by teachers and textbooks, are not likely to function in any reliable way as language production devices or "monitors," since there seems to be no significant correlation between the accuracy of the rule as learned and correct production in the second-language learners he sampled. He does maintain, however, that pedagogical rules can be used successfully as cognitive focusing devices to facilitate acquisition. Specifically, he maintains that they can be useful in language teaching in several ways: (1) they get learners to manipulate, understand, and create with language in an efficient manner; (2) they focus on particular aspects of language that need to be acquired; and (3) they help learners avoid the inefficient testing of false hypotheses as they build their individual grammars of the second languages (i.e., McLaughlin's schemata). This view runs counter to Krashen's assertion that learning grammatical rules and ordering input materials grammatically is of no use in second-language acquisition.

Krashen's critique of Seliger's position brings up the following point: "If rule learning is so often wrong (a point we agree on), how can it be useful as an acquisition focusing device?" (Krashen, 29, p. 121, note 2.) These and other issues must be addressed before we can get a clear picture of how pedagogical rules function in the learning process.

Implicit in the hypotheses advanced by Higgs and Clifford (21) is the belief that teachers need to correct student errors early in instruction if they are to help them avoid early fossilization.

There appears to be a real danger of leading the students too rapidly into the "creative aspects of language use," in that if successful communication is encouraged and rewarded for its own sake, the effect seems to be one of rewarding at the same time the *incorrect* communication strategies seized upon in attempting to deal with the communication situations presented. When these reinforced communication strategies fossilize prematurely, their subsequent modification or ultimate correction is rendered difficult to the point of impossibility. [P. 74]

Although Krashen would not have teachers "push" students into production before they feel they are ready, he does maintain that their efforts at communication should not be corrected when the focus is on meaning. Further, he states that errors will eventually correct themselves. This view clearly runs counter to the hypotheses advanced by Higgs and Clifford.

Until concrete and compelling evidence is provided that accuracy in language production develops without correction of errors and attention to form in adult second-language acquisition, this writer will assume the alternate hypothesis implied in the Higgs and Clifford position: that is, careful error correction and concern for accuracy is important for the eventual development of proficiency beyond Level 2/2+. This means that the teacher who opts for full skill development will need somehow to combine a concern for fostering "communication" with a concern for accuracy early in instruction. This fundamental principle necessarily underlies the design of any approach to language instruction that is truly proficiency oriented.

The Proficiency-Oriented Classroom: Some Preliminary Hypotheses

The first step in characterizing the proficiency-oriented classroom is to examine the guidelines and determine what tasks, contexts, and grammatical features need to be controlled at each level of competence. Such an analysis enables us to form hypotheses about the nature of learning and acquisition activities to be used, and an order in which to use them.

The hypotheses listed below relate to the way classroom instruction might best be organized when the ultimate goal is "Superior" proficiency, i.e., ILR Levels 3–5. In addition, these hypotheses provide a framework around which the activities and materials to be described in subsequent sections can be organized.

The focus of the following sections will be on activities appropriate for Novice, Intermediate, and Advanced levels, though some ideas will be suitable for students at the Advanced Plus Level as well. The discussion will be limited to adult language acquisition and learning, although some parallels can undoubtedly be drawn that will apply to younger learners also. A few ideas for increasing cultural understanding will also be included, although the reader is referred to Chapter 5 for a much more thorough treatment of this topic.

The hypotheses are first listed briefly. Each one is then discussed separately, and model classroom activities are provided that illustrate each principle in operation.

- *Hypothesis 1:* Opportunities must be provided for students to practice using the language in a range of contexts likely to be encountered in the target culture.
  Corollary 1: Students should be encouraged to express their own meaning as early as possible in the course of instruction.
  Corollary 2: A proficiency-oriented approach promotes active communicative interaction among students.
  Corollary 3: Creative language practice (as opposed to exclusively manipulative or convergent practice) must be encouraged.
  Corollary 4: Authentic language should be used in instruction wherever and whenever possible.
- *Hypothesis 2:* Opportunities should be provided for students to carry out a range of functions (task universals) likely to be necessary for interacting in the target language and culture.
- *Hypothesis 3:* There should be concern for the development of linguistic accuracy from the beginning of instruction.
- *Hypothesis 4:* Proficiency-oriented approaches respond to the affective as well as the cognitive needs of students.
- *Hypothesis 5:* Cultural understanding must be promoted in various ways so that students are prepared to understand, accept, and live harmoniously in the target-language community.

Many of the ideas discussed in the next section will be familiar, since this chapter represents an attempt to synthesize existing practice within a proficiency orientation. A few new ideas, recently developed in workshops on proficiency testing, will also be included.

Translating Theory into Practice: Some Sample Activities

Hypothesis 1: Opportunities must be provided for students to practice using the language in a range of contexts likely to be encountered in the target culture. The proficiency-oriented approach will give students, from the beginning of instruction, ample opportunities to learn the language in context and to apply their knowledge to coping with real-life situations.

The first principle is certainly not new in language teaching, at least from a theoretical point of view. Natural language always occurs in some context, both linguistic and extralinguistic. It is obvious that classroom activities and testing procedures should be carried out in a way that resembles real language in use (Wesche, 68; Omaggio, 44).

Slager (62) pointed out a decade ago the need for context and "sentence connectedness" in language practice activities. He quotes Jespersen (24), who in 1904 insisted that "we ought to learn a language through sensible communications" (p. 11). Jespersen saw nearly eighty years ago that "sensible communication" involved a certain connection in the thoughts communicated, implying that language lessons built around random lists of disconnected sentences were unjustifiable. Yet theory is often many years in advance of practice, and many textbooks today present language for practice in non sequiturs. It is certainly the case that a large proportion of classroom tests today still consist of unconnected discrete-point items.

A few sample learning activities, chosen from textbooks, should suffice to illustrate the point that noncontextualized practice is a far cry from "real language." In 1904, Jespersen illustrated this point with the following excerpt from a nineteenth-century French reader:

1. My aunt is my mother's friend.
2. My dear friend, you are speaking too rapidly.
3. That is a good book.
4. We are too old.
5. This gentleman is quite sad.
6. The boy has drowned many dogs.

Contemporary textbooks are certainly much better conceived on the whole than was the one from which the above excerpt was taken. Unfortunately, disconnected and disjointed language practice activities can still be found in abundance in modern texts. The following is an example from a popular French text (Rassius, 50), published only three years ago. The exercise is designed to teach students how to use the subjunctive. A translation is provided below the sample.

Modèle: Il perd son accent. (Il faut que)
         Il faut qu'il perde son accent.

1. Tu attends tes amis. (Je suis content que)
2. Vous étudiez toutes les leçons. (Il veut que)
3. Vous partez avant ce soir. (Il veut que)
4. Il choisit de belles chemises. (N'es-tu pas contente que)
5. Francine remplit la carte. (Il sera absolument nécessaire que)
6. Nous passons l'aspirateur sur le tapis. (Il faut que)
                        etc.

Model: He's losing his accent. (It is necessary that)
         It is necessary that he lose his accent.

1. You are waiting for your friends. (I am happy that)
2. You are studying all the lessons. (He wants)
3. You are leaving before this evening. (He wants)
4. He's choosing some beautiful shirts. (Aren't you glad that)
5. Francine fills out the card. (It will be absolutely necessary)
6. We're vacuuming the carpet. (It's necessary that)
                        etc.

The following exercise from a different recent French text (38) illustrates how essentially the same grammatical exercise can be placed in a larger context. In this text, lessons are organized around a central theme, and all activities, explanations, readings, and cultural commentaries relate to that theme. The larger context for the sample item below is politics.

Une discussion politique. Que peut-on dire à propos du Président, des sénateurs, des députés et de la politique en général? Suivez le modèle.

Modèle: M. Leclerc/souhaiter/que/partis de gauche/être plus/agressif.
M. Leclerc souhaite que les partis de gauche soient plus agressifs.

1. Mme Leclerc/vouloir/les députés/supprimer/impôts.
2. M. Lévêque/exiger/sénateurs/obéir/à/la loi.
3. Mlle Deneuve/préférer/Président/parler/intelligemment.
4. Les Duval/désirer/Président/prendre/électeurs/au sérieux.
5. Mme D'Aubigny/exiger/sénateurs/devenir/plus honnête.
6. M. Duchamp/vouloir/bien/nous/agir/de façon/plus/libéral.

A Political Discussion. What can one say about the President, senators, representatives, and politics in general? Follow the model.

Model: Mr. Leclerc/hope/that/leftist parties/be/more/aggressive.
Mr. Leclerc hopes that the leftist parties will be more aggressive.

1. Madame Leclerc/want/the representatives/eliminate/taxes.
2. Mr. Lévêque/insist/senators/obey/law.
3. Mademoiselle Deneuve/prefer/President/speak/intelligently.
4. The Duvals/want/President/take/electorate/seriously.
5. Madame D'Aubigny/insist/senators/become/more/honest.
6. Mr. Duchamp/really/want/we/act/in a more liberal fashion.

[Muyskens et al., 38, p. 415]

The second sample exercise is roughly equivalent in difficulty and structure to the first. But while the sentences in the first example would hardly be said in sequence in a real-world situation, the sentences in the second could easily be said in summarizing one's political views. The use of the subjunctive to express volition, preference, and other emotions is also bound to occur naturally in a political context. For these reasons, the second activity is much more natural than the first, although it is still highly structured and focused on a particular grammatical point.

Both activities described above could be thought of as "precommunicative." That is, they both focus primarily on forms and are structured to prepare students to use those forms in communicating their own meanings in subsequent language practice activities (see Corollary 1, below). The fundamental difference between noncontextualized and contextualized drills is that the latter link form with meanings that language users might genuinely want to convey in a natural communicative situation. In designing structured, precommunicative practice, contextualized drills are clearly preferable for this reason.

The belief that such structured, precommunicative practice is needed to some extent in a proficiency-oriented approach can be defended if one adopts the positions on language acquisition in adults of McLaughlin (37), Seliger (58), or Higgs and Clifford (21). Higgs and Clifford concluded that if accuracy is one of the goals of instruction, students need to pass first through a period of meaningful, yet structured or "heavily monitored" practice, in order to move toward more open-ended communication. For this reason, they argue against approaches that push too soon for unconstrained communication. This point of view, as well as McLaughlin's (37) hypothesis that language learning involves the gradual shift from conscious control to automatic processing, is echoed by Littlewood (33):

> At first, when a learner needs to communicate through the foreign language, he must search consciously for words in most of the situations he encounters. One reason for this is that many of the lower-level processes are not sufficiently automatic to unfold without his conscious control. . . . Gradually, however, if he gains adequate experience, he increases the range of situations in which he can perform without consciously attending to the linguistic medium. He becomes more capable of devoting his conscious decision-making processes to the level of meaning and of letting the lower-level linguistic operations take care of themselves. [P. 442]

Littlewood suggests that classroom activities be designed to follow a sequence in which meaning gradually plays a greater role. He characterizes linguistic activities along a continuum that progresses through the following types: (1) primary focus on form; (2) focus on form (plus meaning); (3) focus on meaning (plus form); and (4) primary focus on meaning. Type 1 activities should be kept to an absolute minimum in proficiency-oriented approaches. Contextualized and meaningful drills (type 2 activities) allow students to practice specific structures or vocabulary in a way that has some psychological reality and communicative value, and should therefore be used as soon as possible in the early levels of instruction—preferably from the first day of class. Open-ended, creative, and personalized practice (types 3 and 4) should follow this structured practice as soon as possible in a proficiency-oriented approach (see Corollaries 1 through 3).

Higgs and Clifford (21) suggest that this gradual shaping of learners' production can be posited as an "output hypothesis" analogous to Krashen's input hypothesis.

> Students may acquire oral skills when they are encouraged to use the target language in communicative tasks that are just beyond their productive competence. When the communication demands made upon students are too far beyond their current competence, they are forced to adopt or invent communication strategies that lead to fossilization and ultimately prove self-defeating. [P. 78]

Therefore, it is important that the teacher coordinate the communicative tasks with students' current level of linguistic sophistication. This point will be illustrated further under Corollaries 1, 2, and 3.

Some appropriate contexts for structured practice can be gleaned from the ACTFL Provisional Proficiency Guidelines at the Novice, Intermediate, and Advanced levels. In designing language practice activities, it is important to introduce comprehensible material from slightly higher proficiency ranges so that students become familiar with it receptively, prepare themselves to deal with it, and thus anticipate further productive progress. Since comprehension generally precedes production in language acquisition, students can typically understand material that is more advanced than material they can consistently and accurately produce. Some of the contexts to be included in beginning courses can be chosen from the Novice and Intermediate ranges: basic travel and survival needs, daily social encounters, and school- or work-related situations. Students also need to know how to handle simple question-and-answer situations and discuss or write about concrete topics, such as their own background, family, and interests. Additional content areas that might be addressed in beginning and intermediate courses include routine money matters, transportation schedules, prices, understanding and giving directions, and current events. In designing contextualized practice, Slager (62) suggests the following principles.

1. The situation depicted should be relevant and immediately useful to the learners.
2. The content should reflect the level of sophistication of the student and his or her knowledge of the world.
3. The language is, at all times, natural, respecting the "conditions of elicitation" of certain types of structures in natural language use.
4. Answers required of students should have "truth value."
5. Characters used in items are "realistic" in that they have personality and relate to the learners' experience in some way.

6. Items respect sociolinguistic norms.
7. The language sample is short enough so that students have little difficulty in remembering it, but long enough to provide the necessary context.

These same principles should be kept in mind in designing open-ended and creative practice activities also. Some samples of structured activities built around such contexts are illustrated. Hereafter, illustrative examples will be given in English only.

Sample Exercise A

Context: Discussing daily schedules, personal events.
Grammar topic: Practicing times and the past tense.

Activities and Daily Tasks. At the end of the day Sylvaine is telling her husband Jérôme some of the things she has done during the day. Using the cues indicated, describe her activities.

Model: 10:00 / call Suzanne ⟶ At 10:00 I called Suzanne.

1. 9:00 / start to work on my article
2. 11:30 / send a letter to my parents
3. 12:15 / leave the house to go into town
4. 12:30 / eat at the restaurant with some friends
5. 3:00 / correct homework

etc.

[Adapted from Jarvis et al., 22, p. 94]

Sample Exercise B

Context: Social conventions and rules of behavior.
Grammar: The imperative in negative and affirmative sentences.

The Code of Conduct for Guests. Do you know the rules of a very widespread social game—the evening get-together at the home of friends or "important" people of your acquaintance? Here is a list of things to do or to avoid if one is invited to one of these gatherings. Put the rules of conduct in the imperative, using the affirmative or negative, according to your opinion.

1. to arrive on time
2. to bring your dog
3. to put your feet on the furniture
4. to eat everything offered you
5. to drink lots of wine

6. to be in a good mood
7. to tell dirty jokes
8. to act like you're having fun even if you're bored
9. to discuss people who aren't there
10. to leave right after dinner
11. to offer to do the dishes
12. to say "thank you" before leaving

In all of the above examples, the language, though still somewhat stilted because of the focus on structural practice, respects the "conditions of elicitation" mentioned by Slager (62). That is, the forms elicited from students in these precommunicative contextualized drills would naturally occur in those same contexts in normal conversation. The "stiffness" of the structured responses will disappear in the open-ended activities to be discussed in the next sections.

A summary of activity formats for meaningful, precommunicative drilling follows here, with a few sample illustrations, for those interested in designing activities of this type to supplement their own texts. In all these drills, understanding the meaning is necessary in order to carry out the activity. Sometimes students will need more processing time for this type of activity, since choice is often involved—that is, multiple answers within a given range are acceptable. Therefore, the pace of such exercises may be slower than that maintained for "rapid-response" drills of the purely manipulative type.

1. Word association. Given a stimulus word, students are asked to think of related words. This type of exercise is excellent for learning vocabulary in meaningful clusters, for helping students improve their memory for new vocabulary, and ultimately for increasing their fluency and flexibility.

2. Forced choice. Otherwise known as either/or questions, this type of exercise allows students who are not quite ready for open-ended exercises to latch on to appropriate structures in the question to provide their own answer. Such a format can easily be personalized as well as meaningful.

3. Matching. Students match sentences or sentence fragments in Column A with appropriate material (associated words, rejoinders, or completions) in Column B. This requires students to understand the stimulus sentences in order to find the logical match. The following sample activity is used as a comprehension check on a reading in a beginning Spanish text.

1. The popularity of Mexican cuisine in the U.S. is evident	a. is probably the most famous Mexican dish in the U.S.

2. Some Mexican restaurants	b. is used in tacos and enchiladas.
3. The tortilla	c. because there are lots of restaurants that serve it.
4. Chopped meat	d. offer Americanized dishes.
5. Chili sauce is used	e. is the essential part of Mexican cooking.
6. The taco	f. in order to make enchiladas.
7. The Texans	g. are responsible for the invention of the burrito.

[Adapted from Knorre, et al., 28, p. 183]

4. Logical conclusions. In this type of exercise, students read or hear a short passage and decide whether an additional sentence follows logically. Again, the student must understand all the expressions used in order to make the decision necessary in the exercise. The following sample is taken from a series of exercises in which the focus is on university student life.

Logical or Illogical? Correct the sentences that are illogical.

Model: I'm hungry. I ask for a Coke. This is not logical. I'm thirsty. I ask for a Coke.

1. The teacher is very competent. He is always wrong.
2. Paul almost always passes his exams. He's lucky!
etc.

[Adapted from Muyskens et al., 38, p. 99]

5. Logical questions. Students are required to think of an appropriate question for a given statement—that is, to come up with some possible questions that would have *elicited* a particular statement. This exercise type is useful for practicing question formation, an Intermediate Level function (ILR 1).

6. Definitions. A paraphrase of a new vocabulary word is given, and students must identify the word from the definition. A more challenging activity requires the reverse process. In either case, the exercise is good for improving memory for vocabulary, processing information meaningfully, and learning to paraphrase—an Intermediate (ILR 1) function.

7. Completions and cloze adaptations. These tasks require meaningful processing, while affording practice in using specific structures deleted, such as verbs, prepositions, adverbs, and the like.

8. Direct and indirect translation. Translation exercises are valuable for encouraging attention to detail, increasing memory, and providing diagnostic feedback to both teachers and students. Translations can be made to resemble natural interpreting situations that students might encounter in the target culture when traveling with American friends. The example below takes place at a hotel reception desk.

A Message. You are working at an Italian hotel. An English tourist phones the hotel but the proprietor isn't there. Give the message in Italian to the proprietor on his or her return.

"Mrs. Longworth is going to arrive tomorrow with her son and daughter. They plan to arrive before dinner, and they wonder if they can have a connecting room with a bath and twin beds in one of the rooms. . . ."

9. Visual-based exercises. Students can be asked to describe a picture, write captions, answer questions, etc., using a visual stimulus provided by the teacher. Drills of this type encourage vocabulary recall, since no written or oral stimulus is provided as a retrieval cue. They also can be used in open-ended as well as structured practice activities.

10. Slash sentences (telegraphic cues). Sometimes called "dehydrated" sentences, this type of exercise requires students to create full discourse from the essential elements. The activity illustrated on page 53 is an example of this.

11. Sentence combining. Simple sentences must be joined into more complex, "sophisticated" discourse in this type of activity. Students are encouraged to say or write sentences that involve embedded clauses, so that they learn to create natural speech or writing. Research by Cooper (9) and his associates in recent years has shown that practice in sentence combining does indeed help foreign-language learners to develop "syntactic maturity" in their speaking and writing so that they resemble native discourse more closely. It should also be useful in helping students develop oral discourse skills as their proficiency approaches Advanced and Superior levels. The activity types above are described in more detail in Muyskens and Omaggio (39), in Omaggio (42), and in Birckbichler and Omaggio (2).

It is important to remember that sequencing activities for practice is almost as important as designing contextualized practice in the first place. It would be best to integrate the whole sequence of lesson materials into a single theme, context, or situation, at least in designing one class day's work or a unit of study, instead of jumping from one content or topic to another. The latter practice is the norm in many language classes in which course materials are not contextually or thematically organized.

Corollary 1: Students should be encouraged to express their own meaning as early as possible in the course of instruction. Approaches that emphasize the use of rote imitation, extensive memorization, and manipulative practice in the beginning phases of instruction are not as easily adapted to proficiency goals as those that encourage personal expression and early creative language use. Only at the Novice Level do learners work almost exclusively with memorized material. To reach the Intermediate range of proficiency (ILR 1), learners must be able to create with the language and form their own responses and questions.

The activity types illustrated below have as their goal the eventual development of autonomous and creative expression through personalized language practice. In many cases, the practice is still somewhat structured, making it conducive to early use in class following some contextualized precommunicative practice. In other cases, the personalized practice is more open-ended. This latter type of practice is best sequenced after structured activities have been tried, so that students are not led prematurely into communicative situations for which they are not linguistically prepared. The following types of activities represent some of the formats that are conducive to personalized practice.

1. Personalized questions. This is the most familiar format for personalization. Students answer questions directed to them as real people. Questions are normally open-ended, but there is enough guidance provided to help shy or reluctant students to express their point of view. Personalized questions can be asked of individual students in a whole-class format, or by students in pairs or small groups. If the latter course is taken, a followup activity in which answers are reported back to the whole class is useful for several reasons. It encourages students working in small groups to be task oriented. In addition, it shows them that their answers are of interest to others and are to be remembered. Finally, it allows students to transform the answers into the third person, which helps them develop the ability to narrate or report facts, feelings, or preferences—language functions that are important in order to reach Intermediate (ILR 1) proficiency. Ways to encourage group interaction and paired practice are explored in the discussion under Corollary 2.

2. Personalized completion. Students complete a series of sentences or restore a paragraph according to their own point of view. This type of activity can be done as early as the first few chapters of a beginning text if it is quite structured. The more open-ended example given below is structured around reflexive verbs in German and deals with expressing one's personality through feelings and reactions in a variety of circumstances. Students should be encouraged to think of multiple possibilities to complete each sentence.

1. Ich schäme mich über. . .   (I'm ashamed of. . .)
2. Ich beeile mich wenn. . .   (I hurry when. . .)
3. Ich amüsiere mich wenn. . .   (I have a good time when. . .)
4. Ich argere mich weil. . .   (I get angry because. . .)
5. Ich kümmere mich um. . .   (I care about. . .)
6. Ich freue mich auf. . .   (I'm looking forward to. . .)

[From Omaggio, 42, p. 49]

An example that provides a discourse-length frame in which students insert their own elaborative remarks is given in the following example, adapted from one of the early lessons in a beginning college French text (Rochester et al., 54). This example involves description of the student's home and his or her preferred activities in different places in the house.

At my house. Complete the following paragraph to describe your house and family.
The room that I prefer is _____ because _____. I spend a lot of time in _____. I feel very calm in _____ because _____. I work well in _____ and I study in _____ because _____. I eat in _____ and I have a phone in _____. My family spends a lot of time in _____ because _____. [P. 114]

Students can complete the passage using vocabulary for rooms of the house and simple verb phrases; yet the passage is very personal and provides content for comparisons and discussion. A more advanced example, in which students try to persuade others in the class to buy an imaginary product, encourages students to develop their elaborative skills and use their imagination.

Ladies and Gentlemen, I bring you what you've all been waiting for: an elixir for long life that is called _____. This marvelous potion was discovered by _____, the great _____ specialist. This revolutionary product has many advantages and I will only tell you about several of them _____. If you don't believe me, ask _____. Since he's been taking our treatment, he _____. But watch out, this product is very concentrated; only take _____ each day; if not you risk _____.

etc.

[From Jarvis et al., 22, cited in Birckbichler, 1, p. 47]

Students should be invited to share their completions with the rest of the class for each of the activities described in this section.

3. Sentence builders. Using elements of sentences provided in columns, students make their own statements, choosing whichever elements they wish. As Birckbichler (1) points out, the guidance and structure inherent in sentence-builder activities make them especially useful for beginning language classes; students can feel successful at expressing quite a number of ideas and original statements within a very limited grammatical and lexical corpus.

> *Example:* Talk about some of the things you like to do during the week and on weekends by combining elements from each of the columns below. You can also mention things you don't like to do. Feel free to add your own vocabulary to express your meaning.

On Mondays	I like	go to school
On Tuesdays	I love	play tennis
On Fridays	I don't like	watch television
On Sundays	I hate	study
At night	I have	go to the movies
	I want	read a novel
		play the piano
		telephone my friends
		write letters
		do the cooking
		clean the house

4. Personalized true/false. Also known as "agree or disagree," this adaptation of the true/false format allows students to react to controversial statements either by stating simply whether they agree or disagree or by modifying any statement with which they disagree to make it congruent with their own views. Besides encouraging students to process each statement for meaning, this task allows them to respond to terms of the "truth value" the statement holds for them personally. This activity can be used successfully with students who are at Novice or Intermediate levels, as well as with students at higher levels. At the Novice Level, students can simply respond by restructuring the stimulus sentence in the negative, or with substitution of a word or phrase. At higher levels, they can be asked to defend at greater length their point of view, building strategies for supporting opinions—a Superior (ILR 3) function.

The formats mentioned in this section are only a small sampling of possible personalized language practice activities. Ideas for this type of practice abound in the literature, and most are not new to the creative language teacher. Intermediate reading texts with personalized practice have been published in the last several years that contain a wealth of activities, for example, Jarvis et al. (23); Lett et al. (32); and Ratliff et al. (51). Other good sources of personalized practice activities are Boylan and Omaggio (4); Candlin (6); Christensen (8); Joiner and Westphal (25); Kettering (27); Littlewood (34); Paulston and Selekman (45); Stanislawczyk and Yavener (63); and Zelson (70).

Corollary 2: A proficiency-oriented approach promotes active communicative interaction among students. The use of small-group and paired communicative practice has several advantages in terms of building proficiency. First, it allows students more class time to develop oral skills, since everyone is producing language during group work. Second, working with peers takes some of the pressure off students, who often feel intimidated by the need to perform in front of the whole class. Small-group activities can lower the affective filter, hypothesized by Krashen (29) to affect acquisition significantly. Third, group activities can increase the quality of communication by creating legitimate "information gaps," requiring effective, natural communication while encouraging simultaneously the development of certain language functions. A few such examples are given below. The activities illustrated are grouped under three categories: (1) group puzzles, (2) group decision making, and (3) social interaction (mingling) activities. For a description of eleven games and simulations of this type, see Omaggio (43).

Group Puzzles

La ville inconnue (Unknown City)

Purpose: To produce and synthesize multiple clues in the second language in order to solve a problem.
Proficiency goal: To develop skill in giving and receiving accurate information about locations and directions.
Functions: Giving and understanding directions, interpreting and giving instructions, describing locations, reading maps.
Grammatical features: Prepositions of place.
Play: Each student in a group of three is given an incomplete map of La Ville Inconnue (see Figure 1) and one of three information cards. Students must share the information on their cards with one another and then synthesize the group's collective information to locate the missing places on the map. A sample information card is given below. Note that although the activity takes place in French, the card is in English.

Card 1

Using the following words and expressions, give the members of your group the following information in French about locations on the map of La Ville Inconnue.
    1. The post office is next to the Youth Center and across the street from the Café de la Paix.   2. The restaurant "La Tour d'Argent" is across the street from the church on the Avenue du Musée.   3. The movie theater is next to the Maison des Jeunes.

Students will have to pool their information in order to fill out the city map, since some of the information is dependent on what others in the group have to contribute. This give and take of information encourages cooperation and active listening and helps students improve their memory for vocabulary and short phrases, as they are required to retain several facts in their attempt to solve the problem.

Group Decision Making

Le jeu du budget (The Budget Game)

Purpose: To develop fluency and flexibility in speaking, as group members make collective decisions to solve a problem.
Proficiency goals: To increase fluency and flexibility in speaking and develop listening comprehension skills.
Functions: Obtaining and sharing information, dealing with money, persuading and arguing, expressing personal preferences, influencing others' behavior, and responding to others' attempts to persuade.
Grammatical features: Numbers, conditional sentences, subjunctives.
Structure of the game: Students work in groups of three. Each group represents the LeClerc family. The group goal is for the family to come out at the end of the month with the budget in the black. The individual goal for each family member is to be the most influential person by successfully persuading others to spend money as he or she prefers.

Full directions for play, as well as playing pieces and game materials are available from the ACTFL Materials Center (Harbour, 20). This game assumes that students are at the Intermediate High or Advanced level, and that they have been introduced to strategies for reading and understanding classified ads and for writing checks in French. (The game includes lesson materials to prepare students for play.)

Another group decision-making activity, in which students in the role of tourists in a French town must make collective decisions about how to

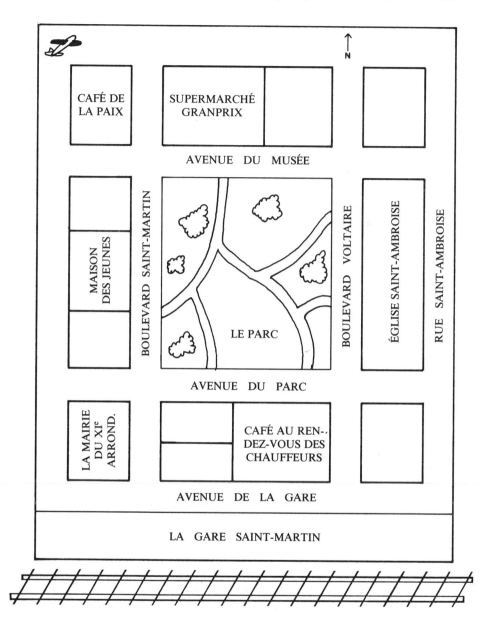

Figure 1. La Ville Inconnue

get French currency, food, lodging, and other survival needs met, will be described under Hypothesis 2.

Social Interaction (Mingling)

Guess Who's Coming to Dinner?

Purpose: To encourage students to use the target language in order to (a) find a dinner partner who has ordered certain foods and (b) convey to others information about one's own menu.

Proficiency goals: To develop vocabulary relating to foods and to build question-asking skills. (Novice and Intermediate ranges.)

Functions: Inquiring about and sharing personal facts and preferences; discussing foods.

Grammatical features: Interrogative words and expressions; partitive vs. definite and indefinite articles in French.

Play: This game is played on the same principle as *Mais vous êtes ma femme!,* developed by Sandra Savignon for the Teacher's Edition of *Voix et Visages de la France* (Coulombe, 10). Students circulate around the classroom in search of someone who has a particular menu matching the one they have on their own playing card. The playing cards, illustrated in the sample below, list foods and beverages ordered by the student himself and by the person for whom he is searching (his "mystery" dinner companion). Students find their dinner partners through questioning one another about each item on the menu. Only when *all* items match has the player successfully completed the search.

Teachers can prepare sets of cards, one for each student in the class, by following the format given in these samples.

Card 1			
You		*Your partner*	
roast beef	baked potato	fish	rolls
red wine	coffee	white wine	coffee
peas	apple pie	green beans	no dessert

Card 2			
You		*Your partner*	
fish	rolls	roast beef	baked potato
white wine	coffee	red wine	coffee
green beans	no dessert	peas	apple pie

For each playing card, a matching card listing the foods in reverse order is needed. Foods can be given on the cards in the native language or in the target language. If the former procedure is used, students need to recall target-language vocabulary. Menus on cards should be quite similar, varying only in one or two details, so that finding one's partner is not too easy. A slightly more complicated version of the game has students locate several other people in their "party," which could include three, four, or five individuals. Obviously, menus should correspond to those typical of the target culture. The above examples have a distinct American flavor and are used to illustrate the concept of the game. In actual play, target-language menus should be designed to help students learn about eating customs and preferences in the target culture. Students should ask questions that show they understand both the typical parts of the meal and the order in which foods are eaten.

Other small-group and paired activities. The above examples provide a sampling of what can be done in groups to increase interaction among students in the classroom. Many good suggestions for creating activities for group practice are available in the literature of the past decade. For example, Lett (31) has created a manual that includes a comprehensive discussion of principles of grouping and guidelines for effective use of small-group instruction in the classroom.

Two more activity formats—interviews and role plays—are mentioned briefly below. They are among the more popular small-group formats currently used by classroom teachers.

Interviews and conversation cards. The use of interviews as a strategy for promoting conversation has been popular in language teaching for many years. Usually, students interview one another in pairs: one student asks questions provided by the text or by the teacher (through indirect translation or directed dialogue) while the second answers according to his or her own thoughts or preferences. Students may then exchange roles. Teachers often have students take brief notes on their partners' responses, or invite several students to report back interesting answers at the end of the interview process.

Bonin and Birckbichler (3) suggest the use of structured interview cards to promote conversation among beginning and intermediate students. Their ideas have led to a variety of adaptations that have proved extremely useful in achieving a blend of "communication" with a concern for accuracy. The following interview cards illustrate how three students can be involved in a conversation that is "self-monitoring." The students holding cards 1 and 2 ask each other the questions they have before them, *as well as any additional followup questions they can think of* once their partner has answered. Student 3 is responsible for checking the accuracy of the questions asked, as well as for providing cues for his classmates when they are unable to formulate their questions, thus serving as the group "monitor." By making students responsible for helping their peers pose accurate questions, the accuracy goal can be fostered in a depressurized atmosphere where communication is also taking place. The cards in this sample relate to the theme of sports and leisure-time activities.

Card 1

Ask your partner . . .
  what sport he/she likes
  if he/she plays basketball
  if he/she prefers skiing or golf
  if he/she plays tennis
Feel free to ask any followup questions
that occur to you during your interview.

Card 2

Ask your partner . . .
  if he/she is athletic
  if he/she likes basketball
  if he/she plays golf
  if he/she prefers tennis or football
Feel free to ask any followup questions
that occur to you during your interview.

Card 3 (Monitor)
Questions for Card 1
1. Quel sport aimez-vous (aimes-tu)?
2. Jouez-vous (joues-tu) au basketball?
3. Préfèrez-vous (préfères-tu) faire du ski ou jouer au golf?
4. Jouez-vous (joues-tu) au tennis?

Questions for Card 2
1. Etes-vous (es-tu) sportif (-ve)?
2. Aimez-vous (aimes-tu) le basketball?
3. Jouez-vous (joues-tu) au golf?
4. Préfèrez-vous (préfères-tu) le tennis ou le football?

Note: Be careful to accept other question types
your partners may use, such as "Est-ce que . . ." or
questions with intonation.

Students should be encouraged to seek help from the teacher, who circulates among the groups working simultaneously on the cards, whenever they need additional vocabulary or have questions about the acceptability of either questions or responses. This interview technique has been used very successfully in beginning and intermediate college classes at the University of Illinois, and students have repeatedly mentioned this versatile activity format favorably in course evaluations.

Situational role plays. Some excellent ideas for using role plays can be found in Zelson (70), as well as other sources mentioned earlier in this chapter. In role plays, a situation is presented to a small group of students who may prepare their parts, if necessary, and then act them out for the rest of the class or record them on videotape for playback later. Role plays can be used with students at virtually any proficiency level. For those at the Novice Level, highly structured role-play cards can be designed with vocabulary hints or partial dialogues given, based on either material already covered in class or the simplest survival situations. For Intermediate learners, role plays can be designed around typical survival situations such as the following.

> You are at the railroad station. You go to the ticket counter.
>
> 1. Ask if there are any trains for Frankfurt.
> 2. Find out when the next one leaves.
> 3. Buy a one-way coach ticket.

One student can play the role of the ticket agent and the other the role of the traveler, or the teacher can play the role of the agent. (For additional ideas about using basic situations, see the discussion under Hypothesis 2.)

At higher levels of proficiency, role plays can introduce a conflict wherein someone has to persuade someone else to act in a certain way, talk his way out of trouble, or make a complaint. Zelson (70) gives the following example.

> Your family and another family have gone on vacation together and rented a cottage. As might be expected, your friendship has been subjected to somewhat of a strain after two weeks of togetherness. At last it is over. Complain to and about each other: i.e., eating habits, housework, children, etc. [P. 52]

As Zelson points out, role plays can be derived from lesson content (themes) and can be either structured around specific grammar points or open-ended. Teachers should be careful to present role-play situations that are at an accessible level of difficulty for students if the activity is to succeed at building proficiency. The ACTFL/ETS guidelines should help teachers make this sort of decision for their classes.

Corollary 3. Creative language practice (as opposed to exclusively manipulative or convergent practice) must be encouraged. Students who hope to advance in their skills beyond the Novice range must learn to create with the language. They must be encouraged to paraphrase, think divergently, and let their imagination and creative ability function as fully as possible within the limits of their linguistic competence. Birckbichler (1) has compiled an extremely valuable set of suggestions for creative language practice. Basing her definition of creativity on Guilford's Structure-of-Intellect Model (Guilford, 17), she posits four types of divergent production factors that relate to the development of creative language behavior: (1) *fluency*, the ability to produce a large number of ideas in a given period of time; (2) *flexibility*, the ability to produce a diversity of ideas belonging to different classes; (3) *elaboration*, the ability to add to or embellish a given idea or set of ideas; and (4) *originality*, the ability to produce uncommon, unconventional, or clever ideas. Drawing on sources from various fields of research on creativity, Birckbichler (1) presents sixty-four classroom activities related to these four factors. Four exercise types illustrating these factors are presented below.

For *fluency*, students make up as many questions as possible for interviewing any real or imaginary person. They can be given a few broad questions as a starter, and then they develop subquestions in each area. For *flexibility*, an isolated sentence such as "Your three minutes are up, sir" is presented, and students think of as many different circumstances as they can in which that sentence might have been uttered. This can be especially valuable when dealing with popular sayings, proverbs, etc. For *elaboration*, students can pick up on a reading or a listening exercise and imagine either what would come next or what might have preceded the anecdote. Throughout these exercises, students can be encouraged to specify sociolinguistic aspects of the utterance such as the tone or mood of the speakers, the setting, the purpose of the utterance, and the status or roles of the speakers involved. For *originality*, a sentence-builder format can be used to create bizarre questions, which can then be used in a question-answer exercise or as the basis for creating a short story, as the following example shows.

Example: The Sentence Inventor

Why did the	put a/an	in his/her/the
1 general	1 five francs	1 pocket
2 president	2 cat	2 motor
3 concièrge	3 tiger	3 drawer
4 dancer	4 kilo of sugar	4 suitcase
5 bandit	5 pistol	5 purse
6 signer	6 billiard ball	6 trunk
7 policeman	7 hard-boiled egg	7 satchel
8 beggar	8 bottle	8 refrigerator
9 plumber	9 hammer	9 toolbox
0 teacher	0 pair of gloves	0 violin case

[Debyser and Laitenberger, 12; in Birckbichler, 1, p. 73]

Students can be asked either to create their own questions by selecting elements from each column or to draw three numbers to determine the question they have to answer. For example, the number 479 would elicit the question "Why did the dancer put a hard-boiled egg in her toolbox?" Students then write a few sentences or even a short paragraph to answer this unusual query. Birckbichler (1) warns, however, that teachers should use such verbal play activities carefully and only occasionally. "Some students may find playing with language to be an interesting and challenging aspect to second language learning, whereas others who tend to view language solely as an expression of reality will be frustrated by verbal play activities" (p. 74).

Many creative writing and guided description activities can be used to encourage autonomous expression in the target language. Students can be asked to generate a context from a list of words, from a picture or series of pictures that may or may not be related to one another, or from a group of random objects. In an activity called *Geschichten aus dem Sack,* Schmidt (55) suggests that a paper bag be filled with disparate objects which students select one at a time for the purpose of generating a connected story, incorporating each new object into the plot as the story unfolds. Rivers et al. (53) suggest an activity called "Gossip," in which a series of questions is typed on a sheet of paper with space left for students to write an answer. As each student answers a question, he hides his answer by folding the paper back and passes it to his neighbor. After the last question has been answered, the story, which is often quite amusing, is read to the class.

These and other similar formats have been used by classroom teachers to help students create with the language in a structured, yet open-ended way. Such activities should continue to be useful in a proficiency-oriented approach to instruction.

Corollary 4: Authentic language should be used in instruction wherever and whenever possible. As much as possible, the contexts for language practice should be devised from culturally authentic sources. The use of real or simulated travel documents, hotel registration forms, biographical data sheets, train and plane schedules, posters, signs, newspapers, and magazines will acquaint the student more directly with real language than will any set of contrived classroom materials used alone. Videotapes of authentic or simulated exchanges involving native speakers, radio broadcasts, television or film, songs, and the like have long been advocated by language educators as stimulating pedagogical aids. The proficiency-oriented classroom will incorporate such materials frequently and effectively at all levels.

It is still not clear how teachers can make the most effective use of authentic language materials in elementary-level (Novice and Intermediate) classes. If Krashen's input hypothesis is true, we might obtain the best results by using simplified versions of authentic materials and gradually move toward incorporating complete, unedited language samples into courses where students are functioning at the Intermediate High or Advanced levels. A second possibility is to provide enough extralinguistic cues to render unedited authentic materials comprehensible to the student at the Novice or Intermediate level. This last option is used, for example, in materials available on ditto masters entitled *The Newspaper* and *The Magazine* (in French by Schulz, 56, and Jorstad, 26; in German by Culver 11; in Italian by Rallo, 49; in Spanish by Seelye, 57), in which unedited materials are presented with English-language comprehension questions and a teacher's guide with cultural notes. The comprehension questions tend to focus on main ideas, directing students' attention toward global meaning rather than details.

When using unedited materials that are beyond the learners' current level of linguistic competence, it is important for teachers to (1) provide guidance in reading or listening that will help students focus on the important features of the text; (2) emphasize any extralinguistic cues to meaning that are available and provide a context in which the material can be situated; and (3) prepare learners to expect and tolerate some ambiguity and uncertainty about details. One excellent way to prepare learners for exposure to authentic materials is to prepare in advance vocabulary sheets and pre-posed questions of a general sort. A short resumé of the content of the material may also be extremely helpful.

Sexton (59) proposes a technique for reading newspaper articles to extract important detail. Students are given four or five short reports of the same incident from different newspapers (authentic or simulated) and are directed to find similarities and discrepancies in the facts reported. As a guide to their reading, a series of questions is provided with space for jotting down notes. The following example relates to a story about a terrorist attack on passengers at an airport.

Questions	Report 1 says. . .	Report 2 says. . .	Report 3 says. . .	Report 4 says. . .
1. How many terrorists were there?				
2. Did the terrorists want to hijack the plane?				
3. What weapons did the terrorists have?				
4. Where was the bomb placed?				

This format encourages students to scan the report for the relevant detail and ignore other detail that is not important for comprehension of the main facts. This type of activity would be suitable for students at the Intermediate High or Advanced levels in reading comprehension, since it deals with narration of events in past tenses—an Advanced (ILR 2) function.

The use of videotaped authentic-language sequences is becoming more popular in second-language classrooms as equipment and resources become more readily available. Renjilian-Burgy at Wellesley College (52) uses local Hispanic television programming as well as "homemade" video programming of various types. Among the ideas she suggests for the latter type of programming are:

1. Interviews with members of the Hispanic community
   a. Questions about their country of origin
   b. Questions about their view of life in the U.S.

2. Materials made on location with a portable camera
   a. Visits to Hispanic agencies
   b. Tapes at Hispanic day-care centers
   c. Visits to bilingual or ESL classrooms
   d. Filming at Hispanic restaurants, such as a videotape of the cook preparing and describing a meal

3. Tapes of language students engaging in various language practice activities, including skits and short plays, "show-and-tell" demonstrations, and interviews with foreign students on campus.

Silva (61) has developed native-speaker interaction videotapes in which particular language functions or tasks are carried out in short segments. One tape demonstrates how to make an apology using both formal and informal registers in sequence. Another demonstrates how to invite someone for dinner or an evening get-together, and how to accept or refuse the invitation. Silva has created a course syllabus based on these tapes and uses the scripts and simplified versions of the dialogues to teach functional English as a Second Language at the University of Illinois.

Omaggio has adapted this idea for supplementing elementary and intermediate French instruction at the University of Illinois with short videotaped exchanges between native speakers in common courtesy and survival situations. Tapes developed thus far include the following exchanges.

1. A split-screen telephone conversation between a student and the owner of an apartment building where student lodging is available

2. Several scenes at restaurants, one demonstrating how to complain about one's food

3. A post-office scene where various transactions are carried out by post-office patrons

4. A short series of invitations to dinner (formal and informal) with acceptance and refusal of invitations, followed by a table-setting scene

at the home of one of the dinner hostesses and the arrival of the guest[1]

5. A hotel registration scene (Ponterio, 47)

6. Transactions at a bank (Ponterio, 47)

7. Buying a train ticket at the station (Ponterio, 47)

8. An airport scene in which an American must deal with the customs agent (Ponterio, 47)

9. A scene in a clothing store where a customer is returning a garment that doesn't fit properly

In situations 5 through 8, an American is involved in a typical survival situation. In the remainder of the tapes, native speakers interact as they naturally would in the target culture.

These tapes have been used successfully in both beginning and intermediate courses at the University of Illinois. Although students in the beginning courses do not understand every word, they are encouraged to get the gist of the message through preteaching activities and replay of the tapes. Scripts are prepared from the videotapes and are made available to students. Comprehension questions, vocabulary lists, simplified scripts, and followup activities are planned for each tape to make this culturally authentic input comprehensible to learners and useful for generating language activities for learning to cope in survival situations. This last goal leads us to a discussion of Hypothesis 2.

Hypothesis 2: Opportunities should be provided for students to carry out a range of functions (task universals) likely to be necessary for interacting in the target language and culture. Traditional classroom instructional settings have been "teacher-centered" and have tended to limit the role of the student to that of "responder." That is, students are most often asked to *answer* questions. In teacher-centered approaches, students are very seldom asked to make inquiries, act out simulated survival situations, narrate or describe events, hypothesize, argue, persuade, provide supporting opinion, or carry out many other language functions that are necessary in everyday encounters with others. In many cases, functional practice of this sort is reserved for advanced conversation courses, which many students never get to take. Proficiency-oriented approaches should introduce students to a variety of functional tasks that have been carefully sequenced to help them cope with the real-world communication demands they will face. The list of task universals that candidates should be able to handle at each level of proficiency on the ACTFL/ETS scale is given in Figure 2. This list should be useful in designing a sequence of functional language practice activities that will build toward these competencies from the beginning of instruction.

---

[1]This videotape was developed by Ulric Chung, a graduate student at the University of Illinois at Urbana-Champaign, as an Individual Studies project.

Figure 2. List of Task Universals

4	Represents point of view Negotiates Persuades Counsels Tailors language to audience	
3	Handles unfamiliar topics or situations Hypothesizes Provides supported opinion	(SUPERIOR)
2	Gets into, through, and out of survival situations with a complication Narrates Describes	(ADVANCED)
1	Gets into, through, and out of survival situations simply Asks questions Answers questions Creates with the language	(INTERMEDIATE)
0+	Communicates with memorized material	(NOVICE MID AND HIGH)
0	Has no functional ability	(NOVICE LOW)

Source: Lowe, 35, pp. 2–13. Reprinted with permission.

Guntermann and Phillips (19) have developed a sourcebook of ideas for adapting existing textbook materials to incorporate functional practice. After reviewing the literature on functional/notional approaches to language teaching, they conclude that work remains to be done before foreign-language courses and materials can be built uniquely around functions.

> Since a great deal of testing of functional-notional approaches has still to be done, it does not yet appear to be feasible to place functions at the center of courses and materials for wide use in schools and colleges. Nevertheless, it is possible to convert structure-based courses to a functional orientation, and textbook writers are seeking systematic means to provide functional practice with grammatical features. [P. 11]

Until such textbook materials appear on the market, however, the teacher must adapt existing materials to incorporate functional practice. Guntermann and Phillips (19, p. 12) outline the stages in which this can be done.

1. Select from the text materials the *essential* grammar and vocabulary that are to be emphasized in the intensive communication practice.
2. Select and sequence the *meanings* that are expressed through the forms chosen in Stage 1.

3. Select and sequence the purposes for practice.
4. Apply appropriate activities to carry out the functions of Stage 3, using the grammar and vocabulary of Stage 1 to express meanings in Stage 2.

In order to help teachers identify the purposes, i.e., the functions, for practice mentioned in Stage 3, Guntermann and Phillips (19) list some common purposes of language use in all four skill modalities. In speaking and listening, for example, they list such macro-functions as socializing; establishing and maintaining closer relationships; placing barriers between oneself and others; influencing others' actions; giving and responding to feedback; arguing; talking one's way out of trouble; requesting, reporting, receiving, and processing information; and several special situations (such as functioning in the classroom, communicating by phone, listening to the radio, and the like). For each macro-function, a variety of subfunctions is given. This inventory should prove valuable to classroom teachers for designing functional language-practice activities for students at all levels of proficiency.

An example of a listening and speaking activity that is focused on both a specific purpose and a grammatical feature is given below:

Purpose: Recounting the events of one's day.
Activity: Students role play in small family groups at the dinner table. Each recounts highlights of his or her day. The others ask questions and make comments. Each may invent or be assigned a personality, attitudes, feelings, and intentions that he or she must express (speaking). The other members of the class may judge the success with which the roles are carried out (listening).

[Guntermann and Phillips, 19, p. 40]

According to Guntermann and Phillips, there are a number of unsolved problems relating to using functions and notions as the organizer or "center" for language course design. A few of those problems are summarized in question from below.

1. If functions and/or notions are to be placed at the center of courses, on what basis should they be selected and sequenced?
2. It is not pedagogically unsound to avoid sequencing grammatical elements according to difficulty? While some linguistic theorists maintain that it is unnatural to separate a language into its smallest parts and then ask learners to build it up again (Newmark and Reibel, 40; Wilkins, 69), there is no evidence that learners can deal with material organized solely by function.
3. If it is necessary to sequence both the functions and the grammar, how can the two be integrated systematically?
4. To what extent is it reasonable to practice the various sociolinguistic

elements of communication? . . . If the circumstances of a speech event are specified (e.g., participants' roles, relative ages, sex, power, attitudes and values, the delicacy or intimacy of the topic), do we not run the risk of overburdening learners with detail, limiting creativity, limiting practice to ungeneralizable material, and overgeneralizing rules of social behavior?

5. How can material be articulated so that it does not appear to be a string of unrelated functions?
6. Will learners acquire language more efficiently and completely through a functional/notional approach?
7. Even if all these questions could be resolved satisfactorily for special-purpose courses, can the same be done for global courses, in which learners' future communication needs may be unknown, varied, or even negligible? (19, pp. 9–10)

These questions are worthy of consideration by those foreign language educators who advocate abandoning a grammatical core syllabus for a strictly functional/notional approach. The issues might be most relevant for designing beginning-level courses; functional/notional texts may be more suitable for intermediate or advanced conversation courses in a foreign-language learning context.

There are a variety of ESL texts on the market that have a functional/notional approach as a basis for presenting course material. Recently, a few intermediate-level foreign language texts have appeared on this same model. One text that seems very promising in this respect for use with Intermediate and Advanced learners is Nusbaum and Verdier's *Parlez sans peur* (41). Language texts of this sort are needed for use either after or in conjunction with basic courses to help students deal with daily situations in sociolinguistically and culturally appropriate fashion.

Teachers can also incorporate functional practice into basic courses by adapting survival situations for classroom use. Situation cards, such as those used in oral proficiency interviews, can be developed for role plays and for simulations to be carried out in small groups in the classroom or on videotape. Ponterio (47) has developed a survival simulation game in which students collectively assume the role of a tourist in a French town. The "tourist" arrives in the town with no French currency and a limited budget and must find the currency exchange office, a hotel, a meal, and information about tourist attractions by carrying out short role plays within a given time limit. This last feature adds a feeling of urgency to the simulation, a feeling not unfamiliar to the uninitiated visitor to a foreign city.

Shinall (60) suggests the introduction into language programs of the "survival lab," a live encounter between language students and native or near-native speakers in survival situations, carried on outside of class. Throughout the semester, several teaching assistants or professors could be on duty for a particular hour to role play survival situations with language students. The lab area could be equipped with realia to make the role plays more realistic. Students would be required to execute a number of survival situations successfully to obtain credit toward their grade. For full benefit of the survival lab concept, classroom instruction would also have to involve practice in such situations. The survival lab concept was initiated experimentally at the University of Illinois with French 102 (second-semester) classes in the Spring of 1983.

Hypothesis 3: There should be concern for the development of linguistic accuracy from the beginning of instruction. This hypothesis is implicit in some of the discussion in previous sections relating to the structuring of communicative and personalized practice around grammatical features of the target language. There are at least two compelling reasons for hypothesizing that some type of monitoring and correction of errors is necessary from the beginning of foreign-language instruction, at least for those learners who want eventually to function beyond the Advanced Level (ILR 2). The first reason has been discussed earlier in this chapter and relates to the phenomenon of the "terminal 2/2+" identified by Higgs and Clifford (21).

The second reason for hypothesizing that error correction is necessary relates to research on native-speaker judgments of second-language learners' efforts at communication. Studies by Chastain (7), Delisle (13), Ensz (15), Galloway (16), Guntermann (18), Ludwig (36), and Piazza (46) have all revealed that lexical and grammatical errors are considered obstructive to communication. In addition, it has been shown that within a given cultural group native speakers tend to have varying levels of tolerance for certain types of errors, and some attempt has already been made to rank error gravity based on these judgments. Furthermore, some language communities may be more tolerant of errors than others: Ensz (15) found that "... the French people ... irrespective of sex, age, occupation, or home region in France, expressed a significant intolerance for grammatical errors ... (p. 138). In her view, students of French must be concerned with developing the greatest possible accuracy during their course of study, although she hastens to add that this should not be incompatible as a goal with the goal of communicating spontaneously and expressing one's own meaning.

It is important to reemphasize here that "building toward accuracy" does not imply that students should be expected to produce *only* correct utterances in the target language or that an optimal language classroom environment should provide "wall-to-wall insurance against error" (Stevick, 64). It is obvious that, at lower levels, learners do not generally produce correct utterances when creating with the language. The proficiency guidelines clearly recognize this fact. In addition, research has repeatedly indicated that errors are useful in diagnosing and determining the learner's current internalized rule system, yielding important information for the teacher. The point is, however, that errors should not be left uncorrected on the assumption that they will all self-correct naturally in time. Neither should they be corrected in a way that puts students on the defensive. Teachers must find ways to monitor and correct errors in a nonthreatening fashion that does not cut off students' efforts to communicate but does provide the feedback they need to make significant progress toward higher levels of proficiency. To this end, the reader is directed to a recent publication by Walz (67) in which a variety of error-correction techniques and practices is discussed. This compilation of ideas represents a careful analysis and synthesis of the existing literature on this issue. An appendix of error-correction and error-monitoring instruments for compositions and other written work is provided, as well as ideas for helping learners correct errors made in oral production activities.

Hypothesis 4: Proficiency-oriented approaches respond to the affective as well as the cognitive needs of students. One of the hallmarks of several recent methodological developments is the greater emphasis placed on the affective aspects of learning and acquisition. Methods, such as suggestopedia, counseling-learning, confluent education, the Natural Approach, and the Silent Way, all emphasize the need to reduce anxiety and tension in the language-learning environment. Stevick (65) emphasizes the close relationship between anxiety and tension and poor performance in language production. This relates to Krashen's filter hypothesis, discussed earlier, which in turn is based on Dulay and Burt's (14) concept of the "affective filter"—somewhat akin to a mental block.

Students will probably become proficient more rapidly in an environment that is accepting, relaxed, personalized, natural, and in which they are not constantly put on the defensive or made to feel guilty for failing to conform precisely to native-language models. This principle relates directly to the issue of error correction discussed above. Teachers can direct the learning process by (1) structuring activities carefully to ensure greater success in communicating one's meaning accurately and (2) providing corrective feedback in a manner that is both nonthreatening and conducive to further acquisition. The use of techniques, such as grouping and interaction activities, can improve the chances of establishing a feeling of community in the classroom, which should in turn depressurize the learning environment considerably. Peer correction and monitoring, as suggested in the discussion of conversation cards (see pages 67–68), should also help increase the feeling of mutual interdependence and cooperation among students, contributing to the creation of a positive affective environment for learning.

Hypothesis 5: Cultural understanding must be promoted in various ways so that students are prepared to understand, accept, and live harmoniously in the target-language community. For many years, foreign-language

educators have been emphasizing the need to incorporate a cultural syllabus into the curriculum and to promote global awareness and cross-
cultural understanding. The use of techniques to increase this type of
understanding should receive a high priority in proficiency-oriented classroom instruction. Such techniques might include the use of culture capsules, culture clusters, culture assimilators, minidramas, audiomotor units,
realistic survival situations, and simulations of cultural events. An example of the last technique was recently developed in a third-semester French
course at the University of Illinois. Ponterio (48) developed a detailed
simulation of a political election in France. Students read political literature about actual candidates in the most recent presidential election in
France, prepared campaign speeches for their particular candidate, and
tried to persuade their classmates to vote for their presidential choice.
Students then voted in the French manner, simulating the election process.
This activity followed a unit on politics in which students had been
prepared lexically and grammatically to handle the situations in the simulation with relative ease. The whole unit integrated the study of grammar,
vocabulary, and culture in a single context, which, though wide and varied, provided the continuity necessary to build toward proficiency.

Many cultural lessons are inherent in the techniques discussed already
in this chapter: the enactment of survival situations through role plays and
the viewing of videotapes, films, and television programming are avenues
to deeper cultural understanding. Interviews with native speakers inside
or outside the classroom can also be structured to help students increase
their awareness of how the target culture operates. Many more ideas
for incorporating cultural understanding in the classroom are given in
Chapter 5.

Summary

The working hypotheses presented in this chapter may or may not represent the best assessment of priorities for designing proficiency-oriented
instruction in the classroom, but they are useful for promoting discussions
of how classroom practice should evolve in the future. As stated in the
introduction, the fundamental question that motivates this chapter is not
answerable within the limits of its pages. Yet it is hoped that from a careful
assessment of proficiency and an understanding of what it means for our
own students we can gain insights into language teaching and how to
organize and plan it effectively. Teachers must have the option to make
their own decisions about which proficiency goals should receive the
highest priority in their own situations, yet they have the responsibility
to do all they can to assure that students can continue in future coursework
or life experience to build their language capabilities. This chapter has
provided some preliminary guidelines for instruction that should make
continued progress possible.

The new focus that proficiency can provide does not need to bring with it a new absolutism. It can bring instead a new freedom, providing us with a means of organizing our thinking so that in the future our many talents, resources, and creative ideas for teaching foreign languages can achieve a renewed viability and purpose. For the first time in many years, the foreign-language-teaching profession is reaching a consensus about a fundamental and far-reaching issue that concerns us all. With that consensus we can achieve the unity of purpose needed to progress toward our common goals.

References, The Proficiency-Oriented Classroom

1. Birckbichler, Diane W. *Creative Activities for the Second-Language Classroom.* Language in Education: Theory and Practice, no. 48. Washington, DC: Center for Applied Linguistics, 1982.
2. _____, and Alice Omaggio. "Diagnosing and Responding to Individual Learner Needs." *Modern Language Journal* 62 (1978):336–45.
3. Bonin, Thérèse, and Diane Birckbichler. "Real Communication Through Conversation and Interview Cards." *Modern Language Journal* 59 (1975):22–25.
4. Boylan, Patricia C., and Alice C. Omaggio. *Strategies for Person-Centered Language Learning.* Hastings-on-Hudson, NY: ACTFL Materials Center, 1979.
5. Canale, Michael, and Merrill Swain. "Communicative Approaches to Second Language Teaching and Testing." *Applied Linguistics* 1. (Spring 1980):1–47.
6. Candlin, C. *The Communicative Teaching of English.* Singapore: Huntsman Offset Printing Pte. Ltd., 1981.
7. Chastain, Kenneth. "Native Speaker Reaction to Instructor-Identified Student Second Language Errors." *Modern Language Journal* 64 (1980):210–15.
8. Christensen, Clay B. *Explorando. Affective Learning Activities for Intermediate Practice in Spanish.* Englewood Cliffs, NJ: Prentice-Hall, 1977.
9. Cooper, Thomas C. "Sentence-Combining: An Experiment in Teaching Writing." *Modern Language Journal* 65 (1981):158–65.
10. Coulombe, Roger, et al. *Voix et Visages de France.* Chicago: Rand McNally, 1974.
11. Culver, Anke. *The Magazine.* Lincolnwood, IL: National Textbook Co., 1977.
12. Debyser, Francis, and H. Laitenberger. "Le Crocodile et le moulin à vent." *Le Français dans le Monde* 123 (1976):14–19.
13. Delisle, Helga. "Native Speaker Judgement and the Evaluation of Errors in German." *Modern Language Journal* 66 (1982):39–48.
14. Dulay, Heidi, and Marina K. Burt. "Remarks on Creativity in Language Acquisition," pp. 95–126 in H. Dulay, M. Burt, and M. Finnochiaro, eds., *Viewpoints in English as a Second Language.* New York: Regents, 1977.
15. Ensz, Kathleen Y. "French Attitudes Toward Speech Errors." *Modern Language Journal* 66 (1982):133–39.
16. Galloway, Vicky B. "Perceptions of the Communicative Efforts of American Students of Spanish." *Modern Language Journal* 64 (1980):428–33.
17. Guilford, J. P. "Three Faces of Intellect." *American Psychologist* 14 (1959):469–79.
18. Guntermann, Gail. "A Study of the Frequency and Communicative Effects of Errors in Spanish." *Modern Language Journal* 62 (1978):249–53.
19. _____, and June K. Phillips. *Functional-Notional Concepts: Adapting the Foreign Language Textbook.* Language in Education: Theory and Practice, no. 44. Washington, DC: Center for Applied Linguistics, 1982.

20. Harbour, Leslie J. *Le Jeu du Budget.* Hastings-on-Hudson, NY: ACTFL Materials Center, 1981.
21. Higgs, Theodore V., and Ray Clifford. "The Push Toward Communication," pp. 57–79 in Theodore V. Higgs, ed., *Curriculum, Competence, and the Foreign Language Teacher.* The ACTFL Foreign Language Education Series, vol. 13. Lincolnwood, IL: National Textbook Co., 1982.
22. Jarvis, Gilbert A.; Thérèse Bonin; Donald Corbin; and Diane Birckbichler. *Invitation.* New York: Holt, Rinehart and Winston, 1979.
23. _____; Thérèse Bonin; Donald Corbin; and Diane Birckbichler. *Connaître et se connaître,* 2nd ed. New York: Holt, Rinehart and Winston, 1980.
24. Jespersen, Otto. *How to Teach a Foreign Language.* New York: Macmillan 1904.
25. Joiner, Elizabeth, and P. Westphal. *Developing Communication Skills.* Rowley, MA: Newbury House, 1978.
26. Jorstad, Helen L. *The Magazine.* Lincolnwood, IL: National Textbook Co., 1977.
27. Kettering, Judith. *Developing Communicative Competence: Interaction Activities in English as a Second Language.* Pittsburgh: University Center for International Studies, 1975.
28. Knorre, Marty; Thalia Dorwick; Francisco R. Ferrán; Walter Lusetti; William R. Ratliff; and M. Stanley Whitley. *Puntos de partida.* New York: Random House, 1981.
29. Krashen, Stephen. *Principles and Practice in Second Language Acquisition.* New York: Pergamon Press, 1982.
30. Laitenberger, Heidi, and A. Lamy. "De certains jeux linguistiques." *Le Français dans le monde* 123 (1976):8–14.
31. Lett, John. "The Communicative Use of Small-Group Instruction." Mimeographed.
32. Lett, John; Patricia Boylan; Marty Knorre; William R. Ratliff; and Aristóbulo Pardo. *Reflejos.* New York: Holt, Rinehart and Winston, 1983.
33. Littlewood, William T. "Form and Meaning in Language Teaching Methodology." *Modern Language Journal* 64 (1980):441–45.
34. _____. *Communicative Language Teaching: An Introduction.* Cambridge: Cambridge University Press, 1981.
35. Lowe, Pardee, Jr. *Manual for LS Oral Interview Workshop.* Washington, DC: DLI/LS Joint Oral Interview Transfer Project, 1982.
36. Ludwig, Jeannette. "Native Speakers' Judgments of Second-Language Learners' Efforts at Communication: A Review." *Modern Language Journal* 66 (1982):274–83.
37. McLaughlin, Barry. "The Monitor Model: Some Methodological Considerations." *Language Learning* 28, ii (1979):309–32.
38. Muyskens, Judith A.; Alice C. Omaggio; Claudene Chalmers; Claudette Imberton; and Philippe Almeras. *Rendez-vous: An invitation to French.* New York: Random House, 1982.
39. _____, and Alice C. Omaggio. *Instructor's Manual to Accompany Rendez-vous.* New York: Random House, 1982.
40. Newmark, Leonard, and David A. Reibel. "Necessity and Sufficiency in Language Learning." *International Review of Applied Linguistics* 6 (1968):145–64.
41. Nusbaum, Marlene, and Liliane Verdier. *Parlez sans peur.* New York: Holt, Rinehart, and Winston, 1983.
42. Omaggio, Alice C. *Helping Lessons Succeed: Activities for the Foreign Language Classroom.* Language in Education: Theory and Practice, no. 36. Washington, DC: Center for Applied Linguistics, 1981.

43. _____. "Using Games and Simulations for the Development of Functional Proficiency in a Second Language." *Canadian Modern Language Review* 38 (1982):517–46.
44. _____. *Testing Language Skills in Context.* Language in Education: Theory and Practice. Washington, DC: Center for Applied Linguistics, forthcoming.
45. Paulston, Christina B., and Howard R. Selekman. "Interaction Activities in the Foreign Language Classroom, or How to Grow a Tulip-Rose." *Foreign Language Annals* 9, iii (1976):248–54.
46. Piazza, Linda Gaylord. "French Tolerance of Grammatical Errors Made by Americans." *Modern Language Journal* 64 (1980):422–27.
47. Ponterio, Marie. Personal communication.
48. Ponterio, Robert. Personal communication.
49. Rallo, John A. *The Newspaper.* Lincolnwood, IL: National Textbook Co., 1977.
50. Rassius, John A. *Le Français: Départ-Arrivée.* New York: Harper and Row, 1980.
51. Ratliff, Wiliam; Patricia Boylan; Marty Knorre; John Lett; and Aristóbulo Pardo. *Cara a cara.* New York: Holt, Rinehart, and Winston, 1981.
52. Renjilian-Burgy, Joy. Personal communication, letter.
53. Rivers, Wilga, et al. *A Practical Guide to the Teaching of Spanish.* New York: Oxford University Press, 1976.
54. Rochester, Myrna; Judith Muyskens; Alice C. Omaggio; and Claudene Chalmers. *Bonjour, ça va?* New York: Random House, 1983.
55. Schmidt, Elizabeth. *Let's Play Games in German.* Lincolnwood, IL: National Textbook Co., 1977.
56. Shulz, Renate. *The Newspaper.* Lincolnwood, IL: National Textbook Co., 1977.
57. Seelye, H. Ned; and J. L. Day. *The Newspaper.* Lincolnwood, IL: National Textbook Co., 1982.
58. Seliger, Herbert W. "On the Nature and Function of Language Rules in Language Teaching." *TESOL Quarterly* 13, iii (1979):359–68.
59. Sexton, Malcolm. *Applying Communicative Concepts to Foreign Language Teaching and Curriculum Development.* Presidio of Monterey, CA: Defense Language Institute, 1981.
60. Shinall, Stanley. Personal communication.
61. Silva, Anthony. "Teaching Language Functions." Presentation at the First Annual Midwest Regional TESOL Convention, Urbana, IL, April 1981.
62. Slager, William R. "Creating Contexts for Language Practice," pp. 71–88 in Elizabeth Joiner and Patricia Westphal, eds., *Developing Communication Skills.* Rowley, MA: Newbury House, 1978.
63. Stanislawczyk, Irene, and Symond Yavener. *Creativity in the Language Classroom.* Rowley, MA: Newbury House, 1976.
64. Stevick, Earl W. *Memory, Meaning, and Method: Some Psychological Perspectives on Language Learning.* Rowley, MA: Newbury House, 1976.
65. _____. *Teaching Languages: A Way and Ways.* Rowley, MA: Newbury House, 1980.
66. Valette, Rebecca, and Jean-Paul Valette. *Contacts,* 2nd ed. Boston: Houghton-Mifflin, 1981.
67. Walz, Joel C. *Error Correction Techniques for the Foreign Language Classroom.* Language in Education: Theory and Practice, no. 50. Washington, DC: Center for Applied Linguistics, 1982.
68. Wesche, M. "Communicative Testing in a Second Language." *Canadian Modern Language Review* 37, iii (1981):551–71.

69. Wilkins, D. A. *Notional Syllabuses.* London: Oxford University Press, 1976.
70. Zelson, Sidney. "Skill Using, Self-Expression and Communication: Exercises in Three Dimensions," pp. 44–56 in Elizabeth Joiner and Patricia Westphal, eds., *Developing Communication Skills.* Rowley, MA: Newbury House, 1978.

3

Curriculum Development at the Foreign Service Institute

Earl W. Stevick
Foreign Service Institute

Introduction

For more than thirty years, the School of Language Studies of the Foreign Service Institute has been directly involved in preparing U.S. government personnel to function successfully in other countries. Our historical focus on proficiency as a goal of instruction is playing a renewed and central role in major curriculum development projects that are currently under way at the Foreign Service Institute. Because each of these projects has arisen in response to a slightly different set of needs, each differs somewhat in scope and purpose, as well as in methodological detail. Nevertheless, they all exploit a shared set of principles which should interest language teachers in other instructional settings.

The Foreign Service Institute (FSI) was founded in 1947. It is the training arm of the Department of State, and as such prepares for overseas assignments employees and family members in most agencies of the United States government: the Foreign Service, the United States Information Agency, the Agency for International Development, and others. The largest single component of the Foreign Service Institute is the School of Language Studies, which works in systematic cooperation with FSI's School of Area Studies.

The School of Language Studies provides instruction in the official languages of all countries with which the United States has diplomatic relations: between thirty-five and forty languages at any given time. Our students fall into two general categories: (1) officers from whatever branch

Earl W. Stevick (Ph.D., Cornell University) is the Senior Training Consultant for the School of Language Studies of the Foreign Service Institute. He is widely published in professional journals, and his *Teaching Languages—A Way and Ways,* and *Memory Meaning and Method* are widely recognized as classics in our discipline.

of the government, by far the largest contingent, and (2) family members and support personnel. Class size varies from one to six students. Courses occupy twenty-seven class hours a week, integrated with three hours a week of area studies. They last from twenty weeks for the more common Western European languages to forty-four weeks for most of the others. The forty-four-week courses in Japanese, Chinese, Korean, and Arabic may be followed by an additional year in one of FSI's field schools.

Overall, we in the School of Language Studies have learned to produce a consistent and serviceable product: on the ILR scale, students at the end of training regularly attain ratings between 2 and 3, or even better for students of reasonably good aptitude. There is, then, some reason for satisfaction.

At the same time, however, careful monitoring of reports from overseas has sometimes turned up facts that keep us from being completely satisfied with the results of our training. We have learned of officers with the "professional working proficiency" rating of S-3 who have felt (or whose supervisors have felt) that "an S-3 is not enough for this job." We have sometimes found that a person who went out with an S-3, R-3 received the same rating or even a lower one when retested after living in the country for two or three years. We have occasionally observed graduates who seemed to avoid using the language except when absolutely necessary. We have also received reports of numerous family members and staff personnel who, having had no language training at all, very much wished they had had a little.

For these reasons, in 1980 the management of the school undertook a survey of fifty overseas posts, checking the linkage between what we had been putting into our training and the actual perceived needs of United States government personnel abroad. This survey generally confirmed the reports noted in the preceding paragraph. Management therefore concluded that the existing curriculum for officers, while basically sound, needed to be altered in some way. Management also concluded that we ought to provide suitable short-term training for the nonofficer clientele who in the past had been excluded from our courses.

These decisions provided the basis for what we have come to call the "New Orientation" of the School of Language Studies. The purpose of this chapter is to describe formats we have used in three types of materials developed under the New Orientation: (1) special units, which we call Bridges, to supplement existing basic courses; (2) a few new basic courses; and (3) "FAST" (i.e., "Familiarization and Short-Term") Courses for family members and support personnel. Each of these types of materials is treated below; thus, the remainder of this chapter is a series of case studies.

Needless to say, the setting in which this work has been done is quite different from the settings in which most readers will find themselves. There may be some value in this very fact, for the differences an opportunity to observe certain familiar but relatively new principles applied on a large scale, in courses of three different kinds, across a wide variety of target languages and cultures. We hope that this observation will lead to new insights into the principles themselves and the nature of the language-teaching task, and that these insights will contribute to our readers' effectiveness in their own professional undertakings.

Emphases Found in All the New Materials _____

Looking back, we can identify five emphases which in one way or another have shaped and structured all of our work during the past two years. These emphases are drawn from, or at least are consistent with, much that is current in contemporary thinking. They are:

1. *Relevance:* close and specific relationship to anticipated needs.
2. *Function:* frequent and clear attention to function as well as to form.
3. *Communication:* consistent effort to make practice activities communicative.
4. *Comprehension:* exploitation of the "comprehension advantage."
5. *Imagery:* systematic development of mental imagery to match the verbal content of the lessons.

Emphasis 1: relevance

The *goals* of the new orientation have been drawn from the needs of our students, virtually all of whom are preparing for assignment to a post outside the English-speaking world. Of course, this had always been true to some extent, but we still often acted as though the only important thing was that students get control of "the Language"—that is, the sounds, basic morphology, sentence patterns, and function words—within almost any basic vocabulary. Then, we assumed, they would be able to add new lexicon as needed after arriving in the host country. Now, by contrast, we are assigning to *immediacy* and *authenticity of content* the same importance that we assign to selection of linguistic elements. In this we are acting consistently with one of the five emphases which are widely discussed in the profession of late: teaching *language for special purposes.*

From this point of view, the kind of proficiency that our students need is communicative—the ability to use language to get things done. Linguistic proficiency in the sense of producing well-pronounced, grammatically correct sentences is still important but only insofar as it contributes to practical, communicative effectiveness.

There is no question that, other things being equal, an S-3 will handle a given situation better than will an S-2. But our experience has also shown that in practice some S-2s are more effective communicators than some S-3s. We have therefore become reluctant to label anything as "an S-4 situation" or "an S-2 situation." Almost any situation can be handled to some extent by officers at almost any point on the speaking scale. *How well* it is handled will naturally depend in part on linguistic proficiency (the S-score). It will also depend in part on the other kind of proficiency with which portions of this chapter are concerned.

What I have just said does not mean that "FSI has stopped teaching for linguistic proficiency." Accuracy in pronunciation, grammar, and vocabulary has always received and continues to receive serious attention in the curriculum of the School of Language Studies. But while the pursuit of linguistic accuracy needs no documentation for this audience, the achievement of global communicative effectiveness is one of the frontiers which the language-teaching profession is still exploring.

Emphasis 2: function

The concern for relevance led us very quickly to a second emphasis that has begun to figure conspicuously in the language teaching of the 1980s: the importance of *function* in its own right, as contrasted with *form* and *meaning* alone; the *tasks* to be accomplished as contrasted with the *mechanisms* for accomplishing them. Indeed, if this emphasis had not been waiting for us in the literature, we would have had to invent it.

The classic examples, "Please shut the door"; "Could you shut the door?"; "It might be better to shut the door"; and "Don't you think it's chilly in here?"—diverse as they are in vocabulary and grammatical structure—all have essentially the same function in that all of them may invite the same act to be performed. Similarly, the one sentence, "What do you know" may function as a request for information, an expression of surprise, or an informal greeting, depending on the context. We wanted to make students aware of the functions of words and phrases—of the tasks which words and phrases help a speaker to accomplish—just as in the past we had made them aware of forms and meanings. To a large extent, I think we have succeeded in doing so. Just how we have done this is detailed in later sections of this chapter.

Emphasis 3: communication

In recent years, much has been said about bringing communication into the classroom, instead of being content with merely preparing students to undertake it after they have left. To say that communication has taken place is to say that (1) one or more of the parties knows or sees something that he or she did not know or see before, (2) the interchange has taken place within a framework of shared information, and (3) the nonshared information has been transmitted for some purpose. Communication practice that lacks even one of these elements can be deceptive. Thus, for example, the reciting of a dialogue—even one that is a transcript of a conversation between native speakers in real life—communicates nothing except whether or not the student is able to recite the dialogue. On the other hand, "The book is in the drawer" communicates nothing to a person who doesn't know which book and which drawer the speaker might be talking about. And unless the speaker has some reason for informing the hearer about the location of the book, the remark will be taken as pointless, and hence unsuccessful communication.

In designing communicative activities, materials writers try to build in some sort of *information gap* that students must close by making use of language. Nonshared information may be about the internal thoughts of the speaker, and in real life, this sort of communication is sometimes very important. More frequently, however, the information that is transmitted has to do with realities which are outside the mind of the speaker and are not entirely under his or her control. This is, of course, more consistent with language use outside the classroom, and for this reason we value this latter type of communication more than we value mere improvised exchanges in which anything that makes sense is acceptable.

We have adopted this view of communication but consider it to be only one special case of the *Principle of Practice: What you practice, you will do more easily in the future, and whatever you want to be able to do more easily, you must practice.* Thus, whoever wants to communicate, in the sense just described, must *practice* communication in that same sense. Concretely, we believe that whoever wants to use language to persuade must practice using it persuasively; whoever anticipates using language under stress is well advised to practice it under stressful conditions; whoever is likely to be inundated by rapid-fire idiomatic language had better accumulate some experience in dealing with it.

Emphasis 4: comprehension

The "comprehension advantage" means that people are generally able to understand more than they are able to produce and much more than they are able to produce correctly. Now and then one hears reports from people who have found that, at one stage in their foreign-language study, they had failed to understand sentences directed at them, even though they would have been able to produce the same sentences themselves. This has occasionally happened to me, in cognate as well as in noncognate languages. I do not, however, think that this experience diminishes either the reality or the importance of the comprehension advantage. In fact, our collective experience with conventional instruction, as well as with the formats described later in this chapter, points in the opposite direction.

It is perhaps worthwhile to distinguish here between complete comprehension and comprehension which is partial but still useful. If a new user of a language feels responsible for complete understanding, this mindset may induce both cognitive and affective impediments as compared with a more practical reaction to aural input. Such impediments will be very costly to our graduates in their life and work at overseas posts. We therefore feel that this decoupling of comprehension and production has been of great importance.

Emphasis 5: imagery

It is a cliché to say that using a language entails moving rapidly and accurately back and forth between what is verbal (sounds, words, grammatical structures, and the like) and what is nonverbal (sensory data and interpretations of these data, as well as feelings, purposes, placement in time, and other elements). Learning a new language, then, means at least forming in one's own central nervous system a new set of connections between the verbal and the nonverbal. During the past two years, the staff of the School of Language Studies has come to realize clearly that *the only verbal and nonverbal elements that students will be able to connect with one another are those which are simultaneously present in their heads.*

Few teachers would deny the truth of this principle stated in this way, yet we sometimes forget it in practice. In particular, teachers must remember that the nonverbal counterparts (pictures, feelings, meanings) which a word, sentence, or story produces in their own minds may not be present in the minds of their students who are exposed to that same verbal material. Therefore, it is worthwhile to ensure that students have ample opportunity to develop rich and well-integrated nonverbal counterparts (pictures, feelings, and meanings) to match the verbal side of a lesson. This is the basis of our fifth emphasis, the "enhancement of imagery."

These five emphases, then, have proved to be corollaries of our "New Orientation." To date, materials produced under the New Orientation include:

- A series of one to seven Bridges in each of thirty-two languages
- New basic courses in Arabic and Russian (A Czech course is also in initial stages of development.)
- A "FAST Course" in each of fourteen languages

We will now discuss each of these types of materials.

Bridges

A Bridge is a training exercise that supplements a regular basic course and is aimed strictly at one or more of our students' professional needs. It lasts for fifteen to eighteen consecutive class hours spread over two and a half class days. One reason for concentrating Bridges into the shortest possible calendar time is that we want to keep the imagery that is generated in one segment (emphasis 5) from evaporating before students reach the next segment. Another reason is that this schedule approximates more closely the conditions and time frame under which the students will work overseas.

Each course now includes from one to seven Bridges. Students meet their first Bridge when they have completed 100–300 hours (the first fifth of their training) and the rest at approximately equal intervals thereafter.

As we began the project, our knowledge of students' probable needs provided us with a range of subject matter which was both broad and specific. Having recognized these needs, however, and even having compiled our preliminary list of them, we found that we were not yet ready to begin writing, for reasons associated with that very same specificity of needs which in some respects we had found so welcome. For example, asking and answering questions about military equipment is all very well for a Military Attaché, but a student who is preparing for service as an Economic Officer or a Consul is likely to see it as a waste of class time. The same applies in reverse, of course, when the Economic Officer or the Military Attaché is asked to work on a dialogue in which a consular employee is trying to get an American tourist out of jail. We had decided that our goal was the kind of proficiency that would lead to effectiveness in a variety of clearly defined tasks. But which functions should we concentrate on?

Fortunately, the curriculum reform team was at that time headed by a Foreign Service Officer who had completed several tours abroad. On the basis of his own experiences and those of other officers whom he interviewed, he drew up a list of "Representative Professional Skills" that are necessary in *all* types of work in the Foreign Service—negotiating, making arrangements, giving a briefing, gathering facts, and the like. These functions were clearly job-relevant, without being job-specific. They are in effect "macrofunctions," which consist of clusters of smaller functions. Thus giving a briefing requires that the speaker bring a meeting to order, announce the topic, give an outline of what he or she proposes to cover, deal with questions, and close the meeting. Each of these may consist of still further layers of subfunctions.

Identifying these Representative Professional Skills turned out to be a breakthrough for us. It puts us in a position to focus the attention of materials writers, instructors, and students alike on words and phrases of the language which are needed for these purposes, regardless of the job specialty of an officer. For example, "I'd like to talk with you for a few minutes about ...."; "Can we come back to that later?"; "If you have further questions ..." all are lines which almost anyone can use. This insight was first and most conspicuously exploited in the construction of the Bridges, but it has also contributed to the work on new basic courses.

Each Bridge concentrates on one of the seven Representative Professional Skills listed below. In general, students meet these Bridges when they have reached at least the ranges on the speaking proficiency scale which are shown in parentheses.

- Dealing with requests (0+ to 1)
- Using language under stress (1 to 1+)
- Getting facts over the telephone (1 to 2)
- Making arrangements (1+ to 2)
- Giving a briefing (2)
- Eliciting an informed opinion (2 to 2+)
- Defending a point of view (2+ to 3)

A Bridge is built around a scenario, generally divided into two or three episodes, which consists of a related series of tasks to be performed by a specific officer in a specific situation. We chose our protagonists from some of the most common categories: Political Officer, Administrative Officer, Cultural Affairs Officer, Commercial Officer, Military Attaché. We also determined to provide practice for a person from any category who is temporarily serving either as a weekend Duty Officer or is in some situation where he or she is being subjected to hostile treatment.

The segments of any Bridge fall into two broad categories, the Main Sequence and the Related Activities. The Main Sequence typically consists of the following segments.

1. Initial briefing
2. Task consideration
3. Key line elicitation
4. Key line practice
5. Sample dialogue A
6. Rehearsal A
7. Further elicitation
8. Further practice
9. Sample dialogue B
10. Rehearsal B
11. Final simulation
12. Microtasks

The most frequent Related Activities are:

1. Work with (usually two) overheard conversations.
2. Work with (usually two) written documents.

In the remainder of this section, we will look briefly at the goals of these segments, the materials associated with them, and the procedures that characterize them.

Segment 1: initial briefing

Goals: (1) To remind students of the form and overall goals of Bridges; (2) to explain the setting and the Representative Professional Skills of the Bridge at hand; and (3) to answer students' questions about the Bridge.

Materials: A briefing paper in English, which sets the background for the scenario of the Bridge.

Procedure: The instructor talks with students in English for a few minutes at the beginning of the first hour, paraphrasing the briefing paper and answering any questions about it. The instructor may also run through the series of activities in the schedule one by one, describing each briefly, particularly with the first Bridge.

Remarks: The scenario is based on a specific professional task the students are likely to face at post. This guarantees relevance (emphasis 1), sets the framework within which functions will have their significance (emphasis 2), and begins to recruit the students' imaginations in generating the mental imagery which must give meaning to the words of the Bridge (emphasis 5).

The Bridge that concentrates on getting facts over the telephone stands second or third in the sequence. It is usually built around a disaster scenario consisting of three episodes. In the first episode, the Assistant Air Attaché receives a call from an officer in the army or the police force. In the second, the attaché makes a call to the same officer for further information. The final episode consists of an unscripted phone call which continues the story line and provides the occasion for an unprepared "simulation" (segment 11). The examples in the following sample briefing paper are taken from German.

Sample Briefing Paper

An American military airplane has crashed in a rural area in southwest Germany during a storm. Some military personnel and civilians may be injured or dead, and there has probably been some property damage. The German police are involved in taking care of the victims.

You are the Assistant Air Attaché in Bonn. You have been assigned to handle communication with the German authorities in this matter and to obtain as much information as possible. You are about to be called by a representative of the German government.

You are aware that:
- *Sembach* is the major rescue headquarters of U.S. Forces in West Germany.
- *Finthen* is the name of a small U.S. airfield.
- *Pferdsfeld* is the name of a German airfield.

- *Wiesbaden* has a large medical facility for U.S. Forces in Germany.

Segment 2: task consideration

Goals: (1) To assemble a set of rather full and vivid mental images, which will be readily at hand and which can be matched up with the words and sentences that students will use in later segments of the Bridge. (2) To list things that the American protagonist of the Bridge will need to get done in the first episode, as predicted by the students themselves on the basis of their past experience. (These "things that need to get done" are what we mean by the "functions" illustrated in the Bridge.) (3) To generate in the students a feeling of personal investment.

Materials: The briefing paper given above.

Procedure: Students list in English things that the American will need to do within the first episode. The instructor goes to the board and writes these "subtasks" as the students call them out. As he writes, he edits any suggestions that are overly specific and states them in general, functional terms. For example, if a student says "The embassy will be open at 8:30 on Monday," the instructor may write "Give information about embassy hours." The instructor does not force students to come up with any preestablished list of subtasks, but he may prompt them if they seem to be overlooking any important areas. This activity continues in English until there are ten to fifteen subtasks on the board.

Remarks: Task consideration helps to ensure maximum relevance (emphasis 1). It also enhances imagery (emphasis 5) because students must imagine themselves in the simulated situation in order to decide what to suggest. Using the students' native language allows fuller access to their store of memories and lets them give full attention to *function* (emphasis 2) without having to worry about the *form* of their utterances. By concentrating on subtasks ("things that the protagonist will have to get done"), this activity lays a strong functional basis for the activities that follow it. Working from the students' collective experience does not lead merely to a "pooling of ignorance," partly because most of them have actually faced comparable situations during their careers, and partly because sample dialogues A and B (segments 5 and 9) provide independent input.

Sample Result of an Actual "Task Consideration" Exercise
Name of interlocutor
Source, organization
Arrange for further contact

Location of crash
Weather conditions
Time of accident
Type of aircraft
Casualties
Cargo
Type of injuries
Type and amount of damage
Assistance at scene
Types of help needed
Thanks and sympathy

Segment 3: key line elicitation

Goals: (1) to mobilize the students' existing resources, and (2) to place at their disposal some utterance-types which will be useful both in the later stages of the Bridge and at post.

Materials: The list of functions created during task consideration (segment 2).

Procedure: For each function, students suggest one or more sentences that might accomplish it. The instructor writes one such sentence on the board in place of the function. The students' suggestions may be in flawless target language (TL), in imperfect TL, partly in English, or (rarely) entirely in English. In any case, if a proposed sentence is culturally appropriate, the instructor writes the correct TL sentence nearest the one proposed by the students. If none of the sentences is appropriate, he indicates this briefly and allows students to try again. He does not make this an occasion either for overt correction or for "teasing" a correction out of students. Students may copy these sentences if they wish.

Remarks: We assume that the verbal side of the ensuing linguistic practice will be more clearly and fully present for students because they themselves have brought both the ideas and many of the words out of their own knowledge rather than simply having followed a prefabricated model. The instructor's unobtrusive editing as he writes down the sentences ensures that students will not end up with a list of incorrect or unidiomatic models to be used in later segments.

Sample of Actual "Key Lines" Based on the "Task Consideration"
Bitte, mit wem spreche ich? (With whom am I speaking, please?)
In welchem Amt arbeiten Sie? (Which office are you with?)
Wie sind Sie zu erreichen? (How can you be reached?)

Wo ist das Flugzeug abgestuerzt? (Where did the plane crash?)
Wieviele Tote und Verletzte gibt es? (How many dead and injured?)
Koennten Sie mich anrufen, wenn Sie mehr Auskunft haben?
(Could you call me when you have more information?)
etc.

Segment 4: key line practice

Goals: (1) To allow students to develop facility in speaking the "key lines" developed in segment 3, and (2) to give students some feeling for the kind of response each key line is likely to elicit.

Materials: The list of key lines from segment 3.

Procedure: If the instructor thinks it necessary, he begins with a bit of conventional pronunciation practice. In the main part of this segment, a student selects any of the key lines and says it to the instructor, who then responds in some appropriate way. If the students seem disposed to stick to the few easiest key lines, the instructor may prompt them with, "Now find out which office I am calling from," etc. If the key line happens to be a question, the instructor's response will probably be an answer. If the key line is a statement, the instructor may come back with a short question about it, or a protest, or a piece of relevant information, etc. Finally, the student gives a minimal response of his own which indicates understanding of what the instructor has said. In the beginning, the instructor's responses are short, simple, and straightforward; but they may become more challenging if the instructor judges it appropriate.

Remarks: We sometimes refer to this activity as a function drill. It provides for repetitive practice of sentences which students are likely to use later on, much as audiolingual mim-mem did. However, the constantly changing form of the instructor's responses, together with the necessity of understanding them, force students to pay attention to the *function* of each key line, as well as to its *form* and *meaning* (emphasis 2). This in turn deepens the verbal-nonverbal nexus (emphasis 5). It also exploits the comprehension advantage (emphasis 4).

Segment 5: sample dialogue A

Goals: (1) To provide for the first episode of the scenario a model produced by native speakers, which is a fully developed discourse rather than a set of isolated key lines. (2) To provide information about how the first part of the scenario might be conducted.

Materials: A dialogue of twenty-five to thirty-five turns, written and tape-recorded in the target language, with a written English version. A "sample" differs from conventional audiolingual dialogues in two respects: (1) it is unbalanced in the sense that the American's lines are kept as short and as versatile as possible, while the non-American's lines are longer and may be more specialized; (2) it is nonreversible in the sense that students do not need to produce the non-American's lines at all, although they do practice the non-American's lines during the rehearsals (segments 6 and 10) and may also find occasion to use them in the simulations and microtasks (segments 11 and 12).

Procedure: With the instructor out of the room and with books closed, students listen to the sample dialogue straight through once or twice. The instructor returns to the room and students tell him what they heard. Everyone listens to it again, referring to the printed text. With help from the instructor if necessary, students answer any questions they may have about the language of the dialogue. Then they go through the sentences looking for function markers, which may be words, sentence fragments, and even whole sentences that will be useful in signaling various functions regardless of substantive content: for example, "That may well be, but ..." or "I see your point, yet ..." as markers for introducing disagreement. For this purpose we frequently make use of worksheets, which are transcripts of the TL on the tape but with most of the function markers obliterated.

Remarks: The first step in this procedure again exploits the comprehension advantage (emphasis 4). The concern for finding markers continues the focus on function (emphasis 2). It also contributes to the internal cohesion of the Bridge itself, since these markers will be useful in simulation and microtasks (segments 11 and 12). As they fill in the worksheets, students sometimes use the tape. Under these circumstances, the worksheets require them to focus only on form. At other times, they attempt to fill in the blanks without the direct assistance of the tape. Under these circumstances, they are focusing on function and frequently come up with acceptable forms that differ from the ones on the tape.

Segment 6: rehearsal A

Goals: (1) To provide an occasion for using material from segments 1–6 in a connected context, and (2) to serve as a controlled first approximation to the performance that will be required in the simulation and the microtasks.

Materials: A functional outline of what happens in the first episode. This is based on the list generated during task consideration and amplified by the students' experiences in the intervening segments. For example:

- Indicating that the briefing has begun
- Stating the topic
- Indicating when questions should be asked
- Giving an outline of the briefing
- Indicating a shift from one point to another
- Dealing with questions
- Closing

In most Bridges, key lines are also available if needed.

Procedure: Students rehearse the first episode, with the instructor taking the part of the non-American. The same student may go all the way through or one student may replace another at some point, but the order of the functions is preserved. After each rehearsal, the instructor comments on communicative effectiveness and cultural appropriateness. Strictly linguistic matters are mentioned in this segment only if they bear on the effectiveness or appropriateness of the message communicated. After the first few rehearsals, the instructor may gradually introduce difficulties of a type which might naturally arise in the kind of encounter being practiced, such as, wandering from the subject, expressing hostility, and the like.

Remarks: Emphasizing the effectiveness and appropriateness of communication over grammatical correctness at this stage of the Bridge is consistent with the concern for job-relevence (emphasis 1). In this sense, Bridges provide a good balance for the main curriculum, where there is necessarily a good bit of attention paid to linguistic correctness. Working from the list of functions is of course another example of emphasis 2. Because both sides are free to improvise what they want to say, the external reality constraint is at a minimum, and so the quality of communication (emphasis 3) may not yet be very high.

Segment 7: further elicitation

Goals: (1) To make students aware of certain types of discourse needs, and (2) to provide linguistic material suitable for meeting those needs.

Materials: None.

Procedure: The instructor goes to the board and asks the students what kinds of difficulty arose during the rehearsal. Depending on the Bridge, difficulties may have included getting the non-American to talk so that the student could understand, getting the non-American back on track, etc. The instructor then elicits suggestions for resources which the students would have liked to have had in order to deal more effectively with this aspect of the discourse. He writes on the board in the TL whatever appropriate suggestions the students make. He is also free to add to the list from his own experience.

Remarks: Because these new sentences correspond to discourse needs, they are functionally strong (emphasis 2); and because they arise in the context of a realistic task, they are highly relevant (emphasis 1). The students have generated this new linguistic material out of the experience of the rehearsal; therefore, they are able to work with a more direct and vivid nonverbal counterpart of the words and sentences (emphasis 5) than if they had merely been provided with a prefabricated list of phrases for the same purposes.

Segment 8: further practice

This activity is similar to segment 7 (rehearsal) in both procedure and rationale.

Segments 9 and 10: sample dialogue B and rehearsal

These segments are similar in procedure and rationale to segments 5 and 6. Sample dialogue B is based on the next episode in the scenario. For example in the Arrangements Bridge, the same officer who held an exploratory meeting with his counterpart in the first episode (sample dialogue A) now gets down to finalizing details.

Segment 11: simulation

Goals: (1) To bring the students in the classroom as close as possible to the kind of field experience for which we have been preparing them; and (2) to provide a culminating event for the Bridge as a whole.

Materials: Separate briefing papers for students and instructor.

Procedure: The simulation is usually an enactment of a third episode in the scenario. For example, in the Arrangements Bridge an emergency back at the Embassy forces last-minute changes in the Ambassador's schedule, which the officer must work out with his counterpart. Each student does the simulation individually, working with an instructor other than the one who had been the instructor for the Bridge up to that point. The student receives a briefing paper that sets forth what he might know as the third episode begins, and the instructor works from a separate paper that provides the facts that might be available to the non-American. The simulation may be tape-recorded for future listening after the Bridge has ended.

Sample Instructions to Students for the Simulation Exercise
Continuing in the role of the American in dialogue A and B, you

telephone the hospital in Bad Kreuznach to find out about the civilians who were injured in the plane crash. Aside from your normal humanitarian motives, it is important for public relations that the United States Government not come across as unconcerned with these people. Therefore, you will want to find out such things as the names and ages of the injured, the nature and extent of their injuries, how long they are likely to be hospitalized, the name of the attending physician, and the addresses of their families. Also, in anticipation of a visit by the Ambassador or his personal representative, you will want to ascertain the visiting hours and the exact location of the hospital in Bad Kreuznach. (Perhaps you will think of other questions.)

Remarks: The change of instructors—together with the absence of suitable key lines, sample, and rehearsal specially aimed at this episode—heightens the realism of this segment (emphasis 1). Instructors commonly get into their roles and display previously hidden dramatic talents which greatly enhance the vividness of the experience (emphasis 5).

Students almost invariably come out of the experience with increased confidence in their ability to deal with the unpredictable (emphasis 4). The disparity of the information in the two briefing papers, and the requirement of reaching some kind of conclusion/agreement/decision consistent with that information, together make for communication of relatively high quality (emphasis 3).

Segment 12: microtasks

Goals: (1) To demonstrate that the *functions* found in the Bridge are independent of the *context* of the Bridge, and (2) to allow each student to practice these same functions in a context that is typical of his or her prospective assignment overseas.

Materials: Separate briefing papers for instructor and student.

Procedure: Follow the same procedures as those for simulations, with the exception that microtasks are usually done with the Bridge instructor and in the presence of the entire class.

Remarks: The results here are similar to those noted for simulations (segment 11), but they are frequently even more dramatic and convincing. It is important that each student receive a microtask that is as close as possible to something he or she expects to face overseas. For this reason, in selecting or designing microtasks for individual students, we feel free to ask them about their own perceived needs.

The microtasks end the Main Sequence of the Bridge activities. At least two kinds of additional activities are interspersed within the Main Sequence. The most frequent of these are "overheard conversations" and "written documents."

Movable segment: overheard conversations

Goals: (1) To provide additional material that contributes to the total picture on which the students will be able to draw in the simulation and microtask segments; and (2) to make it necessary for students to shift out of their customary word-by-word modality and into a style of listening which will serve them well when they are exposed to language that is far over their heads.

Materials: (1) Audio- or videotapes of communication among native speakers with no restrictions on vocabulary, grammar, stylistic level, or speed. These are typically conversations but may also be public addresses, newscasts, etc. (2) Worksheets containing multiple-choice questions. These questions are intended not as tests of comprehension but as attention-pointers to help the students decide what to listen for. There may be two sets of questions about the same tape, one set for most students and another for weaker students: "What, in general, were the speakers complaining about?" contrasted with, "Did the speakers sound pleased or displeased?" The general thrust of all questions is professional rather than linguistic.

Procedure: With the instructor out of the room, the students listen to the tape once without stopping it. They pool their partial understandings of it and try to reach consensus on answering the questions. They listen a second time, again without interruption, and again pool what they have understood of it. At this point, the instructor returns and the students tell him what they have heard. The instructor may answer questions which the students are able to ask on the basis of what they heard, but he does not quiz the students nor discuss the linguistic form of the conversation. At all costs he avoids a sentence-by-sentence translation and prevents the students from reverting to that way of dealing with the TL. If there have been any gross misunderstandings, he may suggest what the students need to listen for and play the tape a third time.

Remarks: This activity has been extremely successful in developing the students' ability to deal with material that is over their heads and in building their confidence in that ability (emphasis 4). It is chosen for its realism and relevance to the task at hand (emphasis 1). The necessity of reaching conclusions that will be consistent with what is on the tape contributes to the quality of communication (emphasis 3). The interesting content and the liveliness of the conversation enrich the imagery which the students can attach to the linguistic side of other segments (emphasis 5).

Movable segment: written documents

Goals: The goals are the same as those for the overheard-conversations segment.

Materials: Authentic materials such as drivers' licenses, public notices, or newspaper articles, or specially written texts such as a press release based on something that has happened in the scenario. Worksheets with multiple-choice questions are sometimes used. In the Facts-over-the-Phone Bridge, one activity involves finding places and following routes on maps of the crash area as the instructor describes them orally.

Procedure: The procedure is similar to that for overheard conversations. Tasks are again professional in nature: "Check this press release for discrepancies with the facts presented in the briefing paper, sample dialogues, etc."

Remarks: Again, this type of activity is closely analogous to its aural counterpart (above), but because the students have the material in written form, the instructor has to be even more careful to prevent this segment from degenerating into conventional translation.

The Bridge ends with a wrap-up session in which students are encouraged to look at the experience of the past two and a half days and examine what they have learned from it—not only the words and sentences but also the insights they have gained into what using a language means and how they themselves go about it.

New Basic Courses

A basic course is just what its name suggests; it underlies the full training program and addresses both the professional and the personal needs of its students, most of whom are officers. There is no need to give a complete description of any of the new basic courses. They do, however, include at least four formats that deserve mention here: "matrix" dialogues, lessons in geography and politics, "question triads," and newspaper articles for beginners. Again, none of these formats is completely original, and insofar as the formats are original, they may not fit the needs of all readers. They have, nevertheless, been quite successful, and they throw additional light on the five emphases listed earlier in this chapter.

All of these formats exemplify the principle of comprehension-based instruction for beginners. For the first 50–100 hours, these courses require little or no production on the part of the student. This obviously puts into practice emphasis 4 (the comprehension advantage). The question was how to preserve the other emphases at the same time, rather than resorting to Styrofoam content. The first two formats address this problem directly.

"Matrix" dialogues

Goals: (1) To accustom students from the beginning to language spoken as they will hear it at post; (2) to develop students' ability to respond to speech as a functional whole, and not merely as a sequence of linguistic units; and (3) to introduce within a realistic "matrix" the general topic of the remaining parts of the lesson.

Materials: (1) A one-to-two-minute tape recording of two or more native speakers engaged in rapid-fire, linguistically unrestricted conversation. The dialogue is on a topic that is generally related to the subject of the rest of the lesson, but it is entirely nondidactic in content and form. (2) A set of questions about the tape, carefully selected to allow the students to respond satisfactorily even within their severely limited capabilities. In the very first lesson, for example, the questions might resemble the following:

- How many speakers are there?
- Do they sound animated? happy? concerned? businesslike? friendly?
- Do you hear any words—proper names, for example—which you think you recognize?

Procedure: With the instructor out of the room, students listen to the tape straight through. As a group they compare their answers to the questions and listen to the tape a second time. Then they discuss the tape briefly with the instructor. The instructor answers no questions about the language— not even questions about the meanings of words, although he may state his own answers to the questions.

Remarks: In the new Arabic and Russian courses, the very first activity on the first day is one of these matrix dialogues. The relationship of this format to the comprehension advantage (emphasis 4) is obvious. We believe also that this experience will help to establish a functional outlook right from the start (emphasis 2). The tape is an interesting artifact which becomes the topic of genuine communication among the students and instructor, even if that communication is in English (emphasis 3). Comparing notes with the instructor about the apparent type of discourse and emotional state of the speakers frequently helps to identify and clear up cross-culturally important differences in perception. It is thus consistent with the emphases on relevance and imagery.

Lessons in geography and politics

Goals: (1) To require students to respond meaningfully to spoken and written utterances in the language; (2) to keep the quality of the communication as high as possible, and (3) to minimize the students' need to produce anything in the language.

Materials: Materials may consist of taped segments, including many names of people and places, and a large geopolitical map.

Procedure: The students listen to the tape and list any proper names they have recognized. Then students are asked in the target language to point out on the map countries and cities whose names they have recognized. Throughout these procedures, students hear but do not produce the target language.

Remarks: There are two quite different reasons, both widely discussed in the current literature, for avoiding production by the students at this stage. First, it reduces the chance of immediate defeat and discouragement, particularly for students with lower aptitude. Second, it allows students time to assemble clear and accurate mental composites of the sounds and the letter shapes without disturbance from listening to their own and their classmates' premature efforts at production.

In our choice of subject matter, we have taken advantage of the fact that the geographical details of the Arab world, the Soviet Union, and Czechoslovakia are not well known to many Americans. These details will, however, be of definite interest and professional relevance to persons living and working in those areas.

Question triads

Goals: (1) To foster the development of rich mental imagery in connection with a dialogue. (2) To provide for high-quality communication in the target language.

Materials: (1) A dialogue of twenty to twenty-five turns. (2) Three questions for each line of the dialogue. The first question in the triad must be answered out of each student's own mental images: "What color is the house?" or "Are there trees between the street and the house?" These questions are ones for which answers cannot be found in, or even inferred from, the words of the dialogue. The second question has to do with the function of the sentence and is usually stated as an alternative: "Was the speaker genuinely seeking information, or was he merely being polite?" and "Was this really a statement of fact, or was it a request for permission?" The third question is generally, "How else might the speaker have accomplished this purpose?"

Procedure: (1) Students listen to the dialogue once without their books. (2) Students listen a second time, noticing points that are not clear to them. (3) Students listen a third time but now interrupt with questions, generally in the TL. The instructor answers questions briefly in the TL until the meaning of the dialogue is clear to all. (4) Students listen a fourth time, closing their eyes or staring at the wall, and watch their own sequence of mental images as these are evoked by the words. (5) The instructor asks the question triads, as described above, and students answer consistent with their own mental images. Conversation is entirely or almost entirely in the TL.

Remarks: One of the first low-aptitude students who used this format was heard to remark, "This is the first time, in any language, that I've known what I was talking about!" We interpret this to mean that for the first time he had a fairly full set of images as nonverbal counterparts to the words of the language sample. If this interpretation is correct, the success of the technique may be due to the time and attention devoted to the images. To use an analogy with photography, images are first developed through the questions and then fixed through comparison and discussion of answers. One university teacher of French reported the following when she began using a similar technique with the dialogues in her textbook:

> The student response was phenomenal. Even my weakest students, who rarely (if at all) try to respond to the traditional questions ("Where are the two friends meeting?" "What did X say to Y?" etc.) were enthusiastically trying as hard as they could to answer the "imagination" questions I posed. The students came alive, each trying to outdo the other with their cleverness, and pulling up from somewhere all kinds of vocabulary they had never had a chance to use before. Dialogue Day became their favorite day of the week, and oral participation improved immediately. . . . The department chairman was delighted.

The job-relevance of this activity (emphasis 1) is derived from the dialogues. Since the images about which the students talk are entirely in their own minds, each person has his or her own set. Conversation is constrained by this reality, and so communication is of relatively high quality. This is particularly true as the students learn from the discrepancies between their own images and those of their instructor (emphasis 3). The images, once established, allow students to do a relatively large amount of interpolation and extrapolation in order to get the meanings of new or partly forgotten words (emphasis 4). Questions of the second and third types are functionally oriented par excellence (emphasis 2).

Newspaper articles for beginners

Goals: (1) To accustom students from the beginning to the kind of printed texts they will be dealing with at post, inculuding the typography. (2) To develop students' ability to look at each newspaper article as a functional whole and not merely as a sequence of linguistic units. (4) To require students to perform, with these articles, tasks similar to those which will be part of their jobs.

Materials: (1) A series of short, generally complete articles photocopied from recent newspapers, and (2) a set of questions or other tasks to accompany each article.

Procedure: Students look at each article, read the questions or tasks, then return to the article and work with it just enough to answer the questions or complete the tasks. The instructor remains present as a resource but does not actively lead the students.

Remarks: In the early lessons, this format is the written counterpart of the matrix dialogues.

"FAST" Courses

"FAST" Courses now exist in fourteen languages including French, Spanish, Thai, Arabic, and German. The acronym FAST stands for "familiarization and short-term," so called because the course is designed for students who would not normally receive full-scale language and area training before going abroad: family members, clerical staff, and others. It is definitely not designed as a beginning course in a coherent sequence of courses.

Like the series of Bridges, a FAST Course places heavy emphasis on proficiency in the practical rather than the narrow linguistic sense. Unlike Bridges but like the twenty- or forty-four-week basic courses, it aims for a kind of comprehensiveness, though on a much smaller scale. A FAST Course in one of the better-known languages lasts ten weeks (approximately 300 hours), while for the less commonly taught ones it lasts six weeks (approximately 180 hours). Students generally emerge with oral proficiency ratings of 1 or 1+, though a few students have done even better.

Each lesson takes place in some very common setting and shows an American dealing with a frequent, often urgent, need. Some examples are: "What if the person who meets me at the airport doesn't speak English?" "How do I go about hiring domestic help?" "What if my car breaks down out in the country somewhere?" Verb forms and pronunciation and sentence patterns come in, but only as they can be shown to contribute effectiveness in dealing with survival situations like these.

The materials, which have been developed for FAST Courses, differ somewhat among themselves. Nevertheless, on the basis of two years experience, we have been able to develop a general methodology that fits most of them and that we recommend for Foreign Service personnel who are using these courses outside Washington. The method consists of nine steps.

Step 1: the night before

Goals: (1) To allow students to see what they can do with new samples of the language before they meet them formally in class, and (2) to save a bit of class time.

Materials: An audiotape, containing at least a dialogue on the topic of the lesson. It may include a TL description of the setting in which the dialogue takes place and possibly other background information as well. The tape may also provide a brief glossary. It does not contain anything resembling pattern drills.

Procedure: The night before the classroom presentation, students take the tape home and listen to it. They are encouraged not to memorize it but to let it sink into their network of unconscious perceptions, to be glad of whatever they happen to understand from it, and to form in their minds questions on the linguistic form or on the content or both.

Remarks: This procedure both recognizes and encourages whatever degree of self-sufficiency each student is able to display. At the same time, it obviates an immediate and public comparison of individuals who are quick at grasping language and those who need a bit more time. It is, of course, also an instance of exploiting the comprehension advantage (emphasis 4). It allows not only for the formation of preliminary mental images (emphasis 5), but also for clarification of the gaps within those images. It thus contributes to students' nonverbal readiness for the formal instruction of the following day.

Step 2: setting the scene

Goals: (1) To develop further the pictorial and other nonverbal resources which students will attach to the words of the lesson. (2) To provide information students would find useful even if they never used a word of the language.

Materials: A description written in English of the setting in which the sample dialogue will take place, e.g., an airport in French-speaking Africa, and an introduction to the situation students will confront in that setting, e.g., the person who will be picking them up does not understand or speak English.

Procedure: The instructor (or the textbook) tells the students in English something of the physical and cultural setting in which the sample dialogue (step 3) will take place: sights, sounds, smells, tastes, temperature, and as many other details as seem to be of interest. He also invites the students to talk about the situation as they had imagined it on the basis of their own past experiences, and to list some of the things they themselves would want to be able to do if they found themselves in that setting.

Remarks: Imagery (emphasis 5) is again conspicuous here. The students' contributions to the discussion also serve to tie the dialogue more closely to their anticipated needs (emphasis 1), and the list of things that need to be done establishes a strong functional outlook for the activities that follow (emphasis 2).

Step 3: hearing it

Goals: (1) To expose students to a sample of how they might deal with the situation on which the lesson is based. (2) To challenge and so to develop and reward the students' ability to pick things up through listening.

Materials: The tape-recorded dialogue used in step 1. The dialogue is unbalanced and nonreversible, as these terms were used in the description of segment 5 of Bridges.

Procedure: Students listen to the dialogue without interruption once or twice, and then they talk—in English, of course—about what they think they heard and about what remains unclear. They are frequently able to work out the answers to these questions among themselves, listening again to the tape if they like, without assistance from the instructor. When they are not able to get what they are after, the instructor is free to give any kind of brief and simple help that seems appropriate. There is, however, no translation of the dialogue.

Remarks: Attention is still primarily on getting the message (emphasis 1) rather than on the language per se, and the channel is still aural comprehension (emphasis 4).

Step 4: seeing it

Goals: (1) To continue the discovery process, now using the visual channel. (2) To allow time for full and accurate composite images of sounds, words, and other features of the language to take shape in the students' minds.

Materials: The tape, together with a TL transcript and an English-language version.

Procedure: The instructor will probably use several techniques during this step. In general, the students listen to the tape, look at the transcript (but not at the English version), and try to figure out as much as they can. This step can be particularly interesting if the language uses an unfamiliar writing system. Then the instructor gives them the English version and lets them repeat the process. They do not read aloud yet, but they may profit at this stage from matching a list of printed words with blanks in a text which is identical with or similar to the sample dialogue. We have also sometimes provided students with the sentences of the dialogue in scrambled order and asked them to renumber them. This has generally worked well.

Remarks: Here is the comprehension advantage (emphasis 4) once more. The blank-filling and unscrambling exercises allow the students to manipulate the linguistic elements relative to each other with reference to the meaningful whole (emphases 1 and 2), instead of requiring reference to English equivalents.

Step 5: taking it apart

Goals: (1) To shift the focus temporarily off the message and onto the form. (2) To take advantage of students' intellectual abilities and build their intellectual understanding.

Materials: The transcript and the English version, accompanied in some courses by a glossary.

Procedure: There are two main types of activity in this step: practicing pronunciation of most or all of the new words, and answering questions. In dealing with questions, the instructor follows two rules: (1) don't answer any question that the students haven't actually asked, and (2) keep each answer under five seconds. If students want to know more, let them ask. (Adhering to rule 2 makes violation of rule 1 less likely!)

Remarks: Although the five emphases that permeate the new materials set them apart from much conventional language teaching of the past, we are not ready to do away entirely with the conscious and intellectual side of language study. We view it as valuable both in its own right and as a means of forestalling anxieties in those who believe it is central to their own best approach to a new language.

Step 6: getting the feel of it

Goals: (1) To allow students to begin flexing their speech muscles on the sample, and (1) to keep each item before the students long enough so they can observe it in multiple ways.

Materials: (1) The sample dialogue again and (2) a few simple pattern drills.

Procedures: Here we use almost the same techniques of choral and individual mimicry and sentence manipulation that have been characteristic of audiolingual instruction.

Remarks: As in step 5, we are unwilling to throw out the baby with the bathwater. We have, however, placed this activity in a supporting role near the middle of our sequence of steps, rather than making it the cornerstone of our method.

Step 7: putting it back together

Goals: (1) To allow students to work with the newly familiar material in another way. (2) To provide both the verification and the satisfaction that are possible only with written output.

Materials: Lists of TL sentences to be expressed in English, identical with or similar to those in the sample.

Procedure: This is usually a group project, the first few minutes of which may be carried out in the absence of the instructor.

Remarks: Notice that we are still working on the nonverbal half of the memory record elaborated in the discussion of imagery (emphasis 5). We assume that the multiple inputs in steps 1–7 reinforce one another and thus help form a mental record which will be relatively accurate, stable, and accessible.

Step 8: making it work

Goals: (1) To shift back from attention on *how* things are said, to a concern with *what* is being said. (2) To wean students from the entirely familiar to the partly familiar.

Materials: The printed sample dialogue.

Procedure: This is a series of many rehearsals with the instructor. As time goes on, these rehearsals change along four dimensions. First, students follow the dialogue on the page; then students keep their books open but look at the page only when necessary; and finally students keep their books closed. Second, the instructor speaks slowly and gradually more rapidly and with some animation. Third, the instructor sticks to the words in the book and then varies them to a lesser or greater degree. Fourth, the instructor preserves the order of the lines in the dialogue, and then changes the order.

Remarks: Whenever the instructor changes the words or the order of the lines or even delivers familiar utterances with unaccustomed dynamics, students must decide whether and how the content has been changed. This brings them back to exploitation of the comprehension advantage (emphasis 4). Because the limits on change are still rather narrow, however, the quality of communication (emphasis 3) remains fairly low.

Step 9: using it

Goals: (1) To come close to and sometimes achieve real communication. (2) Not least, to leave the students with the realization that they have made appreciable progress in their preparation for dealing with everyday life in the host country.

Materials: A series of printed tasks. Examples from the early lessons of one course are:
- Find out what languages the other people in the room speak or have studied. A few minutes later, summarize these same facts in order to verify that you have gotten them correctly.
- If you buy something for 40 francs, how much change will you get from a 100-franc note?
- If your luggage gets lost, how will you describe it?

Procedure: Students and instructor use the language in order to exchange facts, some of which may be new to at least a part of the group.

Remarks: Students are still drawing on their new linguistic ability, yet they are no longer bound by the original sample. An information gap is introduced and filled, and the quality of communication is much higher than in step 8.

Summary

This chapter has been written in consultation with numerous FSI colleagues, and with the helpful comments of Ted Higgs, Alice Omaggio, and Michael McDade. When one writes under these favorable circumstances, one ought to learn something, and perhaps I have. At the School of

Language Studies, we have learned that five aspects of the curriculum development undertaken over the last two years have already made a significant impact on the program. All of them relate directly to specific features of materials design. First is the overwhelmingly positive effect of the overheard conversations (the first movable segment of the Bridge sequence) and the matrix dialogues (the first format mentioned in the description of the new basic courses). We have observed this positive effect in noncognate as well as in cognate languages. Second is the use of task consideration and key line elicitation (segments 2 and 3 of the Bridge sequence) before presenting *any* of the sample dialogues. Third is the early use of authentic and unedited newspaper materials (the fourth format in the description of new basic courses). Fourth is the use of unbalanced and nonreversible dialogues in Bridges and FAST Courses, in order to allow partially spontaneous interchanges between students and instructors even in the very early lessons. The fifth is the use of the question triads (the third format in the description of the basic courses).

A further, more general, conclusion also suggests itself. Looking back at the sections on Bridges, new basic courses, and FAST Courses, I am surprised that one of the five emphases—the emphasis on imagery— appears central with respect to the others. Imagery, remember, does not refer only to visual sensations, which may be quite vivid for some people but almost entirely absent for others. It also includes other physical sensations, awareness of time and purpose, and many other high-level cognitive structures. The emphasis on the comprehension advantage, for example, depends on the fact that images may come even from language that a student could not have produced independently and that he or she may not even understand completely. The emphasis on communication entails the use of a gap in the nonverbal imagery, a gap which is to be filled primarily through exchange of information by means of words. The emphasis on function requires students to take into account aspects of both purpose and setting, beyond the bounds of single sentences. Each of these latter two features is an important, even inevitable, part of what I mean by imagery. Finally, the emphasis on relevance grows out of the concern that the images attached to the words should be appropriate ones.

Although the materials described in this chapter are now two years old and have been used by dozens or, in some cases, hundreds of students, we look forward to developing and refining them further. The Subsaharan French FAST Course is now available through the National Audiovisual Center, and we expect the Spanish FAST Course soon, with others to follow in the near future. Meanwhile, we hope that this report will interest colleagues who, like us, are charged with developing in their students a full range of language proficiencies.

4

Proficiency Testing for the Other Language Modalities

Jerry W Larson
Randall L. Jones
Brigham Young University

Introduction

During recent years language teachers and researchers have invested a great deal of time and effort in the improvement of language tests. Considerable progress has been made, particularly in the area of oral proficiency testing. However, as the emphasis on oral assessment has reached unprecedented heights, development of proficiency-oriented tests for the other language skills and for culture has fallen behind. This lack of evaluation instruments in the other modalities is now of concern to the language-teaching profession. The area of culture is extensively treated in Chapter 5 of this volume. The purpose of this chapter is to discuss some of the issues involved in proficiency-oriented testing of "the other" language modalities, i.e., listening, reading, and writing.

Jerry W Larson (Ph.D., University of Minnesota) is an Assistant Professor of Spanish at Brigham Young University, where he is also Director of Foreign-Language Testing Programs and Director of the Humanities Learning Resource Center. He teaches undergraduate and graduate courses in Language and Methodology. He has published in the *Modern Language Journal* and is an author of *Español a lo vivo,* a college-level introductory textbook. He is a member of the International Association for Learning Laboratories, of AATSP, ACTFL, and UFLA.

Randall L. Jones (Ph.D., Princeton University) is a Professor of German at Brigham Young University, where he teaches undergraduate and graduate courses in Language and Linguistics. He is also the Director of the Humanities Research Center at that institution. His publications appear in a wide variety of professional journals and in the ACTFL Foreign Language Education Series. He is a member of AAAL, AATG, ACTFL, IAAL, and MLA.

What Is Proficiency? ─────────────────────────

Certainly germane to the issue of proficiency testing is an understanding of what is to be meant by "proficiency." Interpretations of the term range from the ability simply to use properly the phonology and structural devices of the language (Fries, 20) to complete mastery of all of the components of communication (Carroll, 8; Hymes, 35; and Jakobovits, 36). Wilkins (73) and others (Harlow, 26; Dobson, 17; Germain, 22) have suggested that language proficiency depends on linguistic functions, situational contexts, and personal needs. For some educators the term *communicative competence* has become synonymous with proficiency. Given the various interpretations of proficiency, it is difficult to settle on one commonly acceptable definition. Jones (39) suggests that perhaps there should not be a single operational definition of language proficiency, since proficiency for placement purposes may be different from proficiency needed for functional purposes. However, in order to serve as a point of reference for the following discussion, language proficiency as used in this chapter will be defined simply as the ability to communicate *accurately* in whichever language modality is pertinent to the communicative requirements of the situation.

Relationship of the four modalities and proficiency testing

To date the commonly used language proficiency tests have been designed to evaluate proficiency in individual language skills, the rationale being that each skill is unique and independent. However, there has also been considerable discussion about the possible interrelationship of skills, which motivates a "unitary factor hypothesis." After analyzing data from the *MLA Foreign Language Proficiency Tests for Teachers and Advanced Students,* Paquette and Tollinger (56) conclude that the intercorrelations of the test parts are sufficiently high to suggest that a large portion of the variance of each skill test is attributable to a common factor of language competence. Oller (50) also asserts that there is substantial empirical evidence to support a general language proficiency factor that accounts for nearly all of the variance in language tests. In another work, he states that this underlying proficiency factor relates to a "psychologically real grammatical system" (Oller, 48). Clifford (15) hypothesizes that this shared common variance may be caused by a redundancy in the aspects of language being tested by each of the skill tests. Oller and Spolsky (49) claim that subscores on any proficiency test are apt to be highly interrelated. They further state that ". . . strong arguments have been developed showing that, from a linguistic point of view, low correlations indicate a lack of validity in the sub-parts of a language proficiency test" (pp. 95–96).

Hosley and Meredith (33), however, reject the unitary factor hypothesis. Based on their analysis of subtests of the TOEFL, they believe that language skills are separate but are hierarchically related—i.e., the skills differ in complexity, with the more complex skills including all or parts of the simpler, more basic ones. Carroll (7) warns against concluding on the basis of high intercorrelations that there is one universal language skill because: (1) high correlations are usually found only in cases where instruction has occurred in all skills, (2) relative levels of proficiency in each of the skills are not accounted for by high correlations, and (3) the language skills being tested are "integrated" skills, which depend on various competencies in particular aspects of the language, e.g., phonology, spelling, grammar, and lexicon. Farhady (18) also cautions that simply because there is a high correlation between two tests, it should not be assumed that the two tests necessarily measure the same thing.

The argument for administering separate skills tests in order to determine proficiency in any given skill is further strengthened when one considers the nature of correlational data. Upshur et al. (67) stress that correlational data are simply incapable of proving causal relationships: "If scores yielded by two measures X and Y are correlated, one does not know whether variance in the underlying variable X produces variance in the underlying variable Y or whether Y produces X, or, for that matter, whether Z is the cause of both, or indeed whether the correlation is better explained by some other, more complex, causal relationship" (p. 99). In a recent research report, Carroll (6) says that while he believes that there is a "general language ability," he also believes that language skills tend to develop at different rates and to different degrees and that this individualized development allows skills to be recognized and measured separately. Oller (48) himself feels that just because part scores on a language test intercorrelate highly, we should not assume that they are redundant and eliminate one of the parts from the test. By doing this, he claims ". . . we would be making a fundamental error in the definition of *reliability* versus *validity*" (p. 194). Nevertheless, because of the great amount of time required to score a nonobjective proficiency test, in certain cases a pretest designed to identify qualified candidates might be considered. If, for example, a test is needed to satisfy the completion of a university foreign-language requirement or to certify a candidate for some other language-related purpose, it would be uneconomical if not impossible to administer an oral proficiency examination to all candidates who presented themselves. A shorter screening test would make it possible to determine who is nominally qualified to take the full proficiency test.

Proficiency testing vs. achievement testing

Before discussing issues related to proficiency testing of the modalities other than speaking, it is first important to make a distinction between "proficiency testing" and "achievement testing." Achievement tests examine specific features of the foreign language and are usually based on a finite corpus of specific instructional materials. They are used mostly for academic purposes such as diagnosis, motivation, grades, and achievement certification. Statistical analysis of this type of test is much simpler than analysis of more global, proficiency-oriented tests. Proficiency tests, on the other hand, are performance oriented, requiring the examinee to apply acquired knowledge to perform designated communication tasks. They are based on functional language ability and are not limited by a closed set of course materials nor constrained by instructional variables.

The language teaching profession continues to emphasize better preparation of students for funcuional, real-life communication. The needs of the world demand it. As this impetus gains strength, the need for valid and reliable performance tests increases. The type of language performance to be evaluated requires that both the nature and design of these tests be different from those of traditional achievement tests. Tests should be constructed in such a way as to cause the student to demonstrate his or her ability to give and receive many different types of information. Jones (41) explains that tests must involve more than simply measuring some one thing or even a few things; they must measure a complex set of sub-abilities which operate simultaneously, and are only partially isolable and distinguishable.

As with achievement tests, proficiency tests also must be valid, reliable, and efficient. In order to develop tests that meet these standards, Jones (41) suggests five conditions that must be met.

- Specification of the significant language criteria to be tested
- Training of judges or scorers with regard to these criteria
- Construction of the test so that it is linguistically realistic and a rational sample of the language being tested
- Proper administration of the test
- Accurate evaluation and quantification of the examinees' performance

Although there has been considerable progress in the development of proficiency tests, much remains to be done, particularly for testing language modalities other than speaking. As Fitzpatrick and Morrison (19) have mentioned, perhaps testers need to be brave enough to experiment with procedures other than the paper-and-pencil type.

Rationale for proficiency testing in all modalities

The need for accurate measures of language proficiency is increasingly evident. The dominant role of English in the world is declining, creating a significant demand for persons who are able to communicate functionally in languages other than English. Secretary of Education Terrell H. Bell commented in a recent interview that "we do not, as a country nor as a people, live in isolation. Learning foreign languages is important. The business of industry and of this country's foreign relations does not occur in just one language; it is conducted in many. . . . As the world grows smaller, . . . we need to know more about the people and culture of other countries. A knowledge of foreign language can help us achieve this" (Garfinkel, 21, p. 64).

In view of the current and future needs for proficiency in foreign languages, the foreign-language-teaching profession is faced with the challenge of both preparing and certifying language-competent students. To assist in the certification process an agreed upon set of national proficiency standards for each of the language modalities is needed. Uniform proficiency guidelines are helpful to both language-training institutions and to employers, in that they serve teachers and learners as yardsticks for measuring progress toward a specific goal of communicative ability. They also serve as screening criteria for employers who must be certain of the proficiency level of their prospective employees. The ACTFL/ETS Provisional Proficiency Guidelines (see Appendix A), in combination with work being done at individual language-training institutions, will ultimately provide a set of standards by which proficiency in a foreign or second language can be accurately determined. Such guidelines will be useful in alleviating many of the current problems of proper placement within academic programs and in outside professions.

Other considerations in foreign-language proficiency testing

Fundamental to testing decisions is a determination of testing needs. Before tests are produced and administered, teachers should decide exactly what the needs of testing are and then be sure that the test meets those needs. If it is determined that a proficiency test is required, the teacher must then decide up to what levels of proficiency the test should be sensitive and for which modalities. It would be unwise, for example, to administer to second-year high school students a proficiency measure designed to identify or to discriminate advanced-level skills. In addition to not providing necessary information, e.g., for making placement decisions, it would have an extremely negative, frustrating effect on the students.

Another area of concern in testing is that of *affect,* or student attitude toward the experience of taking the test. Factors that bear on test affect include testing format and procedures used, tester's personality, physical environment/test location, and the time at which the test is administered. Although relatively little research has focused on test affect, one study conducted by Madsen, Jones, and Brown (46) indicates that there are statistically significant differences in student reactions to different types of tests and that these reactions have an impact on the performance of the examinees. Regardless of how effective a psychometric measurement device appears to be, the affective response to it can influence the validity of that measure.

Testing Listening Proficiency

During the past several years there has been renewed interest among language teachers concerning the role of listening in second-language learning. Krashen (43), Nord (47), Postovsky (58), Winitz (74), and many others have offered compelling arguments that the development of *oral* proficiency is enhanced greatly by systematic training in *listening*. Furthermore, it has been recognized that listening as a skill has been greatly neglected in many second-language programs. Experience has shown that proficiency in listening is not necessarily developed automatically by students hearing pattern drills, dialogues, oral readings, etc. Listening, just as the other skills, must receive its own emphasis in order to be learned effectively. Chastain (12) claims that "in spite of the relative ease with which the native speaker can receive and process oral messages, the assumption that beginning second-language learners leap directly to this ability level on the basis of some extraordinary desire, motivation, or instruction is not justified. A skill as complex as listening comprehension depends upon an acquired series of more specialized, supporting bases" (p. 81).

Perhaps part of the reason that listening has been neglected in so many language-teaching programs is that for so many years it was considered a passive skill. Even though the concept of passive may have been interpreted differently by various language-learning specialists, it nevertheless appears that there has been a common belief that somehow the development and use of listening both in first and second languages require much less active involvement than speaking. Although it is true that listening requires less overt control over grammatical and morphological structures than does speaking, it is also true that the process of listening is a very active, cognitive process. Rivers (60) suggests that it is even incorrect to call listening a *receptive* skill. She prefers instead to look at it as a *creative* skill.

A basic understanding of the process of listening is helpful in determining the most effective methods of teaching and testing it. Rivers (60) differentiates between merely "hearing" a spoken utterance and "comprehending" it, and she suggests that successful comprehension is dependent first of all on three factors: linguistic information, situational context, and intentions of the speaker. Chastain (12) lists four underlying components of listening comprehension in what he feels is an ascending order of difficulty. "One must be able to: (1) discriminate between the significant sound and intonation patterns of the language; (2) perceive an oral message; (3) keep the communication in mind while it is being processed; and finally, (4) understand the contained message" (pp. 81–82).

Basic listening tasks

A brief analysis of the listening situations that are likely to confront the foreign-language (FL) user in a real language situation shows clearly that far more time is spent in listening than in speaking. Most of the listening situations that an FL user experiences will fall into one of the following four categories.

Face-to-face communication.   This kind of personal interaction probably accounts for most of the listening opportunities of the average person. The type of language which is encountered may range from casual to formal, from simple to sophisticated, from regional dialects to standard usage, from brief to extensive. The opportunity to ask for repetition or rephrasing may not be the same in every case. The motivation for being involved in the conversation in the first place may vary widely for each situation. And finally, the amount of anxiety the speaker may experience from engaging in face-to-face conversation will differ vastly from situation to situation, depending on the importance of the situation and the degree of familiarity with the interlocutor. Having casual conversation with a close acquaintance is much less threatening than listening to the response of a bus driver on a rainy day at rush hour, as a crowd of people wait in line behind you.

Formal listening.   There are live but noninteractive listening situations that do not require the listener to respond, e.g., lectures and plays. This type of situation is in some respects less threatening because lack of comprehension is not apparent to anyone but the listener. On the other hand, the transmitted information may be required for future use, as in the case of a university lecture. In most cases formal listening is more difficult than conversational listening. The language is usually more linguistically complex, and comprehension often requires considerable prior knowledge of the topic being treated. Furthermore, the luxury of asking the speaker to repeat or rephrase a sentence is not as available as in the case of face-to-face conversation.

Overhearing. Although it may not be immediately obvious, much of the language that we hear is speech that is not necessarily intended for us. We might be waiting in line to purchase a ticket for the opera and overhear the person at the ticket window tell a disappointed patron at the front of the line that all of the balcony seats for a particular performance are sold out. We may take an interest in the conversation taking place across from us in the bus. Or we stop and listen to a salesperson explaining an item to another customer. Language takes place all around us, and we can benefit from listening to it.

Listening to electronic media. Depending on the needs of an FL user in the foreign environment, there is a very good chance that some listening experiences will involve language that is reproduced electronically, by radio, television, cassette tapes, videotapes, movies, public address announcements, and telephones. Because of the reduced redundancy typical of electronic transmission, comprehension difficulty is increased. It increases even more where the visual component is missing—with radio, telephone, sound recordings, and public address systems—since nonlinguistic information otherwise available for the interpretation of a spoken message—posture, facial expressions, attitudinal indicators, gestures—is missing. Certainly one of the most demanding tasks in second-language use is carrying on a conversation by telephone.

Any kind of functional test that seeks to measure listening comprehension in a natural setting must in some way simulate or otherwise account for the above kinds of tasks. The conditions and requirements are different in each case. It may be misleading to generalize about one's ability to function in a given situation based on conventional listening comprehension tests, arguing that acceptable validity can be achieved only if the testing conditions approximate as closely as possible an authentic listening situation. In some cases tests constructed on this model will not be appealing from a strict psychometric point of view. They will, however, be more appealing in terms of predictive validity, that is, they will be a better predictor of listening proficiency in the real-world situation.

Inhibiting factors

Most recorded material that is used to test listening proficiency has been meticulously prepared under ideal conditions. The language is spoken carefully, and the quality of both the voices and the recordings is very high. In authentic listening situations, however, such ideal conditions rarely exist, and there is an abundance of "channel noise": other people are speaking, dogs bark, doors are opened or closed, phones ring, and traffic noise intrudes. Furthermore, the person who is speaking is rarely as coherent and articulate as the voices on the tape. Other inhibiting factors also intervene. Speed of delivery varies greatly from speaker to speaker. In many languages there is also a wide variation among regional dialects, types and levels of colloquial speech, the use and nature of formal speech, etc. In the past, language testers have rarely attempted to introduce any of these elements of reality into their listening tests. The noise test (Gradman and Spolsky, 24) and the test described by Whiteson (71) are two exceptions. It would seem that for functional listening tests to be valid, the natural environment in which the language is used should be re-created to the greatest extent possible.

Conventional listening tests

The format for the majority of listening comprehension tests has become quite uniform during the past twenty years. Most items used on standard listening comprehension tests are of one of four types:

1. Logical completion
   Right after I arrived home,
   a. the telephone rang.
   b. we lived in California.
   c. her brother is coming.
   d. during the snowstorm.
2. Logical rejoinder
   When would you like to meet for lunch?
   a. Oh, I would love to!
   b. Perhaps right after the lecture.
   c. No thanks, I'm a vegetarian.
   d. I'm sorry that I was late.
3. Logical inference
   I need 10 airmail stamps.
   This sentence was most likely said:
   a. on an airplane.
   b. in a bakery.
   c. in the train station.
   d. in a post office.
4. Content questions
   When Frank told me about the difficulties his daughter had been having, I could understand why he was so upset. He just hadn't been himself for a few days and I was beginning to think *I* was the one who had changed. Fortunately, everything was resolved and he returned to his usual pleasant nature.
   Frank was behaving differently because:
   a. He lost his job.
   b. He was mad at me.

    c. He was having a family problem.

    d. He tends to be moody at times.

The items can, of course, be constructed in such a way as to focus on a particular feature of the language, e.g., phonology, lexicon, or morphology. In general, test items usually succeed at getting at the basic issue of listening comprehension, but they do not address some of the essential needs inherent in *functional* listening proficiency. A person could obtain a high score on the above kinds of tests and still experience difficulties in real-life listening situations.

Other approaches for testing listening

One important reason that the items listed above have been so popular is that they are relatively easy to use. It requires a bit of practice to write good items, but with the proper training and some experience this is not a major problem. The test can easily be assembled, administered, and scored. After a few administrations, test items can be analyzed using standard statistical procedures and can be modified as needed.

More direct approaches to testing listening offer the tester much less security. The tasks are not as easily reducible to neatly defined individual items, and administration is often more involved, sometimes requiring a one-on-one situation. The scoring is frequently less well defined, in many cases necessitating subjective judgments on the part of the scorer. Of course, subjective evaluations are not inherently invalid, and just as with the testing of oral proficiency it is sometimes necessary to sacrifice neatness in the structure of the test in order to obtain more valid results.

Following are some alternative approaches to testing listening. In some cases they have already been used extensively and are now standard testing methods. In other cases they are still tentative, and more work must be done in order to devise more reliable methods of administration and scoring. Imagination is the only restriction on creating unlimited types of testing approaches that will measure functional listening ability.

Dictation. Dictation tests were once very common in second-language programs, but they lost respectability during the 1960s when it was claimed that they were nothing more than spelling exercises. During the past decade the dictation test has been recognized as more than just a mechanical reproduction of spoken language, and in fact, it is said to be an effective and valid integrative test of general language proficiency (Oller, 52). The dictation test can easily be modified to include realistic background noise, thus approaching some of the typical situations faced by everyday users of the language. The response on the part of the examinee is not, however, realistic, i.e., writing down everything that is heard. Therefore, dictation cannot be considered a functional test of listening proficiency.

Aural translation. A listening counterpart to the FSI reading test involves a spoken instead of a written stimulus. The examinee simply listens to a segment of the language and then translates it, either orally or in writing. This kind of exercise, especially in the oral mode, gets at the heart of the matter, and is a common experience for many second-language speakers. One is asked by a monolingual speaker of English to serve as an interpreter in some kind of informal situation. However, oral interpreting usually requires greater precision than is typical in general conversation. The practical limitations of real language situations dictate that we pay close attention not to the *form* of the utterance but to the *content.* Furthermore, we only tune in as closely as is necessary to get the message. Because of the redundancy of language, much of the linguistic material transmitted can be ignored without losing the essentials of the speaker's message. One of the principal problems with aural translation is that it may force the examinee to pay too much attention to the details of the utterance.

Selective listening. It is often the case that we are looking for specific information when listening to language. We want to know if the announcement in the train station concerns our train or if the weather report on the radio forecasts rainy or fair weather. We often tune out or even fail to understand some of the vocabulary or structure. This use of "advance organizers"—i.e., relevant ideas that assist the student in leading up to the task—can be exploited in a listening test by asking only for certain information (Chastain, 12). For example, a short radio message is played and a few questions are asked about the content. The format of the test can range from open-ended to multiple-choice.

Making decisions. Frequently it is necessary to make a decision after we have heard something spoken. If it is announced that my train will be delayed, is there enough time to get something to eat? If someone has given me directions to a certain location, should I walk or take a taxi? After hearing the weather report, do I take an umbrella or not? A variety of testing items can be constructed with this idea in mind. For example, a short message can be played that is typically broadcast in a department store before closing time. The examinee must select from alternatives the most appropriate course of action, e.g., drop everything and get out of the store as quickly as possible, ignore the message and continue shopping, prepare to make last-minute purchases.

Gisting. Sometimes it is important to hear a message and then distill the critical information to a few words or sentences. This, of course, is what we do in taking notes at a lecture. We want to retain only what is necessary in order to jog our memories about the entire message. In most cases key words and phrases are all that need to be recorded (see, for instance, the sections on "key line elicitation and practice" in Chapter 3). Used in a testing context, gisting can indicate if the examinee has understood the general topics of the message and has been able to sort the key ideas from the rest of the accompanying linguistic material.

Reading

Despite the fact that for many years reading has been less emphasized than the oral skills—particularly during the audiolingual era—many educators again recognize reading as a significant communication skill. Henning (30) claims that reading not only is an important objective of language learners but also is a key predictor of overall language proficiency. In separate research studies, Larson (44) and Hosley and Meredith (33) have reported that reading seems to be the most representative of an apparent underlying language proficiency factor. Because of the renewed interest and emphasis on reading, it is necessary for the foreign-language profession to increase its regard for the development of effective and efficient tests of reading proficiency. To understand better the considerations that are involved in testing reading proficiency, some aspects of the reading skill should be discussed briefly.

Reading was once considered a passive skill in which the written language was simply a graphic representation of the spoken language. Behaviorists in psychology and structuralists in linguistics claimed that the reading process consisted merely of learning the grapheme-phoneme correspondences which would in turn allow the reader to recode the visual representation (Hauptman, 28). Later, as more cognitively oriented theories of learning became accepted, reading came to be viewed as an active skill, involving a number of decoding thought processes. Debate still exists in reading theory on whether reading is primarily a language-based decoding skill or a system of processing and organizational skills. There presently remains some emphasis on the traditional view that reading is a decoding process which is dependent on language ability, since limited control of the second language can "short-circuit" a good reader's second-language reading system (Hudson, 34).

Reading subskills

Educators have expressed differing opinions regarding reading subskills. Davis (16) espouses the idea that "reading is meaning." He claims that reading comprehension is based mainly on knowledge of word meanings and on the reader's ability to reason in verbal terms. Clark (14) says there are three levels of skill involved in teaching and testing reading: (1) character recognition (including diacritical and punctuation marks), (2) attachment of semantic meaning to the various combinations and positions of the characters, and (3) ability to infer meaning as a native speaker would. In addition to the subskills mentioned by Clark, Hudson (34) adds sound-symbol correspondence (in oral reading) and recognition of discourse-level linguistic relationships that are present throughout the text.

Riley (59) offers another set of subskills in what she calls "active thought-ful purposeful reading." She asserts that an "intelligent reader" should be able to: (1) select the main idea from the passage; (2) select relevant details to support the main idea; (3) recognize irrelevancies, contradictions, and non sequiturs; (4) use logical connectors and sequence signals; (5) draw conclusions; (6) make generalizations; and (7) apply principles to other instances. She admits that in testing reading some subskills are much more difficult to isolate and test than others.

Goodman (23) explains that reading is an active process of prediction, selection, and confirmation that involves the reader's knowledge of the language plus his or her past experiential and conceptual background. He further states that the reader is continually making educated guesses about the meaning and function of unfamiliar elements encountered in the text. In this hypothesis-formation process, the reader uses graphic, semantic, and syntactic clues in refining or rejecting hypotheses formed during the reading process. Wardhaugh (70) supports the view that reading is an active process in which the reader must use various acquired abilities. He describes reading as giving meaningful interpretation to the text through the use of visual clues of spelling, knowledge of probability of occurrence, contextual pragmatic knowledge, and syntactic and semantic competence.

Smith (65) maintains that reading comprehension depends on three sources: visual information, semantic information, and grammatical knowl-edge. Of the three sources mentioned by Smith, Upshur (68) says that, paradoxically, the visual information contributes the least to reading comprehension. In summary, reading in a foreign-language is a very complex process involving several subskills such as visual perception, vocabulary recognition, structural knowledge, and concept identification and interpretation. A valid test of reading proficiency must account for these subskills.

Difficulties associated with reading

In addition to the various subskills involved in the reading process, other difficulties exist that must be considered in the design and development of reading proficiency tests. Presently, many language programs through-out the United States teach languages that do not use the Roman alphabet. For some of these languages a single character might represent an entire word or phrase. However, despite the difficulties of character or letter recognition and identification, a reading proficiency test transliterated into English certainly would not be valid for these languages. Therefore, the effects of character recognition must be taken into account in the determination of test difficulty levels.

Even when the language being tested uses a familiar alphabet, problems may arise if the text has been handwritten. Many persons who consider themselves proficient in a foreign language have agonized over correspondence handwritten in the target language. Deciphering a handwritten text can be difficult even in one's native language. This difficulty is greatly amplified across languages, since characteristics of handwritten forms often vary among languages.

An additional difficulty associated with reading is that of style. Stylistics can play an important role in reading, particularly if the writing conventions of the target language (TL) differ extensively from the student's native language or from the TL's spoken norms. A student proficient in the target language should be able to read and correctly interpret conventional punctuation, spelling, diacritics, and capitalization. Also associated with style is the manner or tone of the written discourse. Being able to interpret the mood of the author through reading is often difficult in the absence of paralinguistic cues that accompany oral language use. These difficulties associated with reading must be accounted for in valid tests of reading proficiency.

Foreign-language reading tasks

Central to the issue of testing reading proficiency are the kinds of reading tasks that confront foreign-language users and the extent to which the latter need to comprehend printed information. In some cases it is imperative that the reader comprehend fully what is being read, whereas in other instances it is necessary only that the reader understand the gist of the text.

Reading can be divided into two kinds: intensive and extensive. Intensive reading is generally a slower, more deliberate process than extensive reading. It is useful for extracting from the text specific and detailed information. Extensive reading, on the other hand, is reading for more general information. Rivers (61) states that in extensive reading the reader tolerates a certain vagueness, "reading whole sections at a time in order to establish the general meaning so that he can develop his ability to deduce from semantic and syntactic clues the meaning of unfamiliar words and phrases" (p. 206).

Foreign-language reading tasks vary considerably in their nature and purpose, with some being appropriate for intensive reading strategies and others more suited to extensive reading. One may read for interpersonal communication or for personal pleasure, such as when reading notes, letters, stories, or novels. A reader may acquire either general or specific information by reading street signs, ads, train schedules, newspapers, or business reports—all of which vary greatly in form and style from the spoken language. Reading tasks range from understanding simple information like names, addresses, or items on a menu to comprehension of complex passages found in news media, educational writings, or literary works. Tests of reading proficiency should account for the kinds of reading tasks confronting foreign-language readers, and specified levels of proficiency should be based on the relative difficulty of those tasks.

Testing reading versus testing language through reading

Before discussing current and future tests of reading proficiency, it is useful to clarify differences between testing reading per se as opposed to using reading as a vehicle for testing a student's knowledge of grammar, syntax, or vocabulary. Exactly what is to be tested must be determined. Are the examinees to demonstrate their ability to recognize the connotation of certain structures or lexical items *in context,* or are they to show their global competence in comprehending the overall message of the text? Once the answer to this question has been determined, an appropriate test format can be established. It should be remembered, for example, that an examination designed to test the correctness of grammar is *not* a test of reading comprehension.

Reading is commonly used as a means of testing knowledge of structure and vocabulary, since a reading format allows for easy isolation of individual points of grammar, including verb tenses, agreement, and word order. Reading is also extensively used for testing vocabulary concerns such as proper usage and spelling. Reading-type test questions are also amenable to several kinds of testing formats. Multiple-choice, matching, true-false, and translation are among the most popular. Nevertheless, reading comprehension as a skill has a much broader focus than the isolated components of the text. It encompasses a total understanding of the written message. While testing structure and vocabulary through reading is certainly a useful method of determining a student's ability to use or recognize these items correctly, the difference between testing discrete grammatical or lexical points and testing global reading proficiency must be clearly understood.

Conventional methods of measuring reading proficiency

Several testing formats have been used in assessing reading proficiency. Some of the most common techniques are briefly discussed below.

Translation. An extremely popular test of reading ability has been the translation test in which students translate target language passages into their native language. Translation tests may be partial or complete. The former require examinees to fill in missing segments of a partially translated text; the latter require the entire translation. The Foreign Service Institute, however, has used another variety of translation test that could be considered an oral translation. For this test the examinees give in their native language an oral summary of the passage they read.

Translation tests have received both support and criticism from testers. Sewell (64) claims that translation tests provide precise information about the examinee's weak points. Jennings (37) feels that this type of test allows for a check on fine-structure comprehension and points out significant semantic differences that otherwise would go unnoticed. One of the major criticisms of translation tests, however, is that they pose a real problem of reliability of scoring (Jones, 41). This is because of the number of factors involved in judgment, making it difficult to be consistent in assigning scores.

Reading aloud.   Although used primarily as a reading test in the native language, reading aloud has been tried as a measure of second-language reading ability. Valette (69) cautions that this is useful only if the examinee speaks the language with facility. Also, in a study to analyze miscues in oral reading, Allen (3) observes that when reading aloud the reader often operates on a phonic level, paying little or no attention to meaning. He does, however, say that one can both quantify and qualify the kinds of miscues committed by the reader by counting the miscues and judging their seriousness from their nature.

True-false questions.   True-false questions have been used extensively as checks of reading comprehension. They have been popular to a large degree because of the relative ease with which the test can be made and particularly because of the rapidity and reliability of scoring. However, given the indirect nature of this testing technique, the validity of true-false items is questionable.

Multiple-choice questions.   Possibly the most popular testing technique is the use of multiple-choice questions based on specific passages. Questions are designed so that the examinee might choose the item that best expresses the main idea of the passage, or that represents the best paraphrase of specified sections of the passage, or that correctly answers a given content or inference based on the passage. A strong argument for the use of multiple-choice tests is that scoring can be done objectively and rapidly. As with true-false tests, however, multiple-choice tests are indirect measures of reading proficiency. Another concern related to the validity of this type of test is expressed by Upshur (68), who explains that with multiple-choice tests, abilities other than reading ability, such as general knowledge, test-taking strategies, and many other human factors, have a great effect on reading scores.

Question-answer.   The question-answer technique of testing reading ability may employ both a written and an oral response format. However, because of time considerations, the written format is the more efficient one. Sonka (66), explaining various ways to use this technique, says that one procedure is to have the student answer the comprehension questions without referring back to the passage, or, alternatively, to allow the student to refer back to the text as needed. Another variation lets the student see the questions before reading the passage, after which the questions would be answered without further reference to the passage. Similarly, the student might read and underline topic sentences, then reread the entire passage and answer the questions. She claims that the latter two methods emphasize anticipatory reading. An additional approach to using a question-answer technique, she offers, is to have the student read the passage and take notes and then answer questions, referring only to the notes.

Valette (69) recommends another use of the question-answer testing technique. Textual criticism can be used to evaluate reading comprehension by having students answer questions about literary works, for example, questions about the revealed attitude of the author or of certain characters toward the subject of the text. Henning (30), in reporting a study evaluating reading comprehension testing techniques, cautions that regardless of the type of question-answer format used, the grammatical accuracy of the written responses should not be taken into account in assessing reading ability. This is particularly true when trying to obtain a pure measure of reading ability.

Cloze.   The cloze procedure was first used by Wilson Taylor in 1953 in his dissertation study at the University of Illinois and has since become a very common language testing procedure. Cloze tests are prose passages from which every *n*th word has been deleted; the examinee must supply the missing words. Scoring is based either on an "exact" or on an "acceptable" response; the former requires verbatim responses that correspond exactly to the words deleted from the original text, and the latter accepts any response that is grammatical and contextually appropriate.

The cloze procedure as a tool for educational measurement has received a considerable amount of attention. Porter (57) notes that it has been used to measure reading comprehension, global language proficiency, vocabulary, difficulty of reading passages, and IQ. The use of cloze tests for testing language competence is based on the claim that being able to anticipate elements in sequence is the foundation of all language skills, and that cloze techniques are capable of measuring this (Oller, 53). Porter (57) supports this view: "The fact that the ability to predict what lies ahead depends on the ability fully to comprehend the language being 'processed' at any given moment provides the justification for [the cloze procedure] as a test of comprehension" (p. 152). In addition to claims of validity, several researchers have affirmed the reliability of cloze tests (see Oller and Conrad, 54; Hanzeli, 27; and Hinofotis, 32).

Not everyone, however, has totally supported the use of cloze testing. In the late Fifties, the cloze procedure was rejected as a measure of competence on the College Entrance Examination Board's foreign-language tests because it was considered relatively unreliable and too heavily affected by sources of extraneous variance (Carroll, et al., 9). Porter (57), concerned about the fact that cloze tests involve production skills (i.e., writing) as well as reading, proposes a modified cloze procedure that offers multiple choices at each blank from which the examinee selects the correct response. In defense of the recognition nature of the modified cloze procedure, he emphasizes that even though a student might recognize the right word when seen in a list, comprehension of previous text is still required.

Related to Porter's modified cloze technique, is the reading input test, a procedure introduced by Carver (10). The input test provides the reader with a choice between the correct answer and a distractor for every *n*th word. Ozete (55) finds, however, that this technique does not discriminate well among advanced students. Another form of cloze that has been used for testing reading ability is the reverse cloze procedure in which distractors or nonsense words are inserted into the text and must be identified by the examinee. Bowen (4) reports that his "editing task" reading test, a reverse-cloze-type test, correlates highly with other standardized reading measures. Numerous studies have been conducted on the cloze procedure as a viable method of measuring reading and language proficiency in general. Oller (51) has compiled a detailed bibliography of much of this research.

Possible new methods of measuring reading proficiency

The preceding section has discussed several conventional methods used to evaluate reading ability, most of which are indirect, pencil-and-paper measures. While many of these testing techniques have yielded respectable reliability coefficients, their validity has been challenged. Many foreign-language students have not been able to meet the requirements of the "real world" of communication upon finishing their training, although their achievement records indicate that they should be able to. Higgs and Clifford (31) may have assessed accurately the reason for this discrepancy in their claim that our students are working principally in restricted ranges of proficiency, dealing with the simplest of communication tasks. It seems important at this juncture in the development of foreign-language teaching and testing that competence in the various language modalities be evaluated and expressed in terms of actual performance. As implied by Higgs and Clifford, instead of asking if our students are able to read, we should be asking specifically *what* they are able to read, and *how well*. We should be emphasizing *function* and *content* in reading tasks, as well as *accuracy*.

The Foreign Service Institute has developed and used for the past several years a method of assessing *oral* proficiency precisely in terms of these three interrelated categories (i.e., function, content, and accuracy), but not until recently have efforts been expended to include reading in this type of proficiency evaluation. Funded by the Department of Education, ACTFL and ETS have developed a set of provisional proficiency guidelines that will provide for student evaluation and placement on the basis of demonstrated reading performance (1). (See Appendix A.) These global proficiency ratings are based on performance of a specified language function within a specified context with a specified degree of accuracy. In addition to serving as a yardstick for measuring student progress, these guidelines are designed to provide a graduated sequence of learning goals for students and teachers, thus serving as an aid in curriculum and materials development. The ACTFL/ETS reading guidelines are divided into nine levels of proficiency, ranging from Novice-Low (the reader has no functional ability in reading the foreign language) to Superior (the reader can read materials such as newspapers, correspondence, reports, technical information, and novels and other recreational reading materials at a normal rate of speed with almost always a correct interpretation, although at times he or she may be unable to appreciate fully nuance or stylistics). Although these guidelines are provisional and may be revised in the future, the authors believe that they represent an improved method of assessing reading proficiency, since they are based on actual reading performance.

Testing techniques used for verifying levels of reading proficiency are of considerable importance. Since reading mainly takes place in the mind—receiving, analyzing, interpreting, and evaluating the message—it is difficult to devise tests that measure reading directly. Nevertheless, it is possible to employ testing formats that can be considered more direct than others on a continuum ranging from indirect to direct. For example, answering multiple-choice questions about a passage would be viewed as a less direct method of assessing reading proficiency than having the examinee paraphrase, describe, or characterize what was just read. Having the student paraphrase the content of a written FL text in his native language prevents factors other than sheer reading ability from influencing reading scores.

The increased need for adequate tests of reading proficiency demands more research in this area. Further research might be done, for example, to determine the feasibility of using the computer in assessing reading proficiency. Programs might be written that could accurately and objectively evaluate an examinee's reading ability by matching performance on several reading tasks ranging from simple to complex with predetermined proficiency ratings. Current technology would allow the computer to perform and evaluate level checks, provide several probes to determine the upper limits of proficiency, and finish with a wind-down step similar to the procedures recommended for measuring speaking proficiency.

In addition to improving testing techniques for determining levels of reading proficiency, there is a need to focus on the *content* of reading tests. A common tendency has been to overuse stilted or contrived reading passages in assessing reading ability. The main purpose for testing reading competence is to determine how well the examinee uses this skill in actual communication tasks. It is therefore essential to design tests around authentic, real-life reading tasks in the foreign language. The tasks used should, of course, be appropriate to the level of the reader. Lower-level reading tasks might include reading street signs and addresses or brief ads like those found in catalogs and/or shop windows in the target country. Novice-level foreign-language readers should be able to understand informative signs such as no smoking, no parking, and other traffic signs as well as be able to obtain usable information from a telephone book, a train or bus schedule, or a television or movie guide. Students at this stage should be able to read menus and understand maps and application forms.

Intermediate students should understand and interpret newspaper headlines and book titles. They should comprehend simple messages such as those found in greeting cards, get-well and friendship cards, as well as simple narrations of events, biographical information, and personal communications such as letters, invitations, and social notes. Testing the ability to read and follow instructions for assembling simple items like toys would also be appropriate at the Intermediate level.

Advanced tasks might include reading business letters and other types of formal correspondence. Advanced readers should be able to interpret information from cultural sources and promotional brochures, which describe both physical and social aspects of the culture. Reading edited and unedited texts such as essays, short stories, novels, poems, legends, and other prose works are valid Advanced-level reading tasks. For Superior-level readers, interpreting technical materials such as legal briefs and documents, contracts, and conference proceedings are useful tasks for evaluating reading ability. Also appropriate are texts that require the reader to "read between the lines," to understand cultural and literary allusions, to draw inferences, and to interpret idioms, proverbs, and other colloquial materials.

Several reading tasks have been mentioned as possible proficiency test items; many more exist. It is the responsibility of teachers, testers, and researchers within the foreign-language profession to work together to combine appropriate and reliable testing *techniques* with valid and authentic reading *tasks* in order to achieve accurate measures of demonstrated reading ability.

Testing Writing Proficiency

It has been pointed out elsewhere (e.g., Jones, 42) that writing is the least useful and perhaps the most difficult of all of the language skills to master. Perhaps we feel compelled to achieve symmetry in the four skill areas by at least giving some consideration to writing, but in many cases confusion exists about precisely what constitutes writing in a second language. If students write out grammatical exercises to be handed in, can this really be called writing in a meaningful sense? Does the mere use of a pencil and paper necessarily test writing?

Most students have little occasion to write in their native language, and when they write at all they frequently do not write well. In addition to mastery of basic linguistic elements, true *writing* requires a clearly formulated message, precise use of the language, and a keen sensitivity to style and register. There is also the necessity of learning correct orthography and punctuation, and in some languages, a totally different graphemic system.

There is a much greater difference in ability among both first- and second-language users in writing than in any of the other modalities. We should not apologize for the apparent neglect of the testing of writing. For certain special cases it is important, but generally speaking it deserves to be in fourth place, at least at the Novice and Intermediate levels of instruction.

Basic writing tasks

Most of the writing tasks that second-language users face can be classified into one of five areas.

Correspondence.   Whether it be to an acquaintance, to a university professor, or to a business representative, most individuals who spend time in a foreign culture have need to write a letter. Even with the most informal greeting, there are arbitrary conventions in every literate society for opening and closing a letter, as well as for giving and requesting information. The structure of a letter is simply not the same as the structure of a conversation. Few things register as being more foreign than a letter from someone who is writing in one language but using the letter-writing style of another language and culture.

Providing essential information.   Occasionally there is need to write a note informing someone that we will return in an hour or that we can't be at the meeting the next day. Such a task may not be nearly as formidable as writing certain types of letters, but it does require a modicum of precision. In many cases it is permissible to abbreviate the language, using a type of telegraph style: "Back in an hour" or "Can't make it tomorrow."

Completing forms.   Many Americans are not aware that they are denied the privilege enjoyed by most other citizens of the world of filling out seemingly interminable forms which require information ranging from one's mother's religion to one's grandfather's place of birth! In many countries filling out forms is virtually a necessary survival skill. Even in preparing to go abroad, we are sometimes required to complete forms in other languages for such things as visas. In most cases filling out a standard form does not require much more than a few stock phrases. These are easily learned and do not contain sophisticated structures. Perhaps the greatest challenge to most standard forms lies in understanding what they are asking.

Taking notes. The most obvious need for note-taking is for students enrolled in an academic institution. It becomes apparent very soon that listening in the target language but taking notes in the native language does not work very well for most people. Writing in the same language in which the information is conveyed is usually less confusing, *if* one has a sufficiently developed writing proficiency.

But writing down condensed information is not confined to school settings. It is frequently necessary to jot down some information gained from a conversation or observation. It is also necessary at times to write notes to oneself without any external linguistic stimulus, e.g., "Meet Peter at 6:00" or "Get bread and hamburger on the way home."

Formal papers. Students enrolled at a foreign university have an obvious need to develop proficiency in writing. Most courses require at least some written work to be handed in, and in some cases students are expected to write lengthy formal papers. Relatively few American students matriculate in foreign universities, thus such a high level of writing skill generally is not important for them. However, in ESL programs there is great need to teach and test proficiency in expository writing. Indeed, it would be extremely difficult for a university student to survive without being able to write in the language of instruction with a high level of accuracy and fluency.

Conventional writing tests

It might be safe to say that in fact there is really only one conventional method of testing writing proficiency. When it is tested at all, it is usually done directly, using an essay or some other kind of extended prose. Simply stated, if it is necessary to assess the ability of a person to write, then have that person write and let a qualified judge evaluate it.

The testing of writing proficiency has a lot in common with the testing of speaking proficiency. First, a ratable sample must be elicited, then that sample must be scored holistically. There is no good method of scoring the test mechanically, as is the case with certain kinds of reading and listening tests. Each paper must be corrected individually, and scoring can become highly subjective. However, just as with a well-administered oral test, with proper training and with experience it is possible to achieve an acceptable level of scorer reliability (Jones, 42).

Summary ——————————————————————

Language teachers are becoming increasingly aware of the important role testing can play. They are also becoming aware that a good testing program must be flexible, that different kinds of tests may be required for the various needs that exist in a language program. With the growing interest in teaching functional proficiency, it is important that tests be reviewed to make certain they do in fact measure this type of proficiency.

During the past several years significant progress has been made in the development of a model for testing oral proficiency. It is important that similar efforts be made to revise testing procedures in the other modalities, especially in listening and reading. To the extent possible, tests must reflect situations and tasks that are encountered in real life, even though this may mean giving up familiar formats such as multiple-choice and true-false.

A great deal of pioneering work must be done. We need to experiment and determine empirically the best methods of measuring proficiency in all modalities. With a lot of imagination and effort, the language-testing profession will continue to experience the success it has enjoyed during the past decade.

References, Proficiency Testing for the Other Language Modalities

1. *ACTFL Provisional Proficiency Guidelines.* New York: American Council on the Teaching of Foreign Languages, 1982.
2. Aitken, Kenneth G. "Techniques for Assessing Listening Comprehension in Second Languages." *Audio-Visual Language Journal* 17 (1979):175–81.
3. Allen, Edward D. "Miscue Analysis: A New Tool for Diagnosing Oral Reading Proficiency in Foreign Languages." *Foreign Language Annals* 9 (1976):563–67.
4. Bowen, J. Donald. *Testing English Grammar—A Correlation Study.* Paper presented at the TESOL Annual Convention, New York City, March 1976.
5. Carroll, Brenden J. *Testing Communicative Performance.* Oxford: Pergamon Press, 1980.
6. Carroll, John B. "Psychometric Theory and Language Testing," pp. 80–107 in John W. Oller, Jr., ed., *Issues in Language Testing Research.* Rowley, MA: Newbury House, 1983.
7. _____. "Foreign Language Testing: Will the Persistent Problems Persist?" pp. 6–17 in Maureen Concannon O'Brien, ed., *ATESOL Testing in Second Language Teaching: New Dimensions.* Dublin, Ireland: The Dublin University Press, 1973.
8. _____. "Fundamental Considerations in Testing for English Language Proficiency of Foreign Students," pp. 30–40 in *Testing the English Proficiency of Foreign Students.* Washington, DC: Center for Applied Linguistics, 1961.
9. _____, Aaron S. Carton, and Claudia Wilds. *An Investigation of 'Cloze' Items in the Measurement of Achievement in Foreign Languages.* 1959. [EDRS: ED 021 513.]
10. Carver, Ronald. *New Techniques for Measuring and Improving Reading Comprehension.* Washington, DC: American Institutes for Research, 1973.
11. Chastain, Kenneth. *Developing Second Language Skills: Theory to Practice.* Chicago: Rand McNally, 1976.
12. _____. "Testing Listening Comprehension Tests." *TESOL Quarterly* 13 (1979):81–88.
13. Clark, John L. D. "Psychometric Considerations in Language Testing," pp. 15–50 in Bernard Spolsky, ed., *Approaches to Language Testing.* Advances in Language Testing, series I. Washington, DC: Center for Applied Linguistics, 1978.

14. _____. *Foreign Language Testing: Theory to Practice.* Philadelphia: The Center for Curriculum Development, 1972.
15. Clifford, Ray T. "Reliability and Validity of Oral Proficiency Ratings and Convergent/Discriminant Validity of Language Aspects of Spoken German Using the *MLA Cooperative Foreign Language Proficiency Tests: German (Speaking)* and an Oral Interview Procedure." Ph.D. dissertation. Minneapolis: University of Minnesota, 1977. *Dissertation Abstracts International* 38 (1978):5969–A.
16. Davis, F. B. "Psychometric Research in Comprehension in Reading." *Reading Research Quarterly* 7 (1972):628–78.
17. Dobson, Julia M. "The Notional Syllabus: Theory and Practice." *English Teaching Forum* (April 1979):2–10.
18. Farhady, Hossein. "The Disjunctive Fallacy between Discrete-Point and Integrative Tests." *TESOL Quarterly* 13 (1979):347–57.
19. Fitzpatrick, R., and E. J. Morrison. "Performance and Product Evaluation," pp. 237–70 in R. L. Thorndike, ed., *Educational Measurement.* 2nd edition. Washington, DC: American Council on Education, 1971.
20. Fries, Charles C. *Teaching and Learning English as a Foreign Language.* Ann Arbor: University of Michigan Press, 1945.
21. Garfinkel, Alan. "*MLJ* Notes and News." *Modern Language Journal* 66 (1982):60–68.
22. Germain, Claude. "The Functional Approach to Language Teaching." *Modern Language Journal* 66 (1982):49–57.
23. Goodman, Kenneth S. "The Psycholinguistic Nature of the Reading Process," pp. 13–26 in Kenneth S. Goodman, ed., *The Psycholinguistic Nature of the Reading Process.* Detroit: Wayne State University Press, 1968.
24. Gradman, Harry, and Bernard Spolsky. "Reduced Redundancy Testing: A Progress Report," pp. 59–70 in Randall L. Jones and Bernard Spolsky, eds., *Testing Language Proficiency.* Washington, DC: Center for Applied Linguistics, 1975.
25. Groot, Peter J. M. "Testing Communicative Competence in Listening Comprehension," pp. 45–58 in Randall L. Jones and Bernard Spolsky, eds., *Testing Language Proficiency.* Washington, DC: Center for Applied Linguistics, 1975.
26. Harlow, Linda L. "An Alternative to Structurally Oriented Textbooks." *Foreign Language Annals* 11 (1978):559–63.
27. Hanzeli, Victor E. "The Effectiveness of Cloze Tests in Measuring the Competence of Students of French in an Academic Setting." *French Review* 50 (1977):865–74.
28. Hauptman, Philip C. *A Comparison of First and Second Language Reading Strategies among English-Speaking University Students.* 1979. [EDRS: ED 207 324.]
29. Heaton, J. B. *Writing English Language Tests.* London: Longman, 1975.
30. Henning, Grant H. "Measuring Foreign Language Reading Comprehension." *Language Learning* 25 (1975):109–14.
31. Higgs, Theodore V., and Ray Clifford. "The Push Toward Communication," pp. 57–79 in Theodore V. Higgs, ed., *Curriculum, Competence, and the Foreign Language Teacher.* The ACTFL Foreign Language Education Series, vol. 13. Lincolnwood, IL: National Textbook Co., 1982.
32. Hinofotis, Frances B. "Cloze as an Alternative Method of ESL Placement and Proficiency Testing," pp. 121–28 in John W. Oller, Jr., and Kyle Perkins, eds., *Research in Language Testing.* Rowley, MA: Newbury House, 1980.
33. Hosley, Deborah, and Keith Meredith. "Inter- and Intra-Test Correlates of the TOEFL." *TESOL Quarterly* 13 (1979):209–17.
34. Hudson, Thom. "The Effects of Induced Schemata on the 'Short Circuit' in L2 Reading Performance." *Language Learning* 32 (1982):1–31.

35. Hymes, Dell. "Models of the Interaction of Language and Social Setting." *Journal of Social Issues* 23, ii (1967):8–28.
36. Jakobovits, Leon A. "A Fundamental Approach to the Assessment of Language Skills." *Journal of English as a Second Language* 4 (1969):63–76.
37. Jennings, Lee B. "Classroom Translation—A Lesser Bugbear." *German Quarterly* 40 (1967):518–29.
38. Johnson, Keith. *Communicative Syllabus Design and Methodology.* Oxford: Pergamon Press, 1982.
39. Jones, Randall L. "Assessing Second Language Proficiency: Where Are We and Where Are We Going?" pp. 36–52 in James E. Redden, ed., *Proceedings of the Southern Illinois Language Testing Conference.* Southern Illinois University Occasional Papers on Linguistics, no.8. Carbondale, IL: Southern Illinois University, 1980.
40. _____. "Performance Testing of Second Language Proficiency," pp. 50–57 in Eugene J. Briere and Frances B. Hinofotis, eds., *Concepts in Language Testing: Some Recent Studies.* Washington, DC: Teachers of English to Speakers of Other Languages, 1979.
41. _____. "Achieving Objectivity in Subjective Language Tests," pp. 241–53 in Gerhard Nickel, ed., *Proceedings of the Fourth International Congress of Applied Linguistics.* Stuttgart, Germany: Hochschul Verlag, 1977.
42. _____. "Testing: A Vital Connection," pp. 237–65 in June K. Phillips, ed., *The Language Connection: From the Classroom to the World.* The ACTFL Foreign Language Education Series, vol. 9. Lincolnwood, IL: National Textbook Co., 1977.
43. Krashen, Stephen D. *Principles and Practices in Second Language Acquisition.* Oxford: Pergamon Press, 1982.
44. Larson, Jerry W. "Skills Correlations: A Study of Three Final Examinations." *Modern Language Journal.* Forthcoming.
45. Linder, Cathy. *Oral Communication Testing.* Lincolnwood, IL: National Textbook Co., 1977.
46. Madsen, Harold S.; Randall L. Jones; and Bruce B. Brown. "Evaluating Affective Variables in Second Language Testing." Paper presented at the TESOL Annual Convention, San Francisco 1980.
47. Nord, James R. "Three Steps Leading to Listening Fluency: A Beginning," pp. 69–100 in Harris Winitz, ed., *The Comprehension Approach to Foreign Language Instruction.* Rowley, MA: Newbury House, 1981.
48. Oller, John W., Jr. *Language Tests at School.* London: Longman, 1979.
49. _____, and Bernard Spolsky. "The Test of English as a Second Language," pp. 92–100 in Bernard Spolsky, ed., *Advances in Language Testing.* Series 1. Washington, DC: Center for Applied Linguistics, 1979.
50. _____. "Evidence for a General Language Proficiency Factor: An Expectancy Grammar." *Die Neuren Sprachen* 2 (1976):165–74.
51. _____. *Research with Cloze Procedure in Measuring the Proficiency of Nonnative Speakers of English: An Annotated Bibliography.* CAL-ERIC/CCL Series on Languages and Linguistics, no. 13, 1975. [EDRS: ED 104 154.]
52. _____, and Virginia Streiff. "Dictation: A Test of Grammar Based Expectancies," pp. 71–88 in Randall L. Jones and Bernard Spolsky, eds., *Testing Language Proficiency.* Washington, DC: Center for Applied Linguistics, 1975.
53. _____. "Scoring Methods and Difficulty Levels for Cloze Tests of ESL Proficiency." *Modern Language Journal* 56 (1972):151–58.
54. _____, and Christine Conrad. "The Cloze Procedure and ESL Proficiency." *Language Learning* 22 (1972):1–15.
55. Ozete, Oscar. "The Cloze Procedure: A Modification." *Foreign Language Annals* 10 (1977):565–68.

56. Paquette, F. André, and Suzanne Tollinger. *A Handbook on the MLA Foreign Language Proficiency Tests for Teachers and Advanced Students: Their Nature, Uses, and Limitations.* New York: Modern Language Association of America, 1968. [EDRS: ED 074 855.]

57. Porter, D. "Modified Cloze Procedure: A More Valid Reading Comprehension Test." *English Language Teaching Journal* 30 (1976):151–55.

58. Postovsky, Valerian A. "The Priority of Aural Comprehension in the Language Acquisition Process," pp. 170–86 in Harris Winitz, ed., *The Comprehension Approach to Foreign Language Instruction.* Rowley, MA: Newbury House, 1981.

59. Riley, Pamela M. "Specific Reading Skills for Secondary and Post-Secondary E.S.L. Learners." *TEFL/TESL Newsletter* 3 (1977):1–6. [EDRS: ED 200 000.]

60. Rivers, Wilga M. *Teaching Foreign Language Skills.* Chicago: University of Chicago Press, 1981.

61. ———; Milton M. Azevedo; William H. Heflin, Jr.; Ruth Hyman-Opler. *A Practical Guide to the Teaching of Spanish.* New York: Oxford University Press, 1976.

62. ———. *Speaking in Many Tongues: Essays in Foreign-Language Teaching.* expanded 2nd ed. Rowley, MA: Newbury House, 1976.

63. ———. *A Practical Guide to the Teaching of German.* New York: Oxford University Press, 1975.

64. Sewell, Penelope M. "Test Items—Objective and Otherwise." *Audio-Visual Language Journal* 12 (1974–75):147–56.

65. Smith, Frank. *Understanding Reading.* New York: Holt, Rinehart, and Winston, 1971.

66. Sonka, Amy L. "Reading Has to Be Taught, Too." Paper presented at the Annual Conference of the Massachusetts Association for Teachers of Speakers of Other Languages, April 1976. [EDRS: ED 139 297.]

67. Upshur, John A.; William Action; Bradford Arthur; and Alexander Z. Guiora. "Causation or Correlation: A Reply to Oller and Perkins." *Language Learning* 28 (1978):99–104.

68. ———. "A Search for New Reading Tests." Paper presented at the TESOL Annual Convention, Washington, DC, March 1972. [EDRS: ED 061 805.]

69. Valette, Rebecca M. *Modern Language Testing.* 2nd ed. New York: Harcourt Brace Jovanovich, Inc., 1977.

70. Wardhaugh, Ronald. *Reading: A Linguistic Perspective.* New York: Harcourt, Brace, and World, 1969.

71. Whiteson, Valerie, and Herbert W. Seliger. "An Integrative Approach to the 'Noise' Test." *Audio-Lingual Language Journal* 13 (1975):17–18.

72. Widdowson, Harry G. *Teaching Language as Communication.* London: Oxford University Press, 1978.

73. Wilkins, David A. *Notional Syllabuses.* London: Oxford University Press, 1976.

74. Winitz, Harris. "A Reconsideration of Comprehension and Production in Language Training," pp. 101–40 in Harris Winitz, ed., *The Comprehension Approach to Foreign Language Instruction.* Rowley, MA: Newbury House, 1981.

5

Doing the Unthinkable in the Second-Language Classroom:
A Process for the Integration of Language and Culture

Linda M. Crawford-Lange
Blaine Senior High School, Blaine, Minnesota

Dale L. Lange
University of Minnesota

Introduction

(*Scene:* Teacher in an industrial arts course.)

"The focus of study in this course is tools. In this toolbox, there is a hammer. The hammer weighs xxx pounds and measures xxx by xxx. The head is made of steel and the handle is wooden. The head of the hammer is used for hammering in nails. The claw of the hammer is used for pulling nails out. You hammer nails like this. (*Demonstration.*) And you take them out like this. (*Demonstration.*) I will now pass the hammer around the room and you can each practice banging a nail into a block of wood and pulling it out again."

Linda M. Crawford-Lange (Ph.D., University of Minnesota) is Dean of the Blaine Senior High School, Blaine, Minnesota. She has received the Project Award granted by the Central Minnesota Association of Secondary School Principals. She is a recognized authority on the philosophy of Paulo Freire and authored a chapter in Volume 13 of this series. She is a member of ACTFL, Administrative Women in Education, the Minnesota Association of Secondary School Principals, and Phi Delta Kappa.

Dale L. Lange (Ph.D., University of Minnesota) is a Professor of Second Language and Culture Education and Director of Graduate Studies for the Department of Curriculum and Instruction at the University of Minnesota. He has published widely across the full spectrum of professional publications and is a former editor of the ACTFL Foreign Language Education Series. He is a past-president of ACTFL, and is a member of AATF, AATG, AATSP, ACTFL, AERA, and TESOL.

(*Scene:* Teacher in a French course.)

"The focus of study in this course is the French language. In this language, there are regular verbs in three conjugations. The present tense of these verbs is formed by adding endings (a different set of endings for each conjugation) to a root or stem. The present tense is used to discuss actions that are taking place in the present. You form the present tense of regular 'er' verbs like this. (*Demonstration.*) Now, let's go around the room and practice the present tense of 'er' verbs."

These ridiculous vignettes exaggerate a point: Studying an object, such as a language, may result in knowledge of the object, but it does not necessarily result in facile or appropriate use of the object. The analogy to a hammer is intentional. Language is a tool—a tool of communication. Except for linguists, for whom the purpose of language study is examination and analysis, people study language to communicate with and learn about other people. Language learning involves more than study of the tool. It requires use of the tool for its natural purpose, namely communication.

Communicative use of language extends the concerns of a course beyond language per se. At the moment the language student on the first day of class learns how to greet someone in the target language, that student is involved in the target culture. The curriculum may specify that cultural involvement does not begin until Friday's slide-tape presentation or until the end-of-unit cultural episode, but the curriculum is erroneous. Cultural involvement begins as soon as the student, at even the most elementary level, moves from the analysis of language to language use.

The study of language, then, entails the study of culture. Foreign-language teachers have accepted intellectually that language and culture are essentially inseparable. Seelye (73), for example, avows that without a cultural context a word has no meaning. Brooks, in his classic text *Language and Language Learning* (14), advises that linguistic characteristics should be viewed as cultural elements and that culture learning requires the vehicle of language. Further, language teachers have come to understand culture in its anthropological sense as a proper domain of culture instruction in language classes (Brooks, 15; Seelye, 73). To study language without studying the culture of native speakers of the language is a lifeless endeavor.

Despite the intellectual acceptance of the union of language and culture, foreign-language teachers have been criticized for inadequate treatment of culture (Collins, 20). Perhaps one reason they deserve this criticism is because, although culture and language are in reality "married," language curricula respond to them as if they were still only "engaged." Generally speaking, more cultural activities can be observed in foreign language classrooms today than at earlier times. There is a consciousness among teachers that culture should be included in the curriculum; there is even an awareness of the importance of "little c culture" as well as "Big C Culture." Yet, this inclusion of cultural content continues to be seen as an issue separate from that of language. The groom is still waiting at the altar.

Systematic Culture Study: Is It Accomplished? ─────────

Significantly, the culture study which takes place in classrooms usually occurs after or around language learning, without any essential relationship to the learning of language itself. It is rare that the study of culture precipitates language learning. For example, a cultural topic in a foreign-language classroom may be soccer as both a spectator and a participant sport. Ordinarily, the unit begins with a dialogue centered on soccer, moves to grammar study using vocabulary from the dialogue, and ends with a reading on soccer. Students are tested on the grammar and vocabulary, but not on any cultural concepts. How refreshing it might be to open the unit with visuals of soccer as a basis for culturally oriented questions about soccer and the behavior of people at soccer matches, to determine vocabulary and structures for language learning which relate to the language functions and notions of the soccer discussion, and to compare the cultural event with a similar event in the native culture. Students could be examined not only on their linguistic competence but also on their ability to use the language in a culturally appropriate manner.

Why does culture remain peripheral in the foreign-language classroom even when teachers recognize its importance in relation to language? Two explanations may account for this second-class status. First, teachers feel inadequate in their knowledge of the foreign culture. They sense a pressure to dispense culturally accurate information, but they have only limited and time-bound experiences in the foreign culture. Second, teachers may not have been adequately trained in the teaching of culture. They are familiar with a variety of culture-teaching strategies, such as culture capsules, culture clusters, cultural assimilators, and cultural minidramas, but they do not know how to integrate the strategies into a systematic study of culture, nor how to integrate culture study with language learning.

Culture study as information acquisition

Certainly, one who is a student of culture acquires bits and pieces of information about that culture which guide behavior. When the acquisition and dissemination of elements of cultural *information* become the predominant teaching strategy, though, severe limitations are imposed on the learning of culture. An information-centered, culture-teaching strategy implies that the culture under study is closed, final, complete. While such a strategy may correctly identify cultural characteristics that are valid at some particular time, an informational strategy does not adequately prepare students to recognize and understand cultural change over time. This deficit in understanding proves particularly problematic for the person who studies a second culture in high school, but does not actually confront the foreign culture until many years later. For example, having learned thirty years ago, and falsely so, that southern Germans wear *Lederhosen* on a daily basis, an American businessman arriving in Germany immediately buys *Lederhosen,* an alpine jacket, and a green hat to match. He will look extremely strange to his German counterparts when they show up in the latest pinstripe suits. Obviously the example is exaggerated, but the principle holds.

Not only does information-focused culture education inadequately treat cultural changes over time, but also it neglects consideration of individual and regional variations within the target culture. This neglect eliminates consideration of culture at the personal level, where the individual interacts with and acts upon the culture. For example, having learned to drive in Paris at night without headlights, the American driving in Lyon drives only with his parking lights on. The assumption here is that what happens in Paris also happens in the rest of the country. Although most foreign-language teachers intend to diminish stereotypes and generalized biases, an information-only culture-learning strategy may actually *establish* stereotypes, since it provides no means of accounting for cultural variation across individuals or regions at the same point in time.

To learn culture by amassing bits of information leaves the student stranded when facing a cultural situation not previously studied. The student has acquired no tools which facilitate understanding of an unknown cultural situation. This occurs not only within a culture, it arises across cultures as well. Students with much information about the culture of France may behave inappropriately in French-speaking Africa and may possess no skills for understanding and learning the new culture.

Although culture contains knowable facts, these facts are in constant flux. More important to an understanding of culture than the collection of facts is an appreciation of culture as a constellation of phenomena in a continual process of change, brought about by the participants in the culture as they live and work. Culture is in the process of becoming and should therefore be taught as process. To study culture as a body of facts is to study the characteristics of culture; to study culture as process is to study its essence.

Culture study as process

Strides have been made in promoting the systematic inclusion of culture-as-process in language courses. Several persons have contributed significantly to this progress. Nostrand's (61) emergent model organizes human behavior into four subsystems—cultural, social, ecological, and individual—focusing on patterns of behavior shared among participants in a given culture. Thirty headings are cataloged under these four subsystems. For example, culture includes value system and kinesics; society contains family structure and conflict resolution; ecology incorporates technology and attitudes toward nature; the individual subsystem covers status by age and sex as well as personality integration. Nostrand (62) describes techniques for experiencing a culture as well as for collecting knowledge about a culture. Included among eleven experiential devices, Nostrand mentions the minidrama, role playing, native informants, situational dialogue, and pen pals. Among nine cognitive techniques he includes, for example, observation and inference, simulations, and bibliography. A particular contribution of the emergent model is that its organization by subsystem provides a conceptual structure through which a teacher can approach the teaching of culture in a thematic way.

Seelye (73) looks more deeply into the instructional systematization of culture teaching. He identifies seven goals as the fulcrum of culture study. These goals address: (1) culturally conditioned behavior, (2) the interaction of language and social variables, (3) conventional behavior, (4) cultural connotations of language, (5) evolution of generalized cultural statements, (6) cultural research, and (7) attitudes toward other cultures. Seelye proposes that the teacher consciously relate classroom cultural activities to this goal structure in order to assess the purposefulness of activities and to ensure that the full range of cultural goals is being addressed. His procedure for specifying performance objectives for these goals includes a statement of expected terminal behaviors, conditions under which the behavior is to be performed, and the criteria for the determination of behavioral competence. These performance objectives are then related to a variety of learning activities and evaluation techniques.

A State of Minnesota Department of Education document (Committee of Eleven, 21) establishes essential learner outcomes for culture under the headings: (1) process for examining culture, (2) the nature of culture, (3) cultural themes, and (4) discovery and exploration of another culture. Students are expected to gain understandings of the changing nature of culture, the inaccuracy of stereotypes, the sources of cultural patterns, and the recognition of similarities and differences among cultures. Students are also expected to develop in the affective domain by seeking inter- and intracultural differences, valuing cultural contributions, and accepting cultural uniqueness. A seven-step process, known as hypothesis refinement (Jorstad, 39), enables students to achieve the above outcomes: (1) perceive a cultural aspect; (2) make a statement about the aspect; (3) gather information from sources related to that aspect; (4) examine the information and sources, and describe, report, and analyze findings; (5) modify and refine the statement; (6) examine a related aspect in the native culture using the previous five steps; and (7) compare refined statements about the native and target cultures, identifying similarities and differences.

Lange's (49) ten-step process of cultural investigation differs from hypothesis refinement primarily on the following points:

Hypothesis Refinement

1. Any perceived cultural aspect forms the content for study.
2. The statement made by the students is about the culture.
3. No speculative step is included in the process.
4. Related aspects in the native culture are examined.
5. Cross-cultural comparison is made between the target and native cultures.
6. The cultural aspect under study is not specifically viewed in interrelationship with other cultural systems.

Lange's Process

1. Problematic cultural issues experienced by the students form the content of culture study.
2. The statement made by the students includes their experiences with and feelings about the culture as well as their statement about the culture.
3. Speculation on the reasons for the existence of the cultural phenomenon is encouraged and used to identify issues for further study.
4. The process does not specifically address the native culture but could be used to do so.
5. No cross-cultural comparison is included in the process.
6. The particular problematic issue under study is related to the current totality of the target culture.

Each of these four proposals (Committee of Eleven, 21; Jorstad, 39; Lange, 49; Nostrand, 61 and 62; and Seelye, 73) allows for the systematic teaching of culture in the foreign-language classroom. Their existence testifies that language and culture are no longer just "going steady"; they are truly engaged. Marriage has not yet taken place, though, for two reasons. First, such proposals have not been translated into curricular materials. Second, even these four proposals separate culture from the teaching of language.

While language teachers possess the framework for culture teaching, culture has not really been planned for in the curriculum. The Moreau and Pfister (58) analysis of the cultural content of ten second-year college French texts published from 1972–1974 finds only one adequate in its treatment of culture when evaluated for consideration of individualism, common sense, liberty, intellectuality, family ties, youth culture, social stratification, educational system, religion as a social force, man and nature, past versus present, timeposts, Paris versus provinces, and housing design. Their report notes that even where present in the text, cultural concepts are often introduced in an indeliberate manner through dialogues and literature. Levno and Pfister (52) derive a similar conclusion from their study of twenty-one first-year college French texts published from 1972–1978. Analyzed for adequacy in family/personal life, the social sphere, political systems and institutions, the environment, the arts, French-speaking countries, contextual presentation of language, sequential introduction of cultural concepts, distribution of cultural concepts throughout the text, recognition of changing lifestyles, and culturally focused questions, only two texts survived the examination.

Perusal of many contemporary language texts (Kraft, 41; Lohnes and Strothmann, 53; Neuner et al., 59; Oudot et al., 64; Reboullet et al., 66; Sandoval et al., 71; Valdman et al., 84 and 85; Valette and Valette, 96; Weiss, 90) reveal that culture is included as content. Typically, the culture content is presented in forms, such as cultural notes; pictures and illustrations, both captioned and uncaptioned; readings; literature, including prose, poetry, and sayings; glosses in the teacher edition; role-playing exercises; games and songs; and filmstrips. The texts, to varying degrees, show respect for culture in the anthropological sense as well as in avoiding stereotypes and encouraging cross-cultural comparison. However, the culture content is essentially informational. Students are taught *about* culture; they are not taught how to interact with culture. Teacher editions may include cultural concepts in scope and sequence charts, but they do not provide a process for culture learning. In fact, the pedagogical assistance given for the teaching of culture is minimal in comparison to the assistance given for the teaching of language. This lack of assistance leaves teachers, who seriously want to teach culture, dependent on personal experience, supplementary resources, and the weak preparation for the teaching of culture provided by their college language- and teacher-education programs. Some texts are stronger than others in supplying background information and suggestions for cultural activities, but it is disappointing to read that cultural material is included only for fun, enjoyment, and enrichment, or that it is optional, can be done for homework, or can be discussed briefly in class.

Clearly then, culture is still taught separately from language, although some incidental integration of language and culture does occur. For example, Seelye (73) reproduces a culture capsule, written by Marsha Rybski, on setting the French table that incorporates vocabulary study. Oudot et al. (64) describe the manner in which the French complain about poor health, giving both expressions and background information. The four proposals described above organize the teaching of culture, but none of them intentionally integrates language and culture learning. Language is taught on the basis of linguistic analysis; culture is taught on the basis of cultural analysis. Language is taught at one time; culture is taught at another. Language proficiency is evaluated; cultural proficiency is usually not. Language-learning activities are required; culture-learning activities are optional.

The next step

If foreign-language teachers hope to fulfill their promise of developing in students an understanding of and empathy for other cultures, they must upgrade the importance of culture in the foreign-language curriculum. Building on the progress that has been made in this direction, teachers must now seek to construct a process that meets the following minimal criteria.

Does the process:
1. Make the learning of culture a requirement?
2. Integrate language learning and culture learning?
3. Allow for the identification of a spectrum of proficiency levels?
4. Address the affective as well as the cognitive domains?
5. Consider culture as a changing variable rather than a static entity?
6. Provide students with the skill to re-form perceptions of culture?
7. Provide students with the ability to interact successfully in novel cultural situations?
8. Exemplify that participants in the culture are the authors of the culture?
9. Relate to the native culture?
10. Relieve the teacher of the burden of being the cultural authority?

This chapter attempts to move beyond the separate and unequal treatment of language and culture in the curriculum by defining a process that approaches the above criteria. This process is exemplified and related to broad educational goals, as well as to other language/culture learning models. On a practical level, familiar culture-learning strategies and curricular options are situated within the proposed process, and the problem of evaluating proficiency in culture is addressed in light of the ACTFL Provisional Proficiency Guidelines (see Appendix A).

Interactive Language/Culture Learning Process ⎯⎯⎯⎯

Definition

The process described in this section draws upon several sources for its definition (Crawford-Lange, 25; Freire, 27; Jorstad, 39; Lange, 49; Stern, 76). This process is interactive in that it relates target and native languages, cultures, and perceptions (specifically, target language-native language; target culture-native culture; target language and culture perceptions-native language and culture perceptions; target culture-target language). It is also integrative in that it integrates the teaching of culture and the teaching of language. Once defined and exemplified, the process is treated in relation to both cognitive and affective educational goals. Finally, limitations of the process are identified and discussed.

The integrative process incorporates eight basic stages. The first five are largely teacher directed, dealing mainly with the presentation of cultural thematic material, stimulation in the verbalization of perceptions, and the development of language. The final three stages are student directed, relating mainly to the use of language in the verification of earlier-formed perceptions, matters of cultural awareness, and the demonstration of language/culture proficiency. Each of these stages is defined below.

Stage 1: Identification of a cultural theme. In the classroom, the identification of cultural themes may come most readily from two sources: materials yet to be written and those already available. Cultural themes are provocative and perhaps emotionally charged concerns or issues which motivate the culture learner's conduct and the values of the culture. (See Crawford, 22; Freire, 28; Nostrand, 62.) For example, the topic of employment in and of itself may not be a theme, but the issue of the availability of employment for adolescents in a depressed area may well be. The stronger the relationship to the learners' situation, the more powerful the theme will be for language/culture learners. Phenomena are operational elements of the theme. In the theme of employment, phenomena would be the range and kinds of jobs available to adolescents (Where do adolescents work?) and the wages and conditions of employment (Minimum wage? Hours, e.g., late-night shifts? Fringe benefits?). For new materials, the cultural themes to be addressed in the learning process are based either on a systematic view of that culture or on a universal structure of culture, such as the Nostrand emergent model (61), which conceptualizes culture as thematic. Already extant materials can serve as the basis for cultural study. The teacher examines these materials to determine what cultural themes occur or are implied within them. Further development of the themes contained therein are the responsibility of the students and the teacher. For example, a unit dialogue dealing with school may generate themes such as school discipline and attendance codes, required versus elective subjects, and evaluation and grading of students.

Stage 2: Presentation of cultural phenomena. Phenomena are presented to students by means of pictures, bulletin board displays, slides, overhead transparencies, films and filmstrips, videotape, videodisc, audiotape, *and* written text. Other devices, such as culture capsules and clusters, simulations, role plays, critical incidents, minidramas, and the like, may also be used to present cultural phenomena in the target language when the proficiency of students is appropriate for the task. These phenomena represent occurrences of the theme in the target culture. For example, copies of discipline codes or laws governing expulsion from school are phenomena relating to the theme of school discipline. Registration booklets listing graduation requirements are phenomena related to the issue of required versus elective subjects. Sample evaluation instruments, report cards, and grade books serve as phenomena of student evaluation and grading systems.

Stage 3: Dialogue (target/native cultures).   Dialogue between teacher and students or among students discloses the students' initial perception of the cultural theme. The dialogue process focuses on description of the phenomena presented (What offenses are listed in the discipline code? What punishments are given?), analysis of the thematic features (In what ways do the punishments relate to the offenses? How are parents involved? Is there evidence of student input into the discipline code?), and reaction to it in terms of one's own cultural patterns (How does the target-culture discipline code relate to the native-culture discipline code in terms of offenses and punishments? How well do consequences relate to offenses in each? Which do you feel is the more severe? The more effective? Which would you rather live under? Why? What problems are inherent in both? What advantages?). From this dialogue, students state their initial perceptions in written form. Included in this statement are not only the students' perceptions of the cultural phenomena but also their initial reactions to them. Throughout this dialogic stage, teachers may guide students with questioning techniques but accept the students' perceptions even if the perceptions are "wrong." The teachers are neither required to know the "right" answer, nor should the teachers provide it even if they believe they have it. In beginning language classes, this dialogue will be conducted in the students' native language. Use of the target language will increase as language proficiency increases. A thesis of this integrative process is that culture is important enough to include even if in the native language. *Culture is, in fact, the driver of the curricular program.*

Stage 4: Transition to language learning.   Students' first cultural perceptions serve as linguistic motivators. As the need to know more about the culture is developed, the student is required to use the language in order to gain that knowledge. After the initial dialogue, the teacher and students examine language they need in order to proceed: language functions, notions, structure, syntax, registers, and general vocabulary within the cultural theme under study. This transition may be accomplished by questioning students about language needs they may perceive or through the examination of some of the materials they may use in stage 6, the second dialogic opportunity. For example, if you got into trouble in a Spanish school, how could you address your interrogator? Curtly? Politely? What terms for offenses and consequences do you need to learn? If a Spanish exchange student got into trouble in your school, what do you need to know in order to explain to him or her the disciplinary procedures?

Stage 5: Language learning.   With the focus of language learning on the further exploration of cultural perceptions, as in stage 6, both a need and a thematic content for language learning have been provided. The language to be learned is *presented* here with meaningful, representative cultural phenomena. It is then *practiced* using various activities which lead to initial opportunities for language *use,* as the students become ready. The textbook can serve as the source of the language material to be presented and practiced. It can also suggest opportunities to use language for communication. In addition, linguistic content identified in the transition stage can be incorporated with the text material. Identified vocabulary can, for example, be inserted into pattern drills. An identified structure, not included in the current text, can be studied using material from another unit.

Stage 6: Verification of perceptions (target/native culture). Having learned some language, students are thus ready to verify their initial perceptions by examining as many resources as are available to them—print, visual, and human. Different students may pursue different aspects of the theme depending on interest, and different sources may be investigated depending on language ability. The various pieces of information are brought together and described, analyzed, and compared to the original perception. This stage is the second dialogic opportunity for students, and because of the prior language learning, may incorporate increased use of the target language. This opportunity allows those who have been working with different thematic phenomena to combine them into a broader perspective. Within this stage, changes in the perceptions of both the target and native cultures are specifically noted and described, as are positive and negative reactions. Comparison of the perceived phenomena with thematic patterns in the native culture also continue. The investigation of resources can take place parallel to language learning, culminating in the dialogue of stage 6, and could take the form of homework assignments, projects, or group work.

Stage 7: Cultural awareness. Students examine the issues related to their experience with the cultural phenomena, the language learned, and the verification of perceptions. They might relate how their perceptions changed during the process and respond to questions such as: Why are there cultural differences? What effects have geography, time, and people had on cultural evolution? Are there different patterns in different regions? How has the pattern existed in the native culture? What differences exist between the two cultures? Are there any influences of the target culture on the native culture? Has the native culture influenced the target culture in any way? How do phenomena studies in the target culture interact with other systems in the same culture? If your cultural perceptions changed during this unit, what caused them to change? The conclusion of this stage is important because students are conscious of the process they are using and can verbalize their understanding of culture. This process and understanding will be available to them in later life and transferable to other circumstances.

Stage 8: Evaluation of language and cultural proficiency. In order to indicate awareness, knowledge, and appreciation of both target and native cultures, students prepare written and oral materials, using the target language as capacity builds, which demonstrate proficiency in both language and culture. Such demonstrations could include the creation of critical incidents, minidramas, culture capsules and clusters, simulations, or dialogues in the target language. Students may, for example, write a discipline code of a Spanish school, a North American school, and their "ideal" discipline code. They may role play a disciplinary incident in one or both cultures. All of the named devices allow for language proficiency evaluation, as well as evaluation of awareness, knowledge, and appreciation of both the target and native cultures. Because the students create these materials and perform with these devices, they are evaluated on both their use of language and their understanding of culture. Language, of course, can continue to be evaluated in the traditional manner. While the goal is to have cultural evaluation take place in the target language, this goal is progressively achieved as linguistic ability improves. Initially, culture is considered sufficiently important to warrant its evaluation even in the native language.

As the process has been conceived and described above, we have meticulously considered the criteria which we identified earlier as being necessary to upgrade the status of culture in the foreign-language curriculum. We believe that this integrative process approaches a meeting of the criteria. The following example extends meaning to the process, but it also serves as a test to indicate its acceptability in relationship to the stated criteria and its feasibility within the classroom.

Exemplification of the process

(*Scene:* The students in the sophomore class in Johnstown High School are excited about a number of issues: their first year in high school, new friends, a different range of school subjects, extracurricular activities, effects of budget cuts, driving the family car, among others.)

Stage 1: Identification of a cultural theme. The French teacher hears students talking about the kinds of activities in which they participate in school, including sports, clubs, musical organizations, and the like. Some of these activities are threatened by budget cutbacks, and students have expressed concern over this possibility. The next unit in the French text contains a dialogue dealing with sports clubs in a French community. The teacher identifies the theme as "organization of adolescent sports programs."

Stage 2: Presentation of cultural phenomena. Although the theme is identified in the dialogue, other representations of the theme are also brought into the classroom: slides and photographs of adolescents participating in different sports; the school schedule from another unit in the book, which shows the middle of the week free; photocopies of other examples of school schedules collected by the teacher during a recent trip to France; slides and photographs of schools *without* sports facilities; slides and photographs of parks with basketball facilities, soccer fields, and a community swimming pool; slides and photographs of sports clubs; the AFS student; the teacher's culture capsule on sports in France; French school bulletins that do not list athletic activities.

Stage 3: Dialogue (target/native culture). The teacher uses the representations (visual, textual, and real in this case) to focus student attention on the organization of adolescent sports programs. The *first* purpose of the ensuing dialogue among students *and* with the teacher is a description and featural analysis of the representational phenomena. Students would notice the sports in which adolescents participate; that extracurricular activities, including sports, do not appear in the school schedule or in school bulletins; facilities for sports appear in parks, private sports clubs, and community arenas and swimming pools; students pay for their participation in sports activities either as members of a club or by the activity as sponsored by the community. *Second,* the students state their initial reactions to the phenomena and their features, culminating in a short written statement about their perceptions and reactions. An example of such perceptions and reactions might be the following: "French kids don't seem to have sports in the school day. That's not very cool. They study all the time. That must be boring." The teacher's function is to use questioning techniques to elicit description, analysis, and reaction to the phenomena. Examples of elicitation questions might be: What did you see in the photographs and slides? Let's look at them individually. What do they tell you about the organization of sports activities in schools in France? Now that we have described the slides and photographs, what patterns do you see? What are your reactions? What do you feel about the idea of sports activities being organized outside the school? At this point, students also indicate what they wish to know more about this theme since their own activities are threatened by budget reductions. To begin with, the dialogue is in English, but it moves to the target language as the students' competence grows. Certainly, some of the teacher's presentation of cultural phenomena in the target language can appear early in a beginning course to allow for listening comprehension to develop.

Stage 4: Transition to language learning. When the first dialogic opportunity is completed, the next concern, in order to learn more about the theme, is language. Teacher and students together explore the linguistic and communicative needs of the unit: vocabulary, by questioning the extent of different interests; communication (functions, notions), by determining the intent for which language is to be used; and structures and syntax associated with use and interests. The examination of those needs might proceed in the following manner:

TEACHER: Now that we have finished considering our reactions to what we have seen, heard, and read, we need to determine what language needs we have in order to explore these ideas further. What language needs do we seem to have?

STUDENT: I would like to explore soccer as a game that I know little about so that I can teach it to the class.

TEACHER: Then you will need to explore the rules of the game and its vocabulary in French. Since we haven't learned how to give directions yet, you'll need, at least, to give commands as well as to give information if you are going to teach the sport.

STUDENTS: There are several of us who want to do that! Can we do this part together? We want to write to a community organization to find out how they get adults involved. If our clubs get cut, we may need their advice.

TEACHER: You know there are certain formalities for writing letters in French. We'll need to look at them in order for you to put your letter together.

Linguistic needs may also be determined through the examination of potential materials for stage 6. Themes can be examined several times in different ways, thus making it possible to come back to a theme more than once in order to meet the interests and the linguistic and communicative needs of students. Further, students will also have different interests and will therefore wish to become acquainted with different aspects of the theme individually.

Stage 5: Language learning.   The language and communicative strategies to be learned are associated with the representative cultural phenomena used in stage 2. Presentation may be in the form of dialogue, narrative, prepared discussion, or the like from stage 2. It may also be built around existing textbook material. In any case, it is always associated with the cultural theme. The language and communication strategies to be learned are first practiced by a variety of means: drills, games, specially structured activities. Here again, if the textbook is the main source of thematic material, it may substantially supply the language practice. Vocabulary and structures identified in stage 4 are utilized in the drills and exercises contained in the textbook, which will be supplemented by the teacher as the need arises. Initial language use in this case may include simulations and role playing related to joining a community sports club, learning the basic moves in fencing, or teaching a basic swimming stroke, or arguing for or against the retention of extracurricular activities in the school. Evaluation at this point can focus on the parts and pieces of language, employing some of the traditional discrete-point testing devices. However, since language use is also a part of the language-learning phase, testing should also involve situational or global test devices such as interviews, a sample of contextual writing, and recall protocols for listening and reading.

Stage 6: Verification of perceptions.   At this point the language presented, practiced, and used in stage 5 becomes a tool for learning more about the cultural theme and its representative phenomena. Students return to the description and analysis of and reaction to the phenomena. These data are used as the basis for verification. Students seek other sources, as many as possible, to check on the original perception and the data generated from it. In tapping sources, students might write to a French sports club, asking about the nature and kind of activities, its newsletter, or the yearly club schedule. The AFS student could serve as a contact for other French students in the area. Community French-speaking people, both native and nonnative, could be used as sources of information. The coaches in the school could also serve as resources concerning the organization of sports activities for American schools. Library and other written materials, such as popular magazines—for example, *Paris Match*—and teen magazines, may also be explored. Students may wish to examine different phenomena in depth: sports clubs, school schedules, community facilities, different kinds of sports. The information they find is brought together, described, analyzed, and compared to the original perceptions. During this stage, the dialogue among students and with the teacher brings more information together with the original presentation of cultural phenomena of stage 2, thereby allowing more depth of understanding as students compare what they originally perceived as the organization of sports activities in France with new information.

What makes this dialogic opportunity different from that of stage 3 is the depth and expansion of knowledge, as well as more careful comparison with the native culture. For example, some of the kinds of questions to be asked by the instructor at this point could be: What do your observations offer to our particular problem in this school? Faced with budget cuts, should we organize our sports activities differently? How are the two systems different? Could we modify the French system for use in solving our problem? How do you think it could be accomplished?

Stage 7: Cultural awareness.   Students are now ready to examine reasons why their first perceptions may have changed. This may lead them to consider questions like: Why do sports activities play a different role in schooling in France than in the U.S.? What do these differences say about differences between the two cultures? What effect does this organization have upon French people, if any? Are there regional differences related to the role of sports within schools in the U.S.? Other such questions will arise from the nature of the data generated. The purpose of this discussion is for students to become conscious of how their awareness has changed concerning sports in French schools, as well as to examine the process they have dealt with and its application to their own culture and lives.

Stage 8: Evaluation of language and cultural proficiency. It is appropriate that students demonstrate their ability to use language within context. Therefore, emphasis at this stage should be placed on the interaction of language with content. Students could prepare a cultural assimilator with several parts on the organization of sports activities for adolescents in French culture. Some students could teach others a sport not well known in the U.S. Others could contribute to a contrastive study of sports in adolescent culture in France and the U.S. One student might even examine sports in French-speaking or French-influenced cities or regions in the U.S. and/or Canada. Other students may develop a contingency plan for their own school activities, incorporating or adapting some of the aspects of French culture, as the school prepares for the coming budget cuts. The theme in many ways suggests the kinds of activities that could be used in bringing students, language, and cultural content together. Both cultural content and cultural accuracy are determined by what the students have found, as well as by their perceptions of those findings. Evaluation of the cultural aspect must be related to the patterns students found, their reactions, and their perceptions, *not* to a universal pattern for the entire French society or the patterns in U.S. society. Thus evaluation of culture, of necessity, will be limited to the research done by the students. It should be oriented more to *process* than to discrete cultural points. The student's cultural competence should be judged for appropriateness and completeness within the framework in which it was established. Further, some elements of cooperative learning (Johnson and Johnson, 36) may be utilized. In particular, this stage of evaluation may be judged on a group rather than on an individual basis. Language must be judged in this context also from expectations which are related to the language formally learned in stage 5 and to language learned as a tool of discovery. It should be evaluated for appropriateness, accuracy, and completeness as it relates to student need, the activity, and the cultural content. Such evaluation will be global in nature, relating in this case to the expression of the theme, organization of sports activities for adolescents in French schools.

The integrative process in relation to general educational objectives

While the process defined and exemplified above insists on a relationship between language and culture, the two can be untangled from that relationship, examined separately for their contribution to the achievement of general educational objectives, and finally reunited to show how the process joins them together conceptually.

An examination of the tradition of language teaching and learning in the past twenty-five years reveals an ever increasing concentration upon culture as an important element. Language teachers rationalize the inclusion of a foreign language in the curriculum because, "it opens the students' minds to other people's thinking and therefore to a broader world view." The exposure of students to another culture through its language may be an extremely important element in students' general education, but it is not clear what objective is being met. Are students actually learning culture as they are exposed to it through language? How is this learning achieved? Are students learning language in a meaningful way? The present section attempts to answer these questions by clarifying language and culture learning in relation to general educational objectives.

The process of culture learning operates in both the cognitive and affective domains. As defined by Bloom et al. (8), the cognitive domain of general educational objectives consists of six categories arranged in ascending hierarchical order: knowledge, comprehension, application, analysis, synthesis, and evaluation. Organized in the same fashion, the affective domain, defined by Krathwohl et al. (44), is made up of five categories: receiving, responding, valuing, organizing, and characterizing. It is not the intent of this chapter to define or explain these categories; Bloom and Krathwohl have accomplished those goals in publications familiar to most educators. Instead, the discussion turns toward the relationship of these general educational objectives to the learning of culture.

The cognitive domain.   In the literature on the teaching of culture in the second-language classroom (for example, Bishop, 6; Bishop and Undank, 7; Dodge, 26; Ladu, 45; Mead, 55), there is heavy concentration on the facts of culture: history, kinesics, religion, art, architecture, geography, the status of women, economic conditions, courtship, literature, and the like. Many of the culture-teaching activities such as the culture capsule, cultural assimilator, critical incidents, minidrama, and lecture presentations also tend to present cultural facts. From this information and from the observation of teachers and learners in classrooms, it is possible to conclude that although culture teaching and learning in second-language education has progressed from a restricted "Culture" definition to one recognizing all elements of human existence as worthy of a "culture" definition, it still concentrates on information rather than on process. Thus, culture teaching and learning seem to be limited to the lower end of the cognitive domain, i.e., to knowledge and comprehension.

While there is no question that information and the comprehension of the nature of that information are important, learners are capable of higher mental capacities, such as the ability to: (1) apply facts, rules, theories—in other words, learned material—in new situations; (2) analyze or break down related information into component parts, recognize relationships among the component parts, and suggest an organizational structure for the components; (3) synthesize, or organize disparate elements into a new whole; and (4) judge or evaluate the value of elements according to clearly defined criteria. The farther students progress through the hierarchies of the cognitive domain, the more they deal with process. Guntermann (31) provides an example of the hierarchies of the cognitive domain with cultural examples for Latin America.

Culture learning in the language classroom must move beyond the knowledge and comprehension stages into process in order that information become meaningful in a broader sense. For example, it may be important to know and understand the nature and structure of the legally constituted education system in Spain, but that is not enough for the critical thinking required in today's world. One also must be able to show how it is carried out in different regions in Spain, analyze its successes and weaknesses, recommend ways in which it could be more successful, and show why it is successful and why it is weak. When cultural knowledge becomes processed, it begins to carry meaning other than lexical meaning, a meaning of relationships.

Some argue that we live in an age of information; however, it is probably more an age of process than of information. Information is now routinely stored and retrieved electronically. The role of the human is to act on and process information rather than store it. Evidence of the importance of process in culture learning in the second-language classroom is demonstrated in a few sources. Nostrand (62) provides an encompassing view of culture, motivation, and a multiplicity of cultural learning and teaching techniques. In short, he provides the broad frameworks for culture study, but does not link them to any process as such. Seelye (73) adds cultural objectives which are process oriented but which are not connected to an active, conscious process. Jenks (35) suggests that students may use scientific methodology to solve cultural problems. Jorstad (39) adds hypothesis refinement, another adaptation of the scientific method, to the processing of cultural information. Bragaw, Loew, and Wooster (11) discuss a group investigative approach, a social inquiry approach similar to Jenks's and Jorstad's hypothesis refinement model, and an inductive learning model based on work by Taba as ways to cope with culture learning in the second-language classroom. Each of these sources also gives a taxonomy of cultural themes, nodes, or universals. The reader should also examine Brooks's (12) categories which are based on personal and institutional parameters. Yet, in none of these cases is a process built into the language program which offers culture as an integral part of that program.

Conceptually, the integrative process defined and exemplified in this chapter combines cognitive process with both language and culture. Perhaps its most important characteristic is that students use process actively, are aware of its existence, and evaluate its use. Learners are presented cultural information in relation to a theme. They also describe and analyze the representations of the cultural theme presented to them. In this way, students become familiar with the phenomena and the theme; they know and comprehend them. As they learn language related to the theme and the representative phenomena, they become even more familiar with them, know them, and comprehend them. Once the necessary language has been learned, students pursue the theme in depth, bringing in new information, describing it, applying it to what is already known; analyzing relationships among patterns discerned; synthesizing, revising, and reorganizing the relationships; and finally evaluating the patterns and their relationships against patterns and relationships of the same theme in the native culture. The final cognitive manipulation here is the examination of the process itself: What did it tell me (the student) about the two cultures? How can I use it better the next time? What went wrong if it did not work?

By actively using such a process and by making students consciously aware of process as they learn culture and language, students are more likely to arrive at an understanding, at least intellectually, of cultural patterns that are not owned by them, than if they had "learned" culture as a supplement to language learning as in the typical language class. There is a rule of thumb, established by much research in language learning and teaching: "One tends to learn what one has been taught." This applies here. Understanding of other cultures may be learned only if a process attempting to teach understanding is taught. We believe that the integrative process has the potential for allowing for more understanding of other people and cultures cognitively and, as explained below, affectively.

The affective domain.   Learning involves more than intellectual aspects. It encompasses affective ones as well. Culture learning, as is argued by many language teachers, contributes to an interest in and an empathy for people of another culture. The concept, interest in other people, is an important one in learning a second language. Gardner and Lambert (29), after a decade of research in the 1960s, established interest in other people as an element of an integrative orientation which in turn contributes positively to learning a second language. Empathy for another people is the subject of Seelye's eighth cultural objective (73), but he warns that empathy should be developed in careful and rational ways. Guiora et al. (30) report the establishment of a relationship between empathy and the ability to pronounce a language other than English by English-speaking Americans. Yousef (95) shows how negative student attitudes toward cultural behavior other than their own may be modified by training. These examples suggest that affect is both a goal of culture learning as well as an element contributing to language learning.

The process, as defined and exemplified, includes the affective domain as it intermingles with the hierarchical categories of the cognitive domain. The five categories of educational objectives for the affective domain are included in the process in the following ways. As students participate in the presentation of thematic representational phenomena, their attention is drawn to the representations where they *receive,* or show their willingness to attend to them. This attention, or receiving, is the lowest level in the affective domain. As students describe and analyze the thematic representational phenomena, they are *responding* to the phenomena. This response suggests that their attention is being held. Another aspect of response is included when the attention of students in stage 3 of the process is turned toward their personal reactions to the representations. "What is your reaction to sports activities being organized outside the school day and why? Write it down so that we can examine it at a later date." Students' consciousness is specifically directed toward their initial reactions. The recording of those reactions is important in providing personal data which can be further examined as students know and process more about the relationships of the phenomena within the theme. Further response is indicated as students identify the language they will need in order to participate in the verification of perceptions. Attention to learning the language needed is a further indicator of the desire to respond to the theme and the process itself. In verifying original perceptions, students use the language learned to search other sources. Having found a broader spectrum of information, the students must compare what they originally perceived and reacted to with new data. Do their original perceptions and attitudes hold up? How have the perceptions and values changed? Perceptions and values are formally restated. The dialogue of this stage also allows for contrast and comparison of revised perceptions and attitudes with perceptions of and attitudes toward a similar theme in the native culture. In this comparative and contrastive exercise, students bring together and sort out the values they hold of their own culture and also attitudes they have toward other cultures. The integrative language/culture process thus requires them to *organize* their own system of values and attitudes. It also gives them a process for continually developing that system. In the evaluation stage, students demonstrate in the target language their values and attitudes and those of the culture they are studying by participating in activities which bring together language use and cultural processing. These demonstrations show that students have arrived at a point in their development at which they can *characterize* their own values and those of others.

As the process deals with affective learning, several of its strengths appear. First, it is effective in dealing with the personal reactions and responses to the second culture. It requires students to confront their reactions directly by stating them. Reconfrontation with more information from a broader and deeper search tends to modify initial reactions, thereby modifying perceptions and attitudes. The perception and reperception of culture with more information, awareness, and tools can open the minds of individuals to the understanding that they and others together are the makers of culture. Second, as will be developed further below, the intimate relationship of language, culture, cognitive, and affective learning through process has the potential to reduce dramatically motivation problems. Students have a reason to participate. They are responsible for their own learning and are the makers of their own values. Third, conscious attention to the development of affective learning provides outcomes which are no longer hoped-for by-products of language learning but are attainable affective objectives relating to the entire hierarchy of general affective objectives, not just to those at the lower level. Fourth, the process gives active attention to establishing attitudes toward and valuing of the native culture. Many students are not aware even of their own culture and the subcultures within it. The process makes those attitudes and values conscious.

Limitations of the Integrative Process

There are at least three major limitations to the integrative language/ culture process: resources, teacher development, and tradition in language teaching. There is no question that the requirement of a wide fund of resources on current aspects of any chosen theme is perhaps the most striking limitation. Materials (books, magazines, tapes, videotapes, slides, pictures, etc.) and people to offer complete representations of the Nostrand emergent model, for example, are not available. However, the beginnings of such materials are in many textbooks and in teachers' files. They may need reorganization as one way of making them available. Some anticipation of themes and the projected material needed also provides an awareness of what can easily be added to materials already possessed. A survey of the community and the school may turn up undiscovered speakers and those acquainted with the culture. The concepts of a drop-file and word-file (Bragaw et al., 11) are useful in acquiring the necessary material. In short, there are approaches to this limitation that awareness, organization, time, and patience can overcome. In addition, since the primary purpose of the process is to develop the ability to *process information* rather than acquire it, it is necessary only to be aware that additional data may alter perceptions. It is not necessary to provide all existing data in an effort to establish a "correct" perception.

While language teaching is moving more toward the integration of language and culture, the development of teachers seriously lags behind the concept. Institutions of higher education which train language teachers need to integrate culture and language in the preparation they provide. At the University of Minnesota, for instance, a special methods course entitled "Strategies for the Teaching of Culture in the Second Language Classroom" is offered. In the future, this culture-strategies course must be incorporated into the current two-quarter course on "Teaching Second Languages," resulting in a three-quarter course integrating language and culture learning by means of the processes exemplified in this chapter. Those familiar with this integrative process must also train in-service teachers interested in employing an integrative approach. In this regard, a perspective that reaches into language teaching in general and into ESL and writing in the native language in particular, may be useful. Wallerstein (88) provides some insights and sample materials in her discussion of the integration of language and culture in the ESL classroom. Although restricted to the development of writing in English, Shor (74) offers insights into the relationship between the broader culture of North America and its interaction with the development of a written literacy in English, mainly with college students. Until integrative language/culture workshops at institutions of higher education and at professional meetings become more numerous, such publications are a useful source of information.

Traditionally, for more than 2,500 years in fact (Kelly, 40), teachers have focused attention on language, its structure, syntax, and vocabulary, almost to the exclusion of the uses for which language is intended. While the process defined and exemplified in this chapter does not deny the importance of the facts of language, it allies itself with the cultural element to the extent that the cultural element is given as prominent a position as language. It forces consideration of language and its uses within a given content area. As described here, the integrative process does not allow language learning to be superficial or content free. This alliance is natural and reorients the concentration on language to focus on both language and culture. It is expected that those who hold to more conservative views of language learning will have difficulty with the concepts expressed here. These concepts are offered, however, to push even further the dialogue begun in other related publications (Crawford-Lange, 23; Crawford-Lange, 25; and Lange, 49). That dialogue is awaited with anticipation.

Culture within the Language Curriculum

Three somewhat different models of curricular organization may be identified which include culture within the language curriculum, each with varying degrees of success. Those models are the linear model, the communicative model, and the language/culture integrative model. This section will examine the mode used by each model to address the teaching of culture.

The linear model

This model has been described by Wilkins (92) as being synthetic in nature and as one in which the learning of the parts of language, step by step, is supposed to contribute to the learning of the whole of language. Concretely defined by Banathy and Lange (3), the model is based on preestablished objectives which are reduced to learning tasks, based on the nature of the objective and the input of the learner. The accumulation of learning tasks within an objective contributes to the mastery of the objective. The model is simultaneously a "top-down" and a "bottom-up" approach to curriculum development. In this approach, culture is an element outside language learning. While it is a strand of the learning which takes place in the classroom, culture is not integrated with language. It is essentially parallel to language learning. It may be systematic, as in Brooks's (14) five-minute incidental talks on culture which are based on a wide range of topics and which he later (12) classifies as cultural nodes or points of contact between the self and others. In this case, culture probably *is* incidental, an element not specifically treated within the curriculum, an aside, a filler. As an incidental, parallel element to language, cultural objectives take second priority to the language structure which is seen as the major, and sometimes only, concern of a linear curriculum.

The communicative model

Expanded from an incomplete definition by Savignon (72) in the early 1970s, the communicative model concentrates on the use of language in social intercourse where it becomes a tool of communication between or among two or more people. The model considers both usage and use as being primary (Widdowson, 91). The knowledge of structure and the ability to apply linguistic rules in actual communication are considered of equal importance. The concept of language use offers an additional taxonomy of elements to be learned to that of the traditional grammatical taxonomy. The taxonomy of language use displays the categories of communicative functions (imparting and seeking factual information, expressing and finding out intellectual attitudes, expressing and finding out emotional attitudes, expressing and finding out moral attitudes, getting things done, and socializing, for example) which are linked to semantico-grammatical categories or notions (concepts such as, duration, frequency, and dimension). Both categories are related to the purpose for which language is used in a topical situation. The reader should consult Brumfit and Johnson (17), Johnson (37), van Ek (87), and Widdowson (91) for a much more extensive explanation of these concepts.

The main thrust of the communicative model for our consideration here is that it extends language learning beyond structure to the learning of its use in a social context or within a culture. The topics and situations in which functions, notions, and grammar are *used* provide a cultural context for that use. However, the use categories may only be intertwined with grammatical categories, as in the Brumfit visualization of the communicative model (16). They are not fully integrated with one another. Thus, the model may not fully integrate the elements of use and usage, although they are brought into a closer relation. But more important, the full processing of language with cultural information and the valuing of culture is not apparent. The focus is still primarily on language and its development.

The integrative language/culture model

Explained and exemplified in this chapter, this model allows the full integration of language and culture. They are not loosely intermingled but require each other. Without language, culture learning is incomplete because its expression is removed. Without cultural orientation, the language returns to a contentless exercise. In theory at least, this model allows for the most complete relationship between language and culture.

This model has the potential of incorporating the communicative model because it expects the *use* of language as a means of accomplishing perceptions, an understanding, and a valuing of the second culture. It can incorporate many of the recommendations for language development which come from L1 and L2 acquisition research. For example, Krashen's idea of input/intake (Krashen, 42, 43), which suggests that spoken language is ultimately acquired not by the practice of speaking but through the comprehension of input/intake, can be easily accommodated from the very beginning of the process. In stage 2, for example, thematic cultural representations are presented. These representations are easily structured to conform with the requirements of input for both listening and reading as Krashen describes them: comprehensible, interesting or relevant, not grammatically sequenced, and of sufficient quantity. The several recommendations on the development of comprehension in the collection of essays which Winitz (94) has published can also be incorporated, especially those of Nord (60) which attempt to organize a system for the development of listening, and Swaffar and Stephens (80) whose plan for development of language learning involves receiving information, matching input to a set of criteria, problem solving and opinion giving—ideas certainly related to the integrative process. Other elements of the communicative model may also be incorporated: topics, situation, functions, notions, and registers. Grammar is not tightly sequenced, but it is learned as required to be able to process information within a cultural theme. Grammar learning is not the ultimate goal; linguistic and cultural proficiency are. Grammar, therefore, is learned for its appropriate role: providing the structure which contains and communicates ideas. The development of communication thus comes from two sources: (1) the processing of information and ideas and (2) the need to communicate that information and those ideas as students' reactions to culture undergo refinement.

The integrative model proposes the development of cultural proficiency in the target culture through the processing of culture in language. It has one by-product which must also be designated. The process can be extended to the native culture as a means of comprehending the native culture and its many subcultures. Such potential, whether used in or outside the language classroom, may, for example, contribute to a school district's ability to cope with human relations problems in dealing with the many Asian refugees who have entered the U.S. in recent years and who continue to arrive. At a minimum, students utilizing the process should become aware of the pluralistic nature of culture.

Finally, affect toward another culture and cultural change are affiliated in the integrative model. Students must become aware that they do react to cultural information in relation to their own values. In most cases, the level of awareness of such reaction is hidden, probably for many reasons. This model requires conscious and active processing of reactions, attitudes, and values, giving a means whereby once the student has left schooling, reactions toward others, regardless of the context, have a chance to be recognized and dealt with fairly.

The model also prepares students to understand change: their attitudes and values can change with information and time; change is an important aspect of life; and they can have some control over change. The model incorporates some of the basic propositions of Freire's (27, 28) problem-posing education, as explained in Crawford-Lange (25). Freire's approach to education is built on group and individual conscious awareness of people's functions and roles in society and how the individual and group can act with and upon the society to effect change.

Integration of Culture-Learning Strategies

The question addressed in this section is: How do teachers integrate familiar and tried culture-learning strategies into the integrative language/culture process introduced above? These culture-learning strategies include the culture capsule, culture assimilator, culture cluster, audiomotor unit, minidrama, role playing, simulation, and critical incident. Also discussed is the relationship of global education to the integrative process.

Culture-learning techniques

The techniques listed above are defined, described, and exemplified in many places in the professional literature (Hendon, 33; Jarvis, 34; Lafayette, 47; Morain, 56; Nostrand, 62; Seelye, 73; Strasheim, 78; Taylor and Sorenson, 81). The purpose here is to note at what points in the language/culture process these techniques may be most effectively applied, and to identify any modifications that could render a technique more amenable to the process. The selection of a technique for inclusion in this section does not signify that it is the best or the only approach. The various techniques are included because of their frequent recurrence in the literature, with the likelihood that they are familiar to classroom teachers. Table 1 plots the stages at which the various techniques can be most effectively incorporated into the integrative language/culture process.

As is obvious from Table 1, the listed representative techniques apply most appropriately to the presentation, transition, verification, and evaluation stages. The first stage of thematic identification is antecedent to the use of any learning strategies. Dialogue, verification, and cultural awareness center on group interaction, while language learning employs techniques more specific to that task. The audiomotor unit, however, is included under language learning since it is ideal to the development of listening comprehension. All techniques are checked under verification since they can serve as resource material. While reference can be made to the techniques at any stage in the process, the techniques operate most actively and with different emphases within presentation, transition, and evaluation.

The purpose of the presentation stage is to represent cultural phenomena oriented toward a theme in order that the students, in dialogue, can describe, analyze, and interpret the phenomena. With advanced students, this activity, including representation and discussion, would take place in the target language. With beginning students, it would be conducted in the native language. The more a representation avoids drawing conclusions about the cultural theme and, instead, provides materials for the students' description and interpretation, the more useful the technique is at the presentation stage.

At the presentation stage, then, the capsule, incident, minidrama, role play, and simulation can each be used to feature a phenomenon and background information. Through questioning, the teacher leads the students into the dialogic stage of description, interpretation, and analysis. Unless the culture cluster is tightly conceived, it may introduce too much material and thus lose focus. The audiomotor unit is appropriate at the presentation stage, but it is limited in the number of cultural themes it can encompass effectively. The culture assimilator should be revised for use in the integrative process, but the situational introduction should be retained. However, following the setting of the situation, the assimilator typically poses four plausible explanations for the conflict contained in the situation and four feedback paragraphs expressing why the explanation is or is not the correct choice. A more effective format for an *integrative assimilator* would be to follow the setting of the situation with discussion eliciting plausible explanations from the students, to be validated later in the process.

At the transition stage, the techniques provide a reference for identifying language content. If the technique incorporates a visual, the teacher can ask, "What objects do you see in this picture that we will have to know the names of in order to discuss what is happening here?" The teacher

Table 1

Stages

Techniques

	Identification	Presentation	Dialogue	Transition	Language Learning	Verification	Awareness	Evaluation
Culture capsule		+		+		X		+
Culture assimilator		R		+		X		R
Culture cluster		X		X		X		+
Critical incident		+		+		X		+
Audiomotor unit		X		X	+	X		X
Minidrama		+		+		X		+
Role playing		+		+		X		+
Simulation		+		+		X		+

Key: + = strong application   X = applicable   R = applicable with revision could also point to objects in a visual and students could decide whether the vocabulary item is necessary. Language functions can also be noted: "Do we need polite expressions of greeting or leave-taking? Is there an argument going on? How might the people in this situation be expressing their anger/pleasure/impatience?" Even grammatical structures can be highlighted: "Are the people in this situation asking each other questions? Do you know how to ask questions? Are the participants describing a past event or anticipating a future one?" Skillful questions on the part of the teacher can not only guide students toward appropriate linguistic content, but also supply students with a motivational context in which to use the language.

When the stage of proficiency evaluation is reached, the techniques belong to the students for their manipulations. They can write their own capsules and perhaps compare them with the one used in the presentation, showing how their perceptions have changed. The critical incident, mini-drama, role play, and simulation could be similarly adapted. An assimilator could be produced by students in which the four plausible answers are all actually correct and possible. The explanations could specify for whom and under what circumstances each answer is most likely. This structure allows students to demonstrate understanding of individual or regional variations. This same approach could be applied to a culture cluster. A cluster could represent the students' perceptions of the theme across several cultures, including the native one, or demonstrate how the phenomena representing the theme have changed over time.

Inserted into the integrative process, these familiar culture-learning techniques are thus used in a variety of ways. They also can supply materials to the teacher, as the product of the evaluation stage can become part of next year's study or another class presentation. In addition to greater flexibility, the techniques assume greater meaning. As part of a process, they no longer serve as asides or as isolated bits of information. They become powerful stimulators of cultural reflection, as well as motivators for language learning.

The Integrative Process and Global Education _____

The marriage of language and culture proposed in this chapter can be associated with the goals of global education: awareness of the world situation, awareness of the choices people make, understanding of international relationships, consciousness of and respect for alternative world views, and cross-cultural awareness (Hanvey, 32). This association, which is central to the integrative process, occurs through the examination of cultural themes and through the effort, at the stage of cultural awareness, to make students conscious of the process they are using.

The fact that global studies as a pervasive educational concern has migrated from the professional journals and conferences to the minds of educators at the local level is reflected in a recent survey of Minnesota senior high school principals (Crawford-Lange, 24). In this survey, principals were presented a series of ten curricular options, in the form of situational examples, and asked to rate each one as: a good idea they would like to see tried, a good idea but not practical, or not a good idea. Of the respondents, 72 percent thought that an application of global education involving foreign-language classes should be implemented. The example given is that of collaboration between social studies and foreign-language teachers. When social studies classes discuss international trade, the foreign-language classes focus on the role the countries in which their foreign language is spoken play in the worldwide economy. The only curricular concept scoring higher among the principals is career education, accepted for implementation by 76 percent.

An example of such cooperation between social studies and foreign-language teachers was developed in 1982. The University of Minnesota Worldmindedness Project (Mackey et al., 54) examined the relationship of foreign language and social studies within the concept of global education. In this project, Rochester, Minnesota, public school teachers and university staff in social studies and second languages and cultures jointly explored the possibilities of foreign-language and social studies cooperation at a practical level. Two operable modes of cooperation were identified: interdisciplinary and intradisciplinary efforts.

Interdisciplinary efforts included the actual planning by social studies and German teachers of a curriculum to be taught jointly. The units developed relate to World War II and the current peace movement in Europe. Intradisciplinary efforts at applying global education concepts were accomplished by French, German, and Spanish teachers planning to integrate the concept of the World in Minnesota, dealing with language and cultures represented in Minnesota as part of an exploratory course on language. Other efforts involved planning for and using international students in social studies classes; exchanging classrooms during the development of cultural projects, tried by one teacher who instructs both social studies and language courses; exchanging classrooms on the part of two teachers, social studies and Spanish, who lined up their curricula to offer units on Spain and Spanish-American issues, such as the bullfight in Spain, the defeat of the Spanish Armada, and the Falklands/Malvinas crisis.

Into a generalized enthusiasm for global education, Zais (96) inserts a word of caution: global education may become trivialized as "curriculum chic." Zais qualifies this statement, though, both by allowing that concepts which have been usurped as bandwagons may have begun as solid curriculum proposals and by acknowledging that global education may be one of these usurped yet solid proposals. Warriner-Burke (89) clearly disagrees with a global education orientation for language courses, while conceding that all of the reviewed papers addressing curriculum and materials presented at the ACTFL National Conference of Professional Priorities urge improvement in the teaching of culture (Lafayette and Strasheim, 48; Rivers, 67; Stern, 75; Valdman, 82; Zais, 96).

Whatever the fate of global education, passing fad or powerful curricular thrust (and it is too soon to tell which it will be), culture belongs in the language classroom. Culture study enhances the contribution of foreign-language classes to global education (Collins, 20) and to the total school curriculum (Strasheim, 77). The concordance of culture study to the aims of global education is serendipitous. The need for culture study, though, does not originate in global education; culture learning has long been an expressed goal of foreign-language education itself (see, for example, Altman and Hanzeli, 2; Born, 10; Brooks, 13; Dodge, 26; Lafayette, 46; Morain, 57; Rivers, 68; Robinson, 69; Valdman, 83). The promise of cross-cultural understanding can be fulfilled only if culture is actually *taught* in the classroom, and taught with adequate time on task.

Global education pushes language education toward the goal of cross-cultural understanding by validating an increase in time spent on culture learning and by accepting culture as content for foreign-language classes. Not only do global educators stress culture, they specifically ask foreign-language teachers to elevate the place of culture and the time allowed for culture in their classrooms (Bonham et al., 9; Cleveland, 18; Collins, 20; Posvar, 65; Robinson, 70). This increased curricular attention to culture is supported by the finding that foreign-language proficiency does not automatically lead to knowledge of or empathy for global problems (Barrows et al., 4). These issues must be attended to directly in the curriculum if they are to be learned.

Foreign-language teachers respond by setting the development of a cultural syllabus as a professional priority (Lange and Linder, 51). Strasheim (77) is even more radical. She suggests that culture assume a prime role in foreign-language curricula and that culture determine the language skills to be developed. In fact, a unique contribution of foreign-language classes to global education is that in language classes culture can be taught and understood with and through its medium, language. One of the weaknesses of the Worldmindedness Project discussed earlier is that language could be fully associated with culture only in those projects of an intradisciplinary nature. While social studies classes can teach cultural components and language classes could restrict themselves to linguistic components, the picture is whole only when language and culture come together. This merging cannot take place in the social studies course. It can occur only in the language classroom.

Evaluation within the Integrative Process _____

It is not the purpose of this section to enumerate the many kinds of evaluation procedures that could be included in the examination of learning achievement with the integrative language/culture process. Instead, here we wish to draw attention to the categories of evaluation, suggest how they can be utilized within the process, and then examine areas problematic to evaluation within the process.

Since the process is closely oriented toward the development of communication, in culture as well as in language (listening, speaking, reading, and writing), it seems that the standard against which learning and acquisition could best be judged are the ACTFL Provisional Proficiency Guidelines (1). These guidelines suggest nine levels which differentiate developmental proficiency stages in the four language modalities. There are six culture developmental proficiency stages. These proficiency guidelines were developed specifically for the academic and school community from governmental, ILR proficiency descriptions. Although well calibrated, especially at the lower levels, the guidelines are only beginning to become a factor either in developing curricula or in evaluating proficiency. The inclusion of culture-proficiency stages is the first time, for the academic and school community at least, that such proficiencies have been defined. The only proficiency evaluation device currently available to examine language-proficiency stages is the oral interview. It requires some intensive training and retraining for currency, therefore holding off the specific and immediate use of this process on a wide scale. There is no evaluation device available uniquely for culture. The intimate relationship of language and culture in the process described in this chapter and in the real world may suggest that in a future version of the ACTFL guidelines culture be built into the levels of proficiency within a modality rather than stand alone.

How then can evaluation within the integrative process be accomplished? The language and culture proficiency guidelines can certainly be used as the background against which any evaluation can take place. And in general, it is conceivable that the test and evaluation categories we currently use, that is, discrete-point and pragmatic or integrative test types (Oller, 63), are appropriate. There are, however, some cautions which need to be expressed in using these test and evaluation types.

No test is wholly appropriate or sufficient. Each must be carefully planned for and justified within the context in which it is to be used in the integrative process. Discrete-point tests, for example, may be used to check facts, knowledge, and information basic to stage 2 representations, or with a basic understanding of grammar in stage 5. When it has been used for those purposes, the function of such tests is used up. Reliance on discrete-point culture tests, if continued much beyond stage 2, sends the message to students that process is not important, facts are. Similarly with language, if the testing of grammar and vocabulary serves as a measure of students' ability to use language beyond stage 5, then it will be clear to students that only the facts of language, not the use, are important. Development of language proficiency in schools and colleges probably suffers currently from overconcentration on language facts. This process, however, develops language and culture proficiency, thereby going beyond language facts. The tests used with the process must recognize the nature of the process and at the same time send the right signal to students: language proficiency is one of the major outcomes not only to be developed with the process but also to be evaluated.

Some integrative test types related to a communicative task—e.g., an oral interview, a writing task, or even recall protocols for listening and reading events—may be useful in evaluating language proficiency. The oral interview has been documented as useful in a number of governmental contexts, but Cohen (19) shows how it can be used in the classroom. He demonstrates how oral production can be evaluated with a rating system which examines both form (naturalness, style, clarity of expression) and content (suitability, accuracy of information, amount of information related) of a message. A writing task such as a friendly letter or a business letter, a description, or the development of an argument on a particular topic, judged against a set of preestablished criteria for examining the quality of the communication and its quantity, form, and accuracy in language and content, is appropriate for the evaluation of writing proficiency (Winfield and Barnes-Felfeli, 93). Recall protocols related to listening and reading texts have the capacity to examine the amount and extent of students' comprehension after they have listened to a conversation or read a text. Such protocols, written in English, are judged for accuracy and completeness against the original spoken or written text, thereby giving an indication of proficiency in those two modalities (Bernhardt, 5).

The one area of evaluation needing development is the processing of language and culture together. Clearly the direction this kind of evaluation should take is that of judging the process, using the categories of the cognitive and affective domains as criteria, through language/culture activities such as simulations, role plays, debates, monologues, impromptu dialogues based on thematic material, and the like. These activities offer the possibility of evaluating the results of both cognitive and affective learning within the integrative language/culture learning process.

Evaluation, as conceived here, must go beyond facts and information to language use and to the processing of language and culture. Attention to the higher levels of both the cognitive and affective domains extends learning to proficiency and away from concentration on facts and information. The development of effective procedures for these evaluation tasks requires the use of imagination in combination with experience in examining students' abilities by both quantitative and qualitative means. Much of this kind of development remains to be done.

Conclusion

The integrative culture-learning process defined in this chapter certainly alters the complexion of foreign-language curricula. In this process, more time is devoted to culture study, and cultural themes intersect with linguistic objectives. The effect of these changes on the development of language competence is expected to be positive because the changes attend to meaning and, therefore, to motivation.

Student motivation persists as an instructional problem when attracting students into a language program, exciting them once enrolled, and retaining them to the next level. Commonly, teachers attempt to solve this problem by using appealing materials or by making methodological adjustments. Even though harassed by questions such as, "Why are we learning this," and complaints such as, "I don't need to know this," teachers neglect the establishment of meaning or purpose of study as a treatment for motivational problems. The proposed process initiates each progression in language with a discussion of culture that inserts language learning into a meaningful context. Through culture, students discern the "why" and the "in order to" of the language to be studied and used.

Objections may surface regarding the amount of time devoted to establishing meaning, which leaves less time for language study. However, the amount of time devoted to establishing meaning is currently insufficient, as evidenced by the minimal manner in which textbooks address this issue. Lack of attention to establishing meaning, with the time then given to language learning, has not produced students with high language proficiency levels (Lange, 50). In fact, failure to establish meaning may actually inhibit the learning of language as a communicative tool.

Krashen's (42, 43) theory of second-language learning and acquisition codifies what many teachers have observed: when students become so interested in what they are talking about that they forget they are speaking in a foreign language, something seems to click and fluency increases. The opportunities for this lack of linguistic self-consciousness are rare in the traditional language classroom. The proposed process promotes these opportunities. The process: (1) identifies *discussable* themes, not just facts for absorption; (2) *personalizes* discussion by relating to the native culture; (3) *requires* reflection and discussion rather than leaving this interchange optional; and (4) *asks* for students' *emotions, arguments,* and *opinions,* necessitating the teaching of such vocabulary.

Not only does the integrative process support language skills, but it also conveys cultural skills on which students can rely far beyond the classroom. By interacting with culture, accepting culture as changeable and variable, and consciously acknowledging and reflecting on personal reactions to foreign as well as native cultural situations, students internalize the process by which they are being taught. Once the process becomes their own, it facilitates students' interaction with novel intercultural situations and promotes empathic responses to differences across and within cultures. For example, when the former Spanish student arrives in Chile, that student can process experiences in that culture, even if Chile had never been mentioned in class, because the student learned how to observe and interpret situations as well as to relate those situations to personal reactions. In seven years, a French student may not recall the causes of the French revolution, but having internalized the integrative process, may respond more empathically to cross-cultural differences. Rather than cursing the new foreign neighbor's inappropriate (in North American culture) method of garbage disposal, this student may inform the neighbor of available disposal facilities and teach the neighbor how to use them. Empathic understanding of cultural differences extends to intracultural subgroups. The student who has learned language and culture through the integrative process may not so readily dismiss the person with the Southern drawl as unintelligent or conclude that the fast-moving Easterner must be arrogant.

Implementation of the integrative process in the classroom, though, demands adjustments in teacher preparation programs. Most important, since many teachers teach the way they have been taught, teacher education courses and programs must involve the student in an integrative language/culture learning process. Prospective teachers must not merely be told about a process; they must learn with and practice the process. Of course, anthropological culture would then necessarily assume a position alongside, if not in front of, literature study. College students preparing to teach in the public schools will most likely not teach much literature. They will teach mostly communication, including cultural communication. Although literature study should be retained as much for the personal enjoyment it may give preservice teachers as for the elements of civilization and culture it does embody, the study of anthropological culture can no longer be ignored by college language and teacher-education departments if preservice teachers are to graduate with adequate professional preparation.

The foreign-language class structured on the basis of the integrative process would indeed differ from the usual contemporary course. Some teachers fear a loss of identity as language teachers and an absorption into social studies departments. To be sure, the integrative language/culture process does employ concepts and techniques from our cousin discipline. But the integrative language/culture process also allows language teachers to do precisely what social studies teachers cannot do, marry culture to language. With the consummation of this marriage, foreign-language classes evolve. If some would say this development is a revolution rather than an evolution, that will not be denied. It is our opinion that the integration of language and culture is even a more powerful organizing principle for foreign-language education than is language proficiency, because that integration is prerequisite to true language competence.

References, Doing the Unthinkable in the Second Language Classroom

1. *ACTFL Provisional Proficiency Guidelines.* U.S. Department of Education Grant #G008 103203. Hastings-on-Hudson, NY: American Council on the Teaching of Foreign Languages, 1982.
2. Altman, Howard B., and Victor E. Hanzeli, eds. *Essays on the Teaching of Culture: A Festschrift to Honor Howard Lee Nostrand.* Detroit: Advancement Press, 1974.
3. Banathy, Bela H., and Dale L. Lange. *A Design for Foreign Language Curriculum.* Lexington, MA: D. C. Heath, 1972.
4. Barrows, Thomas S., et al. *College Students' Knowledge and Beliefs: A Survey of Global Understanding.* New Rochelle, NY: Change Magazine Press, 1981.
5. Bernhardt, Elizabeth B. "Testing Foreign Language Reading Comprehension: The Immediate Recall Protocol." *Die Unterrichtspraxis* 16 (1983):27–33.
6. Bishop, G. Reginald, Jr.; ed. *Culture in Language Learning.* Reports of the Working Committees of the Northeast Conference on the Teaching of Foreign Languages, 1960. New Brunswick, NJ: Rutgers University, 1960.
7. _____, and Jack Undank, eds. *Culture in Language Learning: Supplementary Report of the 1960 Northeast Conference on the Teaching of Foreign Languages.* Reports of the Working Committees of the Northeast Conference on the Teaching of Foreign Languages, 1960. New Brunswick, NJ: Rutgers University, 1960.
8. Bloom, Benjamin S., et al. *Taxonomy of Educational Objectives, Handbook I: The Cognitive Domain.* New York: David McKay, 1956.
9. Bonham, George W., et al. "Discussion." *Change Magazine* 12, iv (1980): 40–47.
10. Born, Warren C., ed. *Language and Culture: Heritage and Horizons.* Northeast Conference on the Teaching of Foreign Languages. Middlebury, VT: The Northeast Conference, 1976.
11. Bragaw, Donald H.; Helene Z. Loew; and Judith Wooster. "Global Responsibility: The Role of the Foreign Language Teacher," pp. 47–89 in Thomas E. Geno, ed., *Foreign Language and International Studies: Toward Cooperation and Integration.* Northeast Conference on the Teaching of Foreign Languages. Middlebury, VT: The Northeast Conference, 1981.
12. Brooks, Nelson. "The Analysis of Language and Familiar Cultures," pp. 19–31 in Robert C. Lafayette, ed., *The Cultural Revolution in Foreign Language Teaching: A Guide for Building the Modern Curriculum.* Report of the Central States Conference on Foreign Language Education. Lincolnwood, IL: National Textbook Co., 1975.
13. _____. "A Guest Editorial: Culture, a New Frontier." *Foreign Language Annals* 5 (1971):54–61.
14. _____. *Language and Language Learning: Theory and Practice,* 2nd ed. New York: Harcourt, Brace & World, 1964.
15. _____. "Teaching Culture in the Foreign Language Classroom." *Foreign Language Annals* 1 (1968):204–17.
16. Brumfit, Christopher J. "From Defining to Designing: Communicative Specifications versus Communicative Methodology in Foreign Language Teaching." *Studies in Second Language Acquisition* 3 (1980):1–9.
17. _____, and Keith Johnson, eds. *The Communicative Approach to Language Teaching.* London: Oxford University Press, 1979.
18. Cleveland, Harlan. "Forward to Basics: Education as Wide as the World." *Change Magazine* 12, iv (1980):18–22.
19. Cohen, Andrew D. *Testing Language Ability in the Classroom.* Rowley, MA: Newbury House, 1980.

20. Collins, H. Thomas. *Global Education and the States: Some Observations, Some Programs, and Some Suggestions.* A Report to the Council of Chief State School Officers. New York: American Field Service, n.d.

21. Committee of Eleven. *Some Essential Learning Outcomes (Foundation Learnings) in Modern Foreign Languages.* St. Paul: Minnesota State Department of Education, Division of Instruction, 1977.

22. Crawford, Linda M. "Paulo Freire's Philosophy: Derivation of Curricular Principles and Their Application to Second Language Curriculum Design." *Dissertation Abstracts International* 39 (1979):7130A (Minnesota).

23. Crawford-Lange, Linda M. "Curricular Alternatives for Second Language Learning," pp. 81–112 in Theodore V. Higgs, ed., *Curriculum, Competence, and the Foreign Language Teacher.* The ACTFL Foreign Language Education Series, vol. 13. Lincolnwood, IL: National Textbook Co., 1982.

24. _____. *Perceptions of Minnesota Senior High School Principals of Foreign Language Programs: Survey Results.* Mimeo. 1983. (Available from the author.)

25. _____. "Redirecting Second Language Curricula: Paulo Freire's Contribution." *Foreign Language Annals* 14 (1981):257–68.

26. Dodge, James W., ed. *Other Words, Other Worlds: Language-in-Culture.* Northeast Conference on the Teaching of Foreign Languages. Middlebury, VT: The Northeast Conference, 1972.

27. Freire, Paulo. *Education for Critical Consciousness.* Translated by Myra Bergman Ramos. New York: The Seabury Press, 1973.

28. _____. *Pedagogy of the Oppressed.* Translated by Myra Bergman Ramos. New York: The Seabury Press, 1970.

29. Gardner, Robert C., and Wallace E. Lambert. *Attitudes and Motivation in Second Language Learning.* Rowley, MA: Newbury House, 1972.

30. Guiora, Alexander Z., et al. "Language and Person: Studies in Language Behavior." *Language Learning* 5 (1975):43–91.

31. Guntermann, Gail. "A Suggested Procedure for Determining Cultural Objectives." *Hispania* 59 (1976):87–92.

32. Hanvey, Robert G. *An Attainable Global Perspective.* New York: Center for Global Perspectives, 1975.

33. Hendon, Ursula S. "Introducing Culture in the High School Foreign Language Class." *Foreign Language Annals* 13 (1980):191–99.

34. Jarvis, Donald K. "Making Cross-Cultural Connections," pp. 151–77 in June K. Phillips, ed., *The Language Connection: From the Classroom to the World.* The ACTFL Foreign Language Education Series, vol. 9. Lincolnwood, IL: National Textbook Co., 1977.

35. Jenks, Frederick L. "Conducting Socio-Cultural Research in the Foreign Language Class," pp. 95–123 in Howard B. Altman and Victor E. Hanzeli, eds., *Essays on the Teaching of Culture: A Festschrift to Honor Howard Lee Nostrand.* Detroit: Advancement Press, 1974.

36. Johnson, David W., and Roger T. Johnson. *Learning Together and Alone: Cooperation, Competition, and Individualization.* Englewood Cliffs, NJ: Prentice-Hall, 1975.

37. Johnson, Keith. *Communicative Syllabus Design and Methodology.* Oxford: Pergamon Press, 1982.

38. Jonas, Sister Ruth A., S.C. *A Matched Classroom Approach to the Teaching of French in the Elementary Grades.* Final Report, USOE Project Number 6-1944, Contract Number OEC-3-6-061944-1891. Washington, DC: United States Office of Education, 1969.

39. Jorstad, Helen L. "Inservice Teacher Education: Content and Process," pp. 81–85 in Dale L. Lange and Cathy Linder, eds., *Proceedings of the National*

Conference on Professional Priorities. Hastings-on-Hudson, NY: ACTFL Materials Center, 1981.

40. Kelly, Louis G. *25 Centuries of Language Teaching.* Rowley, MA: Newbury House, 1969.

41. Kraft, Wolfgang S. *Deutsch aktuel.* Levels 1 and 2. St. Paul, MN: EMC Corporation, 1979, 1980.

42. Krashen, Stephen D. *Principles and Practice in Second Language Acquisition.* Oxford: Pergamon Press, 1982.

43. ———. *Second Language Acquisition and Second Language Learning.* Oxford: Pergamon Press, 1981.

44. Krathwohl, David R., et al. *Taxonomy of Educational Objectives: Affective Domain.* New York: David McKay, 1964.

45. Ladu, Tora T., et al. *Teaching for Cross-Cultural Understanding.* Foreign Language Curriculum Series, no. 414. Raleigh, NC: State Department of Public Instruction, 1968.

46. Lafayette, Robert C., ed. *The Cultural Revolution in Foreign Language Teaching.* Report of the Central States Conference on Foreign Language Education. Lincolnwood, IL: National Textbook Co., 1975.

47. ———. *Teaching Culture: Strategies and Techniques.* Language in Education: Theory and Practice, no. 11. Washington, DC: Center for Applied Linguistics, 1978.

48. ———, and Lorraine A. Strasheim. "Foreign Language Curricula and Materials for the Twenty-First Century," pp. 29–34 in Dale L. Lange and Cathy Linder, eds., *Proceedings of the National Conference on Professional Priorities.* Hastings-on-Hudson, NY: ACTFL Materials Center, 1981.

49. Lange, Dale L. "Suggestions for the Continuing Development of Pre- and In-Service Programs for Teachers of Second Languages," pp. 169–92 in Jermaine D. Arendt, Dale L. Lange, and Pamela J. Myers, eds., *Foreign Language Learning, Today and Tomorrow: Essays in Honor of Emma M. Birkmaier.* New York: Pergamon Press, 1979.

50. ———. "Using the ILR Oral Interview to Evaluate Proficiency in Secondary Schools." Presentation at the ACTFL Annual Meeting, New York City, November 1982.

51. ———, and Cathy Linder, eds. *Proceedings of the National Conference on Professional Priorities.* Hastings-on-Hudson, NY: ACTFL Materials Center, 1981.

52. Levno, Arley W., and Guenter G. Pfister. "An Analysis of Surface Structure and Its Manner of Presentation in First-Year College French Textbooks from 1972–1978." *Foreign Language Annals* 13 (1980):47–52.

53. Lohnes, Walter F. W., and F. W. Strothmann. *German: A Structured Approach,* 3rd ed. New York: W. W. Norton, 1980.

54. Mackey, James; Edgar Magidson; and Dale L. Lange. *The Minnesota World-mindedness Project.* A Preliminary Report Presented to the Superintendent of the Rochester, Minnesota, Public Schools. Mimeo. March 1983.

55. Mead, Robert G., ed. *The Foreign Language Teacher: The Lifelong Learner.* Northeast Conference on the Teaching of Foreign Languages. Middlebury, VT: The Northeast Conference, 1982.

56. Morain, Genelle. "The Cultural Component of the Methods Course," pp. 25–46 in Alan Garfinkel and Stanley Hamilton, eds., *Designs for Foreign Language Teacher Education.* Rowley, MA: Newbury House, 1976.

57. ———. "Cultural Pluralism," pp. 59–91 in Dale L. Lange, ed., *Pluralism in Foreign Language Education.* The ACTFL Foreign Language Education Series, vol. 3. Lincolnwood, IL: National Textbook Co., 1973.

58. Moreau, Paul Henri, and Guenter G. Pfister. "An Analysis of the Deep

Cultural Aspects in Second-Year College French Textbooks Published from 1972–1974." *Foreign Language Annals* 11 (1978):165–71.

59. Neuner, Gerd, et al. *Deutsch aktiv: Ein Lehrwerk für Erwachsene.* Lehrbücher 1 und 2. Berlin: Langenscheidt, 1979, 1980.

60. Nord, James. "Three Steps Leading to Listening Fluency: A Beginning," pp. 69–100 in Harris Winitz, ed., *The Comprehension Approach to Foreign Language Instruction.* Rowley, MA: Newbury House, 1981.

61. Nostrand, Howard L., ed. *Background Data for the Teaching of French.* Part A, La culture et la société française au XXe siècle. Seattle: University of Washington, 1967.

62. _____. "Empathy for a Second Culture: Motivations and Techniques," pp. 263–327 in Gilbert A. Jarvis, ed., *Responding to New Realities.* The ACTFL Foreign Language Education Series, vol. 5. Lincolnwood, IL: National Textbook Co., 1974.

63. Oller, John W., Jr. *Language Tests at School: A Pragmatic Approach.* London: Longman, 1979.

64. Oudot, Simone, et al. *French Today.* Levels 1 and 2. Boston: Houghton Mifflin, 1982.

65. Posvar, Wesley W. "Expanding International Dimensions." *Change Magazine* 12, iv (1980):23–26.

66. Reboullet, André; Jean-Louis Malandain; and Jacques Verdol. *Méthode Orange.* Levels 1 and 2. New York: Regents, 1978, 1979.

67. Rivers, Wilga M. "Practical Implications of New Trends and Directions," pp. 8–11 in Dale L. Lange and Cathy Linder, eds., *Proceedings of the Materials Conference on Professional Priorities.* Hastings-on-Hudson, NY: ACTFL Materials Center, 1981.

68. _____. *Teaching Foreign-Language Skills,* 2nd ed. Chicago: University of Chicago Press, 1981.

69. Robinson, Gail L. Nemetz. *Issues in Second Language and Cross-Cultural Education: The Forest Through the Trees.* Boston: Heinle & Heinle, 1981.

70. _____. "The Magic-Carpet-Ride-to-Another-Culture Syndrome: An International Perspective." *Foreign Language Annals* 11 (1978):135–46.

71. Sandoval, Manuel G., et al. *Nuestros Amigos: Spanish 1.* New York: Harcourt Brace Jovanovich, 1979.

72. Savignon, Sandra. *Communicative Competence: An Experiment in Foreign Language Teaching.* Philadelphia: Center for Curriculum Development, 1972.

73. Seelye, H. Ned. *Teaching Culture: Strategies for Foreign Language Educators.* Lincolnwood, IL: National Textbook Co., 1976.

74. Shor, Ira. *Critical Teaching and Everyday Life.* Boston: South End Press, 1980.

75. Stern, H. H. "Directions in Foreign Language Curriculum Development," pp. 12–17 in Dale L. Lange and Cathy Linder, eds., *Proceedings of the National Conference on Professional Priorities.* Hastings-on-Hudson, NY: ACTFL Materials Center, 1981.

76. _____. "A Working Paper for a Multi-dimensional Foreign Language Curriculum." The 1983 Reports of the Northeast Conference on the Teaching of Foreign Languages, forthcoming.

77. Strasheim, Lorraine A. "Establishing a Professional Agenda for Integrating Culture into K–12 Foreign Languages: An Editorial." *Modern Language Journal* 65 (1981):67–69.

78. _____. "An Issue on the Horizon: The Role of Foreign Languages in Global Education." *Foreign Language Annals* 12 (1979):29–34.

79. _____. "Language Is the Medium, Culture Is the Message: Globalizing Foreign Languages," pp. 1–16 in Maurice W. Conner, ed., *A Global Approach to*

Foreign Language Education. Report of the Central States Conference on the Teaching of Foreign Languages. Lincolnwood, IL: National Textbook Co., 1981.

80. Swaffar, Janet King, and Don S. Stephens, "What Comprehension-Based Classes Look and Feel Like in Theory and Practice," pp. 254–74 in Harris Winitz, ed., *The Comprehension Approach to Foreign Language Instruction.* Rowley, MA: Newbury House, 1981.

81. Taylor, H. Darrel, and John L. Sorenson. "Culture Capsules," pp. 82–85 in H. Ned Seelye, ed., *Teaching Cultural Concepts in Spanish Classes.* Springfield, IL: Office of the Superintendent of Public Instruction, 1972.

82. Valdman, Albert. "The Incorporation of the Notion of Communicative Competence in the Design of the Introductory Syllabus," pp. 18–23 in Dale L. Lange and Cathy Linder, eds., *Proceedings of the National Conference on Professional Priorities.* Hastings-on-Hudson, NY: ACTFL Materials Center, 1981.

83. ———. "Toward Redefinition of the Basics in Foreign Language Teaching," pp. 1–17 in Reid E. Baker, ed., *Teaching for Tomorrow in the Foreign Language Classroom.* Report of the Central States Conference on the Teaching of Foreign Languages. Lincolnwood, IL: National Textbook Co., 1978.

84. ———, Simon Belasco, and Florence Steiner. *Scènes et Séjours.* Glenview, IL: Scott, Foresman, 1972.

85. ———, Simon Belasco, and Florence Steiner. *Son et sens.* Glenview, IL: Scott, Foresman, 1972.

86. Valette, Jean-Paul, and Rebecca M. Valette. *French for Mastery.* Levels 1 and 2, 2nd ed. Lexington, MA: D. C. Heath, 1981, 1982.

87. van Ek, Jan A. *The Threshhold Level for Schools.* London: Longman, 1978.

88. Wallerstein, Nina. *Language and Culture in Conflict: Problem-Posing in the ESL Classroom.* Reading, MA: Addison-Wesley, 1983.

89. Warriner-Burke, Helen P. "Reactions: Curriculum and Materials," pp. 87–89 in Dale L. Lange and Cathy Linder, eds., *Proceedings of the National Conference on Professional Priorities.* Hastings-on-Hudson, NY: ACTFL Materials Center, 1981.

90. Weiss, Edda. *Deutsch: Erleben wir es!* Levels 1 and 2, 2nd ed. New York: McGraw-Hill, 1980, 1981.

91. Widdowson, Henry G. *Teaching Language as Communication.* London: Oxford University Press, 1978.

92. Wilkins, David A. *Notional Syllabuses: A Taxonomy and Its Relevance to Foreign Language Curriculum Development.* London: Oxford University Press, 1976.

93. Winfield, Fairlee E., and Paula Barnes-Felfeli. "The Effects of Familiar and Unfamiliar Cultural Context on Foreign Language Composition." *Modern Language Journal* 66 (1982):373–78.

94. Winitz, Harris. *The Comprehension Approach to Foreign Language Instruction.* Rowley, MA: Newbury House, 1981.

95. Yousef, Fathi S. "Cross-Cultural Testing: An Aspect of the Resistance Reaction." *Language Learning* 18 (1968):227–34.

96. Zais, Robert S. "Curriculum and Materials Development: A Jeremiad on the Past—A Standard for the Eighties," pp. 24–27 in Dale L. Lange and Cathy Linder, eds., *Proceedings of the National Conference on Professional Priorities.* Hastings-on-Hudson, NY: ACTFL Materials Center, 1981.

6

Preservice and Inservice Teacher Training: Focus on Proficiency

Judith A. Muyskens
University of Cincinnati

Introduction

The current enthusiasm for proficiency-based teaching provides the foreign-language profession a set of common goals that can and should affect all aspects of our work. As stated in the Provisional Guidelines, the focus on proficiency will aid the profession in developing common instructional techniques and curricula. Not only classes, but also teacher-preparation programs will change to reflect the emphasis now being placed on proficiency. Teachers must be trained who will guide students to the highest possible proficiency level in the foreign language (ACTFL Language Proficiency Projects, 1; ACTFL Provisional Proficiency Guidelines, 3).

In order to assess the readiness of the profession to accept the implications of teaching for proficiency, Paul (35) evaluated questionnaires answered by 130 teachers and found that they would in fact use proficiency goals in planning their course curricula, in choosing or designing teaching materials, and in talking to students about their own work. The teachers surveyed also mentioned, although with less frequency, that they would use proficiency goals to choose appropriate teaching methods, plan individual lessons or units, articulate individual courses, and talk to parents about students' work.

Judith A. Muyskens (Ph.D., the Ohio State University) is an Associate Professor of French at the University of Cincinnati, where she supervises the teaching assistants, coordinates beginning and intermediate French courses, and teaches undergraduate and graduate courses in Methodology and French Civilization. Her publications appear in *Foreign Language Annals, Contemporary French Civilization,* and the *Modern Language Journal.* She is an author of *Rendez-vous,* a beginning college French text. Also, she is a member of AATF, ACTFL, MLA, and OMLTA, and is first Vice-President of AAUSC.

In order to help teachers perform these tasks, teacher trainers and supervisors will find it necessary to prepare methodology courses and/or TA training seminars that have proficiency as their organizing principle. This implies that teachers and TAs be trained not only in administering and rating oral proficiency interviews, but also in writing materials and designing activities that revolve around the variables of function, content, and accuracy. In addition, foreign-language educators need to explore the areas of teachers' language proficiency and cultural knowledge. The President's Commission (39) has suggested approaching teacher education on a national level through a national organization. As a result, ACTFL has assigned teacher education a high priority (ACTFL Priorities, 2), and seeks to influence both preservice and inservice education programs. This chapter suggests a model for programs in these areas, with proficiency as its organizing principle.

Preservice Teacher Education

Traditionally, preservice secondary teacher education has been organized around conventional models, competency-based programs, or humanistic programs. Wing (40) and Hancock (17) describe these approaches in detail. Hancock (17) depicts the conventional model as the "widely practiced" program in which students study the grammar, literature, and civilization of the target language, along with courses in general education and foreign-language teaching methods. Although foreign-language educators have discussed systems of "competency-based" certification, few ongoing programs exist that follow this approach. Many of the school systems that attempted competency-based second-language education programs have abandoned them because of the difficulty of measuring intangible competencies (Hancock, 17). The humanistic movement has been primarily concerned with orienting education toward the individual, expanding his affective as well as his intellectual capabilities (Wing, 40; Bailey, 5).

The goals of preservice secondary education vary, but generally they are close to those described by Grittner (13) from working papers on an approved program in Wisconsin. This program adopts the following standards:

1. Development of skills in the use of the target language
2. Development of skills in language analysis
3. Development of knowledge and skills necessary to teach the culture of the target language, using that language as the primary instructional vehicle
4. Development of the ability to plan and implement foreign-language instruction

5. Development of professional awareness and responsibility
6. Development of knowledge and application of areas related to the teaching of foreign languages

The objectives of TA training programs differ from those intended for secondary teachers. In fact, for many years TAs were not even trained. "It is clear that over the last two decades more and more colleges have become aware of the importance of TA training" (Ervin and Muyskens, 8, p. 335). In 1979 Schulz (37) reports that 69 percent of these universities responding to her survey required some formal preservice orientation for their TAs, and 38 percent required a methods course offered concurrently with the first year of teaching experience. Previous studies had revealed fewer universities which trained TAs (MacAllister, 26; Hagiwara, 16). The professional literature reveals numerous descriptions of TA training programs, with methods courses and orientations taking many forms. Most of the programs are practical and strive to meet the "immediate needs of TAs" (Nerenz et al., 31).

In an attempt to determine the most necessary aspects of TA training, Ervin and Muyskens (8) surveyed preservice TAs nationwide. Included in the top quartile of the priorities, inexperienced TAs cited needs for gaining experience and self-confidence, learning practical teaching methods and techniques, making classes interesting, making the best use of class time, making presentations, organizing and planning lessons, and inspiring or motivating students. The authors presented procedures for setting priorities for TA training. Although this questionnaire was not designed around proficiency principles, it is easy to see that many of the concerns expressed by the surveyed TAs can be directly addressed by incorporating these principles in TA training programs.

The goal of any teacher-training program is to shape effective foreign-language teachers. Moskowitz (27) has identified the following characteristics of exceptional high school teachers: The exceptional teacher has a thorough knowledge of the subject matter, is very well prepared, is fluent in the foreign language, enjoys teaching, is willing and able to answer students' questions, is fair, has well-organized lessons, has good classroom control, conveys self-confidence, and is dedicated and hardworking.

Moskowitz has also attempted to identify the classroom interaction patterns shown by outstanding teachers. Among the interaction traits mentioned were the following: The target language dominates the classroom interaction, whether teachers or students are talking; the teachers have an excellent command of the target language; the amount of teacher talk is less; the teachers are expressive and animated and they move around the class a great deal; the climate is warm and accepting; the teachers personalize the content; less classroom time is devoted to students doing silent reading and written tasks; there is greater amount of warm-up questions, review, and focusing on the skills of the speaker; there is a greater number of different activities per lesson; the pace of the lessons is generally more rapid; and the teachers have excellent classroom control. This list of interaction patterns is interesting in that although Moskowitz's research was not explicitly conducted from a proficiency perspective, precisely the kinds of behavior that she identifies are most likely to encourage language acquisition by providing extensive comprehensible input in a low anxiety environment. "Acquired competence" almost certainly leads to higher proficiency levels than does "learned competence."

The past teacher-training and TA training programs have lacked coherence, as has the discussion of competencies. Joiner (21) states that professional standards need to be established for foreign-language teachers. At present, however, our knowledge of teacher proficiencies is limited. Problems arise in identifying and evaluating desired competencies; however, the movement toward proficiency provides an axis around which foreign-language educators will be able to conduct teacher-training programs. It also gives new impetus to reevaluating and improving teacher standards (Joiner, 21).

Language skills and cultural knowledge of future teachers

Implementation of proficiency goals addresses the issue of the language level of the prospective teacher or TA. Since Carroll's study (6) in 1967, which showed that the average proficiency level of foreign-language undergraduate majors was 2 to 2+ on the FSI scale, educators have been concerned with upgrading the proficiency level of prospective teachers. Many foreign-language educators have suggested that future teachers be required to spend time abroad. The language curriculum of majors who want to teach must be reorganized so that students learn to communicate in the target language. Grittner (13) states:

> High school teachers are influenced directly and indirectly by the situation in higher education. First, they tend to teach as they were taught by literary specialists in higher education who may or may not use the foreign language in a communicative way in their own teaching. Second, they are exposed to a professional environment in which it is often clear that cultural knowledge and language teaching are at a lower prestige level than literary and linguistic research. [P. 73]

Proficiency guidelines can provide the necessary rationale for organizing culture and language courses at the undergraduate level. Standardized guidelines can aid foreign-language departments in developing curricula to meet the needs of students. Such guidelines may not remedy the overemphasis on literature in most foreign-language programs, but they will help professors to be more realistic about the language proficiency of the students they are training.

On the other hand, how many foreign-language methodologists teach their courses in the target language? Even if we cannot teach our methodology courses in the target language because we prepare teachers of different languages in a single class, the level of those students' proficiency could surely be improved by providing opportunities to peer teach using materials that students have prepared.

The goal of undergraduate teacher-training programs should be to train future instructors for the Superior Level of proficiency (see Appendix A for description). It is clearly unrealistic to require that nonnative instructors achieve native-like proficiency in the foreign language. Nevertheless, it is vital that instructors model the language accurately and fluently so that their students will be in an acquisition-rich environment. An instructor whose proficiency is at the Advanced or Advanced Plus Level may feel too inhibited to use the language naturally and may run the risk of teaching "about the language." At the Superior Level, while the instructor's speech and writing may be obviously nonnative, there will be no patterns of errors. The control of grammar and the breadth of vocabulary associated with this proficiency level allow for the spontaneous and natural use of the language so critical to the successful progress of students through the low proficiency levels.

The departments in charge of teacher education should administer proficiency tests to prospective foreign-language teachers. Those not meeting required levels would enroll in remedial classes until they met the required proficiency level. If prospective teachers have difficulty attaining required skill levels, providing additional classroom experience may not be sufficient. Jorstad (22) concludes that improvement in teachers' ability is directly related to study abroad. Even after spending time in the target country, however, some future teachers may still not attain the required level of proficiency. They should be encouraged to seek the help of native-speaker assistants in the classroom and to use audiotapes, videotapes, and structured activities for building the proficiency skills of their students, which focus on accuracy of communication. If the teacher plans an "accuracy first" program, the students may well acquire the necessary foundation to surpass the teacher's skills at a later stage (Higgs and Clifford, 19).

In order for prospective teachers to exhibit an advanced appreciation of culture according to the ACTFL Provisional Proficiency Guidelines, time abroad in a target country would again seem desirable. Students should live through situations in which they apply common rules of etiquette and learn to avoid taboos. They should be prepared to fit their behavior to the audience and should be able to discuss in the target language the current events, political realities, and institutions of the target country. Culture courses can provide some of the *facts* but may not allow prospective teachers to discuss abstract ideas relating the foreign to the native culture. Jorstad (22) describes a workshop that helps inservice teachers to develop and practice refining hypotheses. Teachers or students perceive aspects of culture by using learning materials on culture. A course of this nature could be adapted for preservice teachers. Lange and Jorstad (25) discuss a contract program which unites curriculum development procedures with cultural experience in the country, language practice, and purposeful travel. Although this program was specifically intended for inservice teachers to design supplementary materials such as cultural units, capsules, clusters, and assimilators, it could serve as a model for undergraduate study abroad so that those preparing to teach would plan materials before they entered the classroom. In case opportunities to study abroad are not available to future teachers, courses following a similar model could be planned using native contributors. Chapter 5 in this volume outlines a model program to this end.

The Methods Course

Omaggio (33) suggests beginning the methods course with the question, "What does it mean to know another language?" The ensuing discussion invariably leads to identification of the tasks to be accomplished, the topics addressed, and the accuracy conveyed by the nonnative speaker. After this introduction, students see the importance of the ACTFL Provisional Proficiency Guidelines for describing language skills. The models of subskill factors which contribute to global language proficiency, presented by Higgs and Clifford (19) and discussed in the introductory chapter of this volume, serve as an effective means of orienting students to the relative importance of skills in vocabulary, grammar, pronunciation, fluency, and sociolinguistic appropriateness.

After the introduction of the guidelines and the subskill models, demonstrations and interviews can be given that illustrate language in use. Nonnative speakers of English may be used first, followed by demonstrations and interviews in the target language. These interviews can be videotapes or live demonstrations. Methods students will learn to gauge the appropriateness of different question types at different levels of proficiency if they see interviews of speakers whose proficiency ranges from the Novice through the Advanced levels.

The theme of proficiency can subsequently be used as the organizing principle of the methods course. Upon presentation of the history of methodologies, students will easily see how the proficiency guidelines serve as a means of conceptualizing and understanding all of the disparate methodologies of previous years. Omaggio (32) suggests evaluating current methodologies—such as the Natural Approach, the Silent Way, suggestopedia, and counseling-learning—from the standpoint of proficiency. The methods instructor may lead students in discussions wherein the students determine which methodologies stress accuracy and which ones focus on content or function, and which ones attempt to account systematically for all three variables.

Using a proficiency-oriented approach in the methods course

Discussion of teaching pronunciation, grammar, the four skills, culture, lesson planning, classroom management, testing, and choosing and adapting texts can all be organized around proficiency criteria. The methods course that is proposed in this chapter is organized in three stages: (1) acquainting the students with a concept, (2) demonstrating the concept's practical application, and (3) asking students to prepare materials and demonstrations for their peers. Inherent in the makeup of the course is the improvement of the methods-students' language skills by preparing and presenting activities for pronunciation, vocabulary, grammar, and the four skills.

Teaching pronunciation.   Methods students can be presented with a rationale for teaching pronunciation by stressing the difference between the short-run need for minimally acceptable production of crucial phonemic distinctions in the target language, i.e., the threshold of comprehensibility, and the long-run goal of achieving near-native phonetic accuracy. Sounds will always be presented for mastery in a communicative setting and never as isolated units. Achieving perfect pronunciation is neither possible nor necessary for beginning students, and excessive time should not be spent correcting pronunciation errors. Playing recordings of beginning language students reading phrases or answering questions in the target language, and then asking students to indicate which phonological errors they would and would not correct can provide valuable practice in dealing with beginning language students. The methodologist can demonstrate a pronunciation lesson and should have the students prepare one as well.

Vocabulary.   Vocabulary acquisition demands close attention at the Novice Level (see the introductory chapter of this volume, and Higgs and Clifford, 19). Methods teachers should remind inexperienced teachers to reenter vocabulary and to prepare vocabulary supplements for their teaching materials which help to express facts; get and give information; and provide information about past, current, and future activities. To discuss subject matter in which students are interested, teachers must be prepared to teach vocabulary related to student background, home, school, and basic survival needs. This will require that methods teachers work with their students to identify and present vocabulary helpful in dealing with basic survival needs and minimal courtesy requirements. Methods students require guidance in selecting supplementary vocabulary and putting it into context. To warn prospective teachers against overwhelming their students with lists, the methods instructor must give techniques for entering vocabulary in contexts and in "real-language" situations. Future teachers can be taught to prepare dialogues, videotapes, or audiotapes of situations that reflect or simulate a legitimate information gap in order to motivate students to learn vocabulary in meaningful contexts. Following practice in preparing such approaches, methods students can practice by writing activities for students to use actively, i.e., to express their own meanings. For example, prospective teachers can prepare a vocabulary unit on the location and description of the home. This would include teaching vocabulary in context and presenting followup activities for students to use the vocabulary as it relates to their own lives.

Grammar. Because grammatical accuracy is crucial to successful communication at the higher proficiency levels, and its attainment may be thwarted by deemphasizing its importance in the formative stages of the acquisition process (Higgs and Clifford, 19), even beginning students must be provided with a solid structural base on which to build. Higgs and Clifford hypothesize that students in "accuracy first" programs can continue to build on the skills they already possess and later acquire the additional skills necessary to progress beyond the 2/2+ level. Those, however, in "communication first" programs, may be "either unsuccessful at extending their linguistic ability or tend to show improvement only in areas in which they had already shown high profiles" (p. 74). Prospective teachers must, therefore, realize the importance of linguistic accuracy in successful communication. Their students cannot, however, assimilate and correctly use all grammar within a short period of time. Techniques for teaching grammar should be presented to prospective teachers, whether the approach be inductive or deductive. Stress in the section on grammar teaching should fall on the communicative value of grammar, i.e., on the ways the grammar converts meaning into speech. The categories used in Chapter 2 of this volume provide a structure for activities appropriate for methods students to develop: drills in context, personalization, communication and interaction, and creative language use.

Following a grammar-presentation assignment and a demonstration by the methods teacher, students should write their own exercises in context. Giving a context provides students not only with motivation for doing the exercise but also with an understanding of the topics which can be addressed using the grammar point. (See Chapter 2 for examples.)

Another segment in the teaching of grammar will include personalization activities in which the language learner tells something about himself. Future teachers will use a grammar point that they had previously presented and write related personalized activities. The formats can include sentence completion, sentence builders, agree/disagree statements, and personalized questions. (See Chapter 2 for examples.)

The use of grammar to stimulate communication and interaction would constitute another segment of the grammar unit. Activities in small groups would play a role here. Methods instructors would ask future teachers to practice developing interview or fact-finding situations. Omaggio's chapter demonstrates several activities of this type.

Creative language use of a structured nature minimizes student errors so that communication *through* rather than *in spite of* language occurs

(Higgs and Clifford, 19). The role of the teacher's own creativity can be stressed in activities whose goal is to have students create with the language in response to their own needs. Prospective teachers should practice identifying situations in which students can express themselves with minimal guidance.

The focus for grammar, then, is not only on accuracy but also on its role in transmitting content and expressing communicative functions. The role of abstract grammatical constructs and manipulation exercises is diminished if not eliminated entirely. Instead, the teacher connects a grammatical concept to a student's knowledge of a subject (Higgs, 18).

The four skills. From the point of view of teaching for proficiency, methods students must think about developing the functions, content, and accuracy inherent in each of the four skills—speaking, listening, reading, and writing—at each proficiency level. Grammar and vocabulary are no longer the main focus but rather what students *do* with the language is (Guntermann and Phillips, 15). Freed (11) reports that the proficiency requirement at the University of Pennsylvania has helped carry both the student and instructor beyond concern with sentence-level production to focus on language skills that are more comprehensive, such as sustained conversation and listening comprehension.

Oral proficiency is the skill most sought after by students and should, therefore, be the one most stressed in the methods course (Guntermann, 14). Students must practice tasks that upgrade their own communication skills. Future teachers need an array of functions in order to set up practice situations. These functions can be taken from materials on notional/functional concepts, as described in Chapter 2, and in Guntermann and Phillips (15). Methods teachers will give their students practice in associating these functions with topics which interest their students. This may be done in elementary classes by generating lists of everyday survival topics and basic courtesy formulas. Other topics of interest to students include family, school, work, travel, and current events, or topics which require an exchange of simply factual or personal information. After the functions and topics are identified and the methods teacher has some representative activities, methods students are asked to prepare materials for their prospective students. Role-playing activities are especially valuable in this regard. Guntermann and Phillips (15) suggest, for example, having students make a list of questions they would like to ask others in the class about their daily lives or giving students the name of another person in the class and asking them to pay a compliment to that person.

Because many textbooks and supporting materials do not include sufficient listening materials, prospective teachers require instruction in designing such activities. The parts of the methods course dedicated to listening comprehension could provide opportunities for future teachers to prepare materials that emphasize spoken daily language with simple questions or statements about autobiographical information. As the guidelines suggest, comprehension activities should contain language in contexts demonstrating basic survival needs, such as ordering meals, securing lodging, giving and receiving simple instructions, and giving commands. Prospective teachers can prepare materials that require recognition of future and past references, among other things. What is important is that they prepare activities that entail listening to "real language" in context. These may take the form of audiotapes, videotapes, or passages read by the instructor or a native speaker.

Reading skills are often treated superficially. Traditionally, the teaching of reading skills has consisted of giving the assignment: "Read pages 1–9 for tomorrow and answer the comprehension questions." Reading is indeed more than recognizing a transcript of speech. Future teachers need to view reading as a communicative skill (Phillips, 36). Therefore, they require experience in presenting schedules, timetables, signs, and texts of more complexity than simple messages or greetings. Teachers in training can collect public announcements, magazines, and newspaper headlines. They will learn to provide practice to their students in interpreting negation, interrogatives, and time frames in order to develop reading comprehension. After demonstration by the methods instructor, students present materials they have created for building the reading proficiency of Novice- and Intermediate-Level students.

In order to prepare teachers to adapt materials for writing proficiency practice, the methods instructor will give demonstrations using realia such as forms to be filled out by the students. Methods students can create forms for registering in a hotel or school and models for writing short notes or letters. They should prepare topics for short compositions in which their own students will be able to ask for food, lodging, or transportation and can meet routine social demands. Techniques for expanding circumlocution skills can be demonstrated as can assigning functions to the activities so that students have the opportunity to express their own attitudes.

A methods course which requires its students to read information on the culture and daily life of the target country will prepare them to upgrade the cultural proficiency of their own students. Prospective teachers can present situations in which students enact leave-taking, shopping, getting a hotel room, going to the bank, writing requests, and declining invitations. Although sociolinguistic factors in communication present complex questions in foreign-language methodology, Higgs and Clifford (19) report that, at the Superior Level (ILR 3 and beyond), they play a role which is increasingly important.

Some methods professors may find a reorganization of the methods course desirable, making the four skills subordinate to the more general classifications of function, content, and accuracy.

Lesson planning

Foreign-language methodologists will want to train prospective teachers or TAs in writing objectives for proficiency and in setting proficiency goals for courses. In addition, to evaluate their immediate progress, future instructors will learn to prepare daily and weekly goals. They will prepare lesson plans which not only include variety, the four skills, culture, presentation of new material, and review of old material, but also the functions on which they are working and the contexts in which they are important. Furthermore, teachers will learn how to include periodic checks for students' accuracy in communication and to judge whether their students are progressing satisfactorily. Periodic proficiency tests or survival laboratories, such as the one devised at the University of Illinois, provide techniques for continuous evaluation of progress (Omaggio, 32).

The following self-evaluation checklist may prove helpful to methods students in verifying whether their lesson plan aims toward proficiency each day.

Checklist for daily progress toward proficiency
1. Did I include a warm-up activity which asked students to perform a function or a contextualized or personalized activity?
2. Was most classroom interaction in the target language?
3. If I presented vocabulary or grammar, did I do so in context?
4. Were any exercises I did contextualized or meaningful?
5. Did I include some speaking practice which required students to interact or be creative with the language?
6. Was small-group work included in the class hour?
7. Did the students participate in some type of role-playing activity?
8. Did I include sufficient listening practice to help my students understand utterances in situations?
9. Did I include or assign writing practice which gave students practice in writing on topics of interest to them?
10. Did I provide a context for culture and an opportunity for students to express a culturally appropriate act?
11. Did I correct students in a way that was helpful to them?

Teachers may not be able to include all of these areas each day because of time constraints, but the checklist will provide a reminder of their daily goals. Moreover, other factors may be important in individual cases. Grittner (13) provides a comparable checklist. Freed (11) reports that TAs who teach to the proficiency requirement at the University of Pennsylvania provide "for more situational or contextual activities which recognize functional aspects of language use as well as the occasional introduction of sociolinguistic aspects of language." Moving toward the proficiency goals will, without a doubt, encourage foreign-language instructors to make adjustments in daily class preparation and implementation.

Choosing and adapting materials

Few materials for teaching for proficiency have been published to date. Prospective high school teachers can be guided in their selection of textbooks that complement their efforts at emphasizing proficiency. Methods professors can provide such guidance by analyzing existing texts from a proficiency perspective. Some questions arising in text selection for proficiency follow.

1. Does the first third of the book provide simple survival situations where students are asked to work with basic courtesy formulas and simple vocabulary groups such as colors, days of the week, months of the year, and kinship terms?
2. Does the first third provide simple question words and use of the present tense, near future, and recent past? Are useful irregular verbs presented?
3. Does the second third of the book provide topics for description of family members and friends, location and description of home or school, and other topics that involve an exchange of simple factual information? Are situations set up so that students can express their needs for ordering a meal, getting a hotel room, and asking for directions?
4. Are the past tenses presented in the second third?
5. Does the last third of the book present more abstract topics for discussion allowing students to discuss opinions, leisure-time activities, and topics of current public interest?
6. Is a way provided for students to discuss future plans? Is the subjunctive presented in a manner which allows students to support opinions and describe emotions and personal reactions?
7. In general, is vocabulary useful and practical? Are the cultural themes in the book realistic and useful without stereotyping? Are students taught about everyday life in the target countries?
8. Are listening activities provided in the teacher's edition that will help students understand utterances about basic needs and minimum courtesy and travel requirements?
9. Are realia included with which students can practice reading, e.g., songs, menus, timetables, maps, and schedules?
10. Are composition topics included which guide students in writing simple biographical information, short messages, descriptions, and narrations?

If the response to most of the questions is affirmative, the textbook under consideration can more easily be adapted to a proficiency approach (Muyskens and Omaggio, 30).

Flynn (9) states that "while every textbook has some valuable drills, exercises, explanations, and readings, none will be suitable to every teacher's needs" (p. 39). Adapting and supplementing texts should, therefore, play a role in the training of preservice teachers and TAs.

"One of the first steps that every teacher takes, consciously or unconsciously, is to choose which parts of a lesson to drop, combine, or emphasize" (Flynn, 9, p. 39). In adapting or supplementing books for proficiency goals, the teachers must first look at the grammar and vocabulary presented in the book. From there the teacher will decide what to delete or supplement. Flynn says that the "need to supplement arises whenever important program goals are not being realized . . ." (p. 40). This will often be the case in the proficiency-oriented program.

After inspecting the grammar, themes, and vocabulary, the teacher will want to take the following steps.

- Prepare materials using real language in context to demonstrate the functions and content to be added. This can be done with videotapes, audiotapes, or written dialogues.
- Gather the needed materials, e.g., realia, handouts, and visuals, to help students practice.
- Allocate class time so that students practice the language activities, which may include small-group work and interviews, games, minidramas, filling out forms, and listening to tapes (Guntermann and Phillips, 15; Ariew, 4; and Flynn, 9).

Homework assignments should also be stimulating and should reflect the goals of the teacher. In other words, they should continue the proficiency orientation. For example, teachers may ask students to interview native speakers, prepare dialogues, describe pictures, design advertisements, write short letters, prepare descriptive narratives, plan an event, listen to tapes of conversations, and read short messages, newspaper ads, magazines, or poetry (Guntermann and Phillips, 15).

Although the task of textbook adaptation and supplementation is time-consuming, prospective teachers can realize that their job is "to provide what the textbook fails to provide" (Ariew, 4, p. 31). If the text does not entirely meet program goals, teachers need to adapt it themselves.

Classroom management

Class organization can evolve efficiently if proficiency goals are taken seriously. Teachers will conduct their classes more often in the target language, doing administrative matters in the language, joking, and even disciplining students in the target language. Such behavior is identified by Moskowitz (27) as a characteristic of outstanding classroom interaction. In addition, students will feel the need to speak the target language more often to gain as much practice as possible. Guntermann and Phillips (15) state that "a great deal of communicating takes place among students, and some teachers are able to establish a psychological atmosphere—through encouragement, insistence, and creating a special physical environment—in which much of the extraneous communication is conducted in the target language" (p. 34).

Prospective teachers can be given hints on ways of rewarding students for their target-language efforts and gently pushing students to do their classroom communication in the target language. Stevick (38) suggests that the interpersonal relationships teachers establish with students will "either kill their taste for speaking the language or whet their appetites for more" (p. 127). Moskowitz's studies (27) on the classroom interaction of outstanding teachers support Stevick's assertion that the teacher should be warm and accepting so that students feel more secure. Thus, the way in which teachers set up classroom activities will determine whether students are willing—or possibly able—to implement what they are learning about the foreign language.

An example of this is the teacher's handling of error correction. The way errors are corrected will affect students' attitudes toward themselves and the target language. Future teachers should be taught to correct errors by guiding their students to accuracy without intimidating or discouraging them. Awareness of proficiency goals will change teachers' expectations; they will not expect beginning students to assimilate all of the grammar immediately. They will be aware of the need to reinforce accuracy without stressing skills and grammar points that can only be expected of more advanced speakers.

Techniques for error correction such as those given by Joiner (20) will show future teachers how to make corrections without embarrassing students. These techniques include rephrasing a question, giving a model answer, providing options or prompting, repeating an answer correctly, using gestures, and writing a word on the board. Each of these techniques will help students to monitor their language and will aid in the development of linguistic and communicative competence. Stevick (38) reminds teachers that each correction strategy has its advantages and disadvantages. He states, "You yourself, from day to day and from moment to moment, will have to balance speed, rhythm, depth, and anxiety against one another and make your own choices" (p. 15).

Motivating students to study should be less difficult using a proficiency approach in the classroom. Guntermann (14) summarizes surveys which suggest that cultural understanding and communication are still the two major goals of language study. Students should find, therefore, that the proficiency goals meet their needs. Freed (11) reports that a sample of students' opinions at the University of Pennsylvania, where there is a proficiency requirement, shows them "to be more motivated than in the past because of the emphasis on spoken language. Others commented that increased motivation was due to more lively and varied classes." Resentment toward the proficiency test was expressed, however, even though enrollments did not decrease. In addition, Freed mentions that students are more outspoken about what they are not getting from a class as a result of pressure from the proficiency standard. The proficiency goals answer student needs and may, as a result, make teaching less difficult for the inexperienced teacher. If, however, teachers choose to institute proficiency-based language requirements, they must verify that this goal is reflected in their classes each day.

Prospective teachers should also recognize the usefulness of proficiency guidelines when counseling students who are frustrated with their inability to communicate immediately in the target language. This will aid students in setting more realistic goals. Teachers can explain the progressive nature of proficiency and the interaction of various grammatical concepts with linguistic functions, thus maintaining students' momentum in their foreign-language study.

Advanced students

Teaching advanced high school students and intermediate college students is often excluded from preservice methods courses. Future teachers who will teach more advanced students will find great advantages in the proficiency guidelines. Proficiency tests can be used to determine the level of competence of intermediate and advanced students; this will enable teachers to select appropriate materials. Freed (11) reports that the implementation of a proficiency requirement at Penn has resulted in a more integrated sequence of courses and a smoother integration of materials. In addition, the guidelines will also help teachers to be more aware of the capabilities of these students.

Prospective teachers also need motivational techniques for students at these higher levels. Activities appropriate for third- and fourth-year high school classes and intermediate college classes would include *sustaining* general conversations and initiating questions, handling simple description and narration about present, past, and future events. Students should be able to use the past and future tenses but will have difficulty expressing doubt and supporting opinions. Students should also be exposed to cultural situations at the Intermediate and Advanced levels of the guidelines through videotapes or visits by native speakers to the classroom. Methods teachers can demonstrate materials for this level and have students prepare and demonstrate their own activities for speaking, listening, reading, writing, and culture using the guidelines.

Testing

Clark (7) states that "in *direct* proficiency testing, the testing format and procedure attempt to duplicate as closely as possible the setting and operations of the real-life situations in which the proficiency is normally demonstrated" (p. 10). Future teachers trained for a proficiency-oriented classroom will recognize the need to test for samples "of the real-life language situations in question . . ." (p. 11). As previously mentioned, methods students would be exposed to demonstrations of oral proficiency tests at the beginning of the methods course. In order to prepare them to conduct and rate oral proficiency interviews, they must first be tested themselves and only then trained. To practice giving oral proficiency interviews, future teachers can test beginning students from the university. This implies that the methods professor will be a certified trainer. If he or she is not, training sessions by ETS or by a certified trainer from the area can be organized.

Proficiency tests for listening, reading, and writing are still being developed. Chapter 4 in this volume discusses testing techniques in these modalities in detail.

Once prospective teachers are aware of the proficiency goals, they will no longer want to give only traditional discrete-item achievement tests. Omaggio (34) has proposed that "revisions in curriculum and instruction are too often made without concomitant changes in evaluation procedures" (p. 47). She proposes ideas "for achievement testing that are based on the assumption that 'real communication' involves a blend of communicative and linguistic proficiency" (p. 48). Omaggio also describes tests "in which natural communicative language is used as much as possible, tested along a continuum of grammatical and/or lexical specificity ranging from the discrete-item to the integrative or global-item type" (p. 48). She proposes techniques for testing listening, reading, and writing in contexts so that the language is presented naturally. If real language is used in evaluation, students will take proficiency goals more seriously.

In order to gain experience, teachers should be asked to prepare several contextualized achievement tests. It should be emphasized to future teachers that these tests are only one part of a comprehensive testing program that will include frequent oral proficiency interviews which serve to inform students, parents, and the administration of the students' progress in language proficiency.

Student teaching

The student-teaching experience is one of the most valuable elements in the preparation of teachers. It is a time for prospective teachers to practice what they have learned in methods courses and to learn about teaching

(Knop, 23, 24). If methods students are prepared to teach for proficiency, their experience in student teaching should reflect this emphasis. Ideally, only coordinating teachers who have training in oral proficiency testing should be chosen. However, this may not always be possible, and a lack of common goals calls for even closer coordination. Knop (23) says that if supervising teachers "are going to depend more and more on coordinating teachers for training and supervision, we must assume the responsibility of helping these teachers understand their roles and responsibilities . . ." (p. 627). She suggests inviting coordinating teachers to inservice workshops. In the case where the master or coordinating teachers do not have training in proficiency testing, they should be invited to sessions on proficiency testing and proficiency-oriented classroom activities. These master teachers must be willing to allow the student teacher to experiment with proficiency techniques in the classroom.

On the other hand, it is entirely possible that a coordinating teacher who is interested in proficiency goals will be assigned a student teacher who has no knowledge of these goals. In such a case, the coordinating teacher can share goals, materials, and techniques with the student teacher and the university supervisor. These situations require trust, understanding, and communication. Muyskens and Berger (29) note that since our discipline values communication and understanding among peoples, it follows that these same values should be reflected in our professional life. The common goals of all involved should be emphasized in the process of familiarizing one another with the proficiency guidelines.

Inservice Teachers

"Effective inservice education for language teachers can renew and invigorate progress at all levels, and it is thus one of the most crucial issues in language teaching today" (Jorstad, 22, p. 81). With the focus on proficiency, the time has come to reevaluate and possibly redefine our roles as foreign-language teachers. Jorstad feels that institutions of higher education can contribute greatly by providing teachers with varied experiences and continued training. She suggests courses in language, linguistics, literature, and culture which are geared to the needs and schedules of inservice teachers. Furthermore, she provides approaches for improving language proficiency and cultural knowledge. Higgs (18) reminds teachers that the best way to improve their students' proficiency is to improve their own. Nevertheless, many teachers may not be able to improve their language competence by traveling abroad. If that is the case, Jorstad (22) suggests the organization of inservice summer workshops or weekend retreats for language practice. Further possibilities include obtaining grants or working as interns in commercial firms abroad. Higgs (18) proposes becoming a chaperone or organizer of student trips abroad. Teachers can be trained and updated in their cultural knowledge through courses designed especially for them or through travel programs designed to focus on culture.

Many teachers are not yet acquainted with proficiency goals or tests. Interested teachers may attend workshops organized by ACTFL or ETS, or projects funded by the Undergraduate International Studies and Foreign Language Program of the U.S. Department of Education. David Hiple at ACTFL and Judith Liskin-Gasparro of ETS can inform those wishing training about future workshops. Such workshops will train teachers in applying oral testing techniques to secondary schools or universities. Area language supervisors or universities training teachers may wish to familiarize classroom teachers with proficiency goals and oral proficiency testing through workshops or summer programs. The development of curricular materials appropriate to proficiency goals and activities for the proficiency-oriented classroom would offer other topics of discussion. The state supervisor can identify school districts where proficiency is a goal and ask teachers in these districts to make presentations at state or regional meetings. Videotapes of proficiency-oriented classrooms would also help teachers to understand the new approaches (Jorstad, 22).

Inservice teachers who wish to familiarize themselves with current developments in proficiency can do so by reading materials in the *Modern Language Journal, Foreign Language Annals, Canadian Modern Language Review, The ADFL Bulletin,* and the publication of their AAT organization. In addition, teachers who have developed classroom materials with proficiency goals should share them through these journals. The "local collaborative groups" being organized under the national project developed by Gaudiani (12) may be opportunities to share ideas for and progress in proficiency programs. Special sessions focused on proficiency testing could be planned.

Some teachers may perceive themselves as isolated in their attempts to develop a proficiency orientation. The first step toward change is to inform colleagues of the proficiency goals and testing techniques. In order to introduce others to the idea, the instructor interested in proficiency can share reading materials and invite colleagues to videotaped sessions of oral proficiency testing.

Even those professors who are not methodologists can understand the value of proficiency goals. Citing Carroll's study (6) on the proficiency of the typical undergraduate major will help them to realize that proficiency goals can improve the quality of their majors and graduate students. The guidelines will also make instructors more aware of levels of student abilities after completing beginning and intermediate classes. Colleagues made aware of such facts will realize their significance and potential for benefit. The guidelines serve as a "common yardstick" so that academic goals are shared.

Those of us in teacher training programs need to reevaluate our methodologies, language proficiency, and cultural knowledge. This means frequent contact with native speakers and visits to appropriate foreign countries. Inservice meetings can be organized for teacher trainers to share materials and ideas for training teachers in order to emphasize proficiency and discuss teacher competencies. It is time for us to offer the most practical methods courses possible—asking teachers what their priorities are and planning inservice workshops to meet the needs of teachers who wish to take refresher courses. Methodologists must give the prospective teachers an opportunity to practice the skills they believe are appropriate for themselves, to upgrade their language proficiency and cultural knowledge, and to practice techniques which will be useful to their proficiency-oriented classroom later.

Summary

In this chapter we have seen that TA training, methods courses, and inservice workshops all have as their major goal the reorientation of foreign-language teachers. Traditional training programs in these areas have tended to focus on specific techniques for teaching and testing specific aspects of the target language, usually grammatical structures. With proficiency as the organizing principle, both what teachers think and what they do in the classroom can and must be viewed from this new perspective.

We have mentioned some of the more obvious applications to which proficiency evaluations can be put, e.g., certification standards for both students and instructors, establishing criteria for completing a language requirement or for entering and exiting a higher-level program, designing guidelines for vertical and horizontal articulation, etc. But what we really have is an orientation that finally allows us to place nonnative speakers of a language—both students and instructors—within a global framework of foreign-language learning/acquisition. As Omaggio stressed earlier in this volume, many activities that instructors have used in the past are immediately applicable to language courses taught from a proficiency orientation. The same is true for much of what has been recommended and practiced in teacher-training programs at all levels. However, it is now possible to interpret every aspect of a program—materials and activities, student and teacher behaviors—into a larger conceptual framework. Such a framework not only constrains what we do in the classroom, it allows us to interpret this in terms of what students who are to become competent foreign-language users must eventually know.

Perhaps the simplest way to underscore the impact of the proficiency movement is to point out that in addition to suggesting to the profession *what* should be happening, it also allows us to say *why,* and perhaps even *how.* A proficiency orientation can make everyone a more critical and hence a more productive reader of textbooks and professional literature.

Central States Conference on the Teaching of Foreign Languages. Lincoln-wood, IL: National Textbook Co., 1982.

30. _____, and Alice C. Omaggio. *Instructor's Manual for Rendez-vous.* New York: Random House, 1982.

31. Nerenz, Anne G.; Carol A. Herron; and Constance K. Knop. "The Training of Graduate Teaching Assistants in Foreign Languages: A Review of Literature and Descriptions of Contemporary Programs." *French Review* 52 (1979):877-81.

32. Omaggio, Alice C. "Methodology in Transition: The New Focus on Proficiency." *Modern Language Journal,* in press.

33. _____. Personal communication, 1983.

34. _____. "Priorities in Classroom Testing for the 1980s," pp. 47-53 in Dale L. Lange and Cathy Linder, eds., *Proceedings of the National Conference on Professional Priorities.* Hastings-on-Hudson, NY: ACTFL Materials Center, 1981.

35. Paul, Regina H. "Needed: Stepladders for Foreign Language Learning." *Foreign Language Annals* 14 (1981):379-84.

36. Phillips, June K. "Reading Is Communication, Too!" *Foreign Language Annals* 11 (May 1978):281-87.

37. Schulz, Renate A. "TA Training, Supervision, and Evaluation: Report of a Survey." *ADFL Bulletin* 12 (September 1980):1-8.

38. Stevick, Earl W. *Teaching and Learning Languages.* Cambridge: Cambridge University Press, 1982.

39. *Strength through Wisdom: A Critique of U.S. Capability. A Report to the President from the President's Commission on Foreign Languages and International Studies (1979).* Reprinted in *Modern Language Journal* 64 (1980):9-57.

40. Wing, Barbara H. "Free to Become: Preservice Education," pp. 285-335 in Gilbert A. Jarvis, ed., *Perspective: A New Freedom.* The ACTFL Foreign Language Education Series, vol. 7. Lincolnwood, IL: National Textbook Co., 1975.

7

Proficiency Projects
in Action

Reynaldo Jiménez
University of Florida

Carol J. Murphy
University of Florida

Introduction

The first Foreign Service Institute (FSI) Testing Kit Workshop, held in early 1979, marked the beginning of the current trend toward proficiency-based foreign-language teaching and testing in the nation's high schools, colleges, and universities. The passage of the oral proficiency interview (OPI) from government hands to academia, as detailed in Chapter 1, has in just a few short years sparked a burgeoning revitalization in foreign-language education. With encouragement and support from the Department of Education, the cooperation between government agencies—especially the Interagency Language Roundtable (ILR)—ACTFL, and ETS has made possible two separate but related projects which stand as the cornerstones of the current proficiency movement: the offering of familiarization workshops in oral proficiency interviewing, and the

Reynaldo Jiménez (Ph.D., University of Illinois) is an Assistant Professor of Spanish at the University of Florida at Gainesville, where he trains teaching assistants and coordinates the elementary Spanish language program. He teaches foreign-language and literature courses, and also Spanish for native speakers. He has published in professional journals in the United States and abroad, and is the author of *Guillermo Cabrera Infante y Tres Tristes Tigres*. He is a member of ACTFL, LASA, and MLA.

Carol J. Murphy (Ph.D., University of Pennsylvania) is an Associate Professor of French at the University of Florida at Gainesville. She supervises the French teaching assistants; does research in twentieth-century French novel, criticism, and film; and teaches undergraduate and graduate courses in French language and literature. She is the author of *Alienation and Absence in the Novels of Marguerite Duras*. Her professional affiliations include AATF, ACTFL, and MLA.

articulation of proficiency guidelines for speaking and for the related areas of listening, reading, writing, and culture.

The first projects—the familiarization workshops—began in 1979 and 1980 when three FSI Testing Kit Workshops and their followup sessions brought FSI interviewers and raters together with postsecondary language teachers. These first steps toward the application of oral proficiency testing to the academic world were further pursued and reinforced by ACTFL's decision in 1981 to make language proficiency a primary goal of their organization. Collaboration with ETS and continued grants from the Department of Education led to the first ACTFL/ETS Oral Proficiency Interview Workshop held in Houston, Texas, in February 1982. Thirty instructors, fifteen in Spanish and fifteen in French, from postsecondary institutions were trained in administering and evaluating the oral proficiency interview. In February 1983, a second intensive workshop was held in Washington, D.C., for college teachers of German and Italian.

A followup to the 1982 Houston intensive workshop, held in Miami, Florida, in April 1983 furthered the spread of ACTFL/ETS-approved oral proficiency interviewing by training eleven French and nine Spanish instructors who would eventually become certified ACTFL/ETS oral proficiency raters and workshop trainers. The Miami trainers' workshop focused on vigorous review of the ACTFL scale, elicitation techniques, and rating skills. The twenty participants conducted two one-day familiarization workshops with forty Miami high school teachers of French and Spanish, who were introduced to the history and principles of the oral proficiency movement. Afternoon sessions were devoted to interviewing and to critiquing elicitation technique and rating skills. Followup work for trainers and trainees included written evaluations by trainers of trainees' performance on taped interviews conducted within a month after the workshop. Quality control and objectivity in proficiency testing have thus been critical concerns in the dissemination of the OPI techniques.

The second proficiency project, involving the development of proficiency guidelines in speaking and the other language modalities, was also supported by the Department of Education and resulted in a provisional set of guidelines written by a group of educators involved in the early stages of oral proficiency testing. These proficiency guidelines have already begun to exert an influence not only on testing but also on curriculum planning and classroom teaching.

The purpose of this chapter is to acquaint the profession with a representative though certainly not exhaustive sample of proficiency-related projects in action. It is divided into two parts. The first, a report on the state of the art, is the result of many telephone conversations and correspondence with educators who have described programs, grants in progress and/or plans to implement proficiency-based language teaching. This report is very encouraging. We find that ACTFL and ETS have provided the nucleus for a communication network which has resulted in a snowballing of efforts to measure and improve language skills. The individuals that we contacted have participated either in the FSI Testing Kit Workshops, the ACTFL/ETS intensive workshops in Houston and/or in Miami, or in ACTFL/ETS familiarization workshops. We have transcribed their accomplishments and/or goals. The second part of this chapter is a summary of findings from a questionnaire distributed by ETS to the thirty participants in the 1982 Houston workshop. It promises exciting developments in language teaching and serves as a barometer of present trends in and philosophies of language acquisition.

Proficiency Projects in Action

Among the first participants in the FSI Testing Kit Workshops were Howard T. Young, Chairman of the Department of Modern Languages and Literatures and Professor of Spanish at Pomona College in Claremont, California; and Francis Johnson, a colleague in the French section.· Upon returning to Pomona College after the 1979 workshop, Young administered oral proficiency interviews to twenty-five students, sharing the taped results with the FSI examiners. At the 1980 followup workshop in Washington, D.C., Young spoke at a session of the Georgetown University Roundtable on Languages and Literatures about the need for oral proficiency guidelines, paving the way for the development of the present ACTFL Provisional Proficiency Guidelines. Young delivered a similar talk at the ADFL Summer Seminar West at the University of Southern California in July 1980, which was subsequently published (13).

Pomona College has maintained an active interest in the oral proficiency movement, sending two additional faculty members to participate in oral proficiency workshops held at ETS in Princeton in 1981. The department also plans to establish a proficiency-based foreign-language requirement using the modified ACTFL/ETS rating scale. In addition, the department sponsored an OPI workshop in September 1983.

James Graham, Chairman of the Division of Cross Cultural Studies and Professor of French and Spanish at Central College in Pella, Iowa, participated in the FSI Testing Kit Workshop II, in Washington, D.C., in January 1980. Graham reported that since Central College's general prestige and recruiting strategies are intimately tied to foreign-language excellence, they are currently using the ILR proficiency-based examination procedure to evaluate the effectiveness of their programs.

Among the several uses of the ILR procedures at Central College, Graham referred to its use in evaluating students in Study Abroad and Language House programs through entry-exit oral proficiency interviews. In addition, the ILR scale is used to place entering students having two or more years of high school language study. Graham has identified four general areas of application of the training received: (1) as an administrative tool in the evaluation of the effectiveness of the college's language programs; (2) as a pedagogical tool which incorporates a series of clearly defined tasks and objectives, thereby stimulating the students to reach the objectives; (3) as a measure of the students' gains in the target language after a Study Abroad or Language House program; and (4) as a counseling mechanism for prospective participants in these programs.

Barbara Freed, Assistant Dean for Language Instruction and Lecturer in French in the Department of Romance Languages at the University of Pennsylvania, along with Lucienne Frappier-Mazur in French, also attended Testing Kit Workshop II and the followup session held in May of the same year. At Penn, Freed has established oral proficiency in the 1+ (Intermediate High) range as one exit requirement for the two-year language-requirement program. The Intermediate High oral proficiency requirement initially applied only to French students, but during academic year 1982–83, German and Russian students were also required to attain this level of proficiency. Currently the Spanish section is considering the adoption of a comparable oral proficiency requirement for its majors.

Freed conducted a study at Penn which correlated CEEB scores and FSI (ACTFL/ETS) scores. She tested twenty-four students in a third-semester French course, and the results of the oral testing showed a high degree of correlation among students earning a score of 1+. Her methodology and results appear in a recent edition of essays devoted to oral language proficiency measurement (Freed, 2).

Freed's other projects have included an articulation conference for high school teachers, held in the Spring of 1983, which acquainted them with the oral proficiency model and the language requirement at the University of Pennsylvania. A more detailed explanation of the Penn program can be found in *The ADFL Bulletin* (Freed, 3).

Alice Omaggio, Assistant Professor of French at the University of Illinois at Urbana-Champaign, has been involved in oral proficiency testing since she participated in the third FSI Testing Kit Workshop, held in 1980. She also took part in a two-week intensive session at the Defense Language Institute in the Summer of 1982. A collaborator in the formulation of the ACTFL Provisional Proficiency Guidelines, Omaggio also conducted training sessions for college language teachers at the November 1982 ACTFL preconference and assisted in training postsecondary teachers from Maine, New Hampshire, and Vermont during Project OPT (Oral Proficiency Testing) which is discussed below in this chapter.

Omaggio's experience with the proficiency guidelines has resulted in curricular and testing changes at the University of Illinois, where she supervises the French teaching assistants and the elementary and intermediate language program. Oral testing is a major component of the two-year language requirement. In their methods course, as well as in special workshops, teaching assistants are trained to administer and grade two oral exams per semester for each student. The results, according to Omaggio, have been gratifying. Most students after the first year of the elementary program test in the Intermediate (ILR 1) range. Omaggio has written an extensive manuscript (7) on proficiency testing in the classroom. She has coauthored two elementary French textbooks (6, 12) which reflect, at least in part, her FSI/ACTFL/ETS training, and is working on an intermediate French text which is even more directly inspired by the oral proficiency rating scale (8).

At the University of Minnesota's Twin Cities Campus, Dale L. Lange, Professor of Second Languages and Cultures Education, has been conducting research in secondary schools to examine the correspondence between proficiency levels and number of years of language study. He conducted twenty-four interviews in three different secondary schools at four different levels of instruction: French 2, 3, 4, 5 (the numbers correspond to years of instruction). His findings reveal that, with the exception of three students (one at level 4, two at level 5), everyone tested out at the same level of Novice High (ILR Level 0+).

Lange, who was trained at the third FSI Testing Kit Workshop, reported on the outcome at the November 1982 ACTFL meeting. A tape of his report can be obtained from ACTFL. Having answered the question which motivated his study—that is, "What constitutes language proficiency at the secondary level?"—Lange plans to go beyond his initial data to determine the relationship of teacher and curriculum to development of proficiency. He will focus on the three exceptions identified in his survey to account for the difference in their level of proficiency.

Lange intends to use the results of his study to investigate the "terminal 2" performance profile as it is treated by Higgs and Clifford (4) in their seminal article "The Push Toward Communication." Lange hypothesizes that a surplus of grammar, rather than a lack of it, hinders effective communication, at least at the high school level. Before publishing the results of his survey, Lange will be doing further reliability studies.

Barbara H. Wing, Assistant Professor of Spanish in the Department of Ancient and Modern Languages and Literatures of the University of New Hampshire, obtained a one-year grant from the International Studies and Research Programs of the Department of Education, Title VI, to carry out a research project on oral proficiency testing ("Project OPT"). The principal objective of this project is to determine the feasibility of incorporating specific techniques of oral proficiency evaluation in foreign-language courses at the college level. As presently envisaged, OPT will produce three results: (1) a final report, describing all aspects of procedures and results of the investigation; (2) a handbook of guidelines and techniques for developing locally produced oral proficiency tests; and (3) a network in northern New England of foreign-language professors who are working to improve proficiency evaluation in their institutions.

Project OPT involves thirty professors of Spanish, French, German, and Russian from Maine, New Hampshire, and Vermont. A training workshop held in January of 1983 introduced participants to the oral proficiency interview. A participant project involving the use of the OPI in an ongoing foreign-language course and a followup workshop for evaluation purposes complete the program. The participant project served as a focal point for the followup workshop held in Durham, New Hampshire, from August 5–8, 1983. Previous to this meeting, participants had been asked to complete and submit a questionnaire about the impact and implications of using the ACTFL/ETS rating scale in foreign-language courses.

Research questions associated with determining the feasibility of incorporating specific techniques of oral proficiency evaluation into ongoing foreign-language classes include the following.

- Can foreign-language professors who complete an intensive four-day training workshop in the Foreign Service Institute model for oral evaluation successfully adapt those techniques to a course they are currently teaching?
- What demands, in terms of time needed for preparation, administration, and scoring of oral tests, does the use of these techniques make upon the teacher?
- What conditions and facilities are needed by professors to implement an oral testing component in a foreign-language course?
- What adjustments must be made in the curriculum to accommodate the oral testing component?
- What context variables are associated with successful implementation of an oral testing component?
- What problems do professors encounter when developing and implementing an oral testing component?
- What further training is necessary to help instructors develop an oral testing component in their language courses?
- What differences, if any, appear in the interviewing and rating techniques of professors when interviewing their own students and students they do not know?
- What proficiency levels are associated with typical levels of instruction (beginning, intermediate, advanced) at the college level?

Dixon Anderson, Chairman of the Spanish Department of Brigham Young University, attended the first ACTFL Oral Proficiency Workshop in Houston. He later organized a two-day workshop at BYU, in cooperation with ETS, which involved thirty-five secondary and postsecondary teachers and included two general information sessions on the history and methods of the oral interview procedure as well as practice in interviewing and rating. Postworkshop activities included once-a-week practice sessions. More recently, he has been involved in interviewing public school teachers as part of an ETS national proficiency project involving secondary school teachers. He also attended the Miami workshop. He is currently developing a set of vocabulary and grammar materials tailored along the lines of the situations and role playing suggested by the oral interview procedure which will be used in the Spanish program at BYU.

Luz Berd, Assistant Professor of Spanish and Coordinator of the Foreign Language Department at George Williams College in Downers Grove, Illinois, also attended the ACTFL Houston workshop. Following her workshop experience, she received a three-year grant from the U.S. Department of Education's Title VI program to train postsecondary teachers of Spanish and French throughout Illinois. The grant provides for two five-day workshops to be held in each of the three years. Information about the workshops and application forms were sent to junior college, college, and university language teachers through the Illinois Foreign Language Association.

The first workshop was held December 8–12, 1982, at George Williams, and was coordinated by two ETS trainers. The second workshop took place March 2–6, 1983, with equal numbers of French and Spanish teachers. The third workshop, scheduled for November 1983, will address teachers of German, Italian, and Spanish. During the third year, the language-specific training groups will be determined by the needs of the state.

At the University of Rhode Island in Kingston, proficiency testing has been a key factor in formulating grant proposals, according to Joseph G. Morello, Associate Professor of French in the Department of Languages. URI is now in the second year of a two-year Title VI grant for International Education and Foreign Language Improvement. The grant involves five faculty members from three departments (Political Science, History, and Languages) and was proposed by Project Director Michael Honhart of the History Department.

The grant aims to internationalize curriculum in the university's General Education program in three ways: (1) by setting an oral proficiency standard for the foreign-language requirement; (2) by developing "culture cluster courses," which would be an alternative to a foreign-language requirement for students in the Bachelor of Science program; and (3) by internationalizing the professional schools. Regarding the last, the College of Business Administration is currently working on a proposal for a major in International Business and Foreign Language.

Morello, along with Remo Trivelli (Italian) and John Grandin (German, Project Director), have submitted another proposal to the Department of Education Title VI that aims to set up the ACTFL Provisional Proficiency Guidelines as a point of articulation between high schools and universities. The project contains both training and research phases. The former would allow for two intensive workshops in consecutive summers to train a total of fifty French and Spanish teachers in public and private high schools in the administration of the oral proficiency interview. The latter would provide released time to test French students throughout the state to determine existing proficiency norms. By familiarizing high school teachers with the proficiency definitions and by assessing the prevailing level of oral proficiency in high schools, the project coordinators hope to make concrete suggestions for curricular revision at the secondary level.

Claus Reschke, Associate Professor of German at the University of Houston, organized an oral proficiency familiarization conference and workshop for September 15–17, 1983, with support from the University of Houston and the Goethe Institute in Chicago. Thirty members of the German section of the American Association of University Supervisors and Coordinators of Foreign Language Programs (AAUSC), who usually hold their annual meeting in Chicago, were instead invited to the two-day conference at Houston. There, representatives from various universities which have been successful in instituting oral proficiency testing in their language courses outlined the problems and successes of their programs. On September 17, the workshop sessions of the conference were opened to secondary school and college teachers of German, Spanish, French, and ESL in the greater Houston area. Participants received experience in oral proficiency testing. Among the workshop directors was C. Edward Scebold, Executive Director of ACTFL. Raymond Clifford of the Language School at the Defense Language Institute (DLI) and Pardee Lowe of the CIA Language School instructed teachers of German; Judith Liskin-Gasparro of ETS and Theodore Higgs, Associate Professor of Spanish at San Diego State University, trained participants in Spanish; and both Higgs and Frances Hinofotis of the Department of English at UCLA worked with ESL teachers. Training in French was handled by Alice Omaggio of the University of Illinois at Urbana-Champaign.

Reschke has been associated with oral proficiency testing for several years. In addition to his work on the ACTFL Provisional Proficiency Guidelines, he has published several articles and presented several papers on the subject of proficiency testing (9, 10, 11).

At the University of Texas at El Paso, Armando Armengol, Assistant Professor of Spanish in the Department of Modern Languages, organized a four-day intensive oral proficiency workshop for faculty members in Spanish and English as a Second Language. This workshop was funded by the College of Liberal Arts and included a total of twelve faculty members. The workshop's followup sessions included regular meetings to refine elicitation techniques, interviews in Spanish with fourteen applicants for summer intensive courses, and interviews in English with foreign teaching assistants in the university.

Theodore V. Higgs, Associate Professor of Spanish and Hispanic Linguistics at San Diego State University, was a participant in both the Houston and Miami workshops. He has offered numerous familiarization workshops throughout California, and assisted Armando Armengol in the El Paso workshop mentioned in the preceding paragraph. In October 1983, he and Armengol offered a five-day intensive workshop to graduate teaching assistants, part-time instructors, and full-time faculty of the Spanish Department at San Diego State. The workshop, which included more than twenty participants, was funded through a grant from that university's Latin American Studies Center.

H. B. Dyess, State Coordinator for Foreign Languages and Bilingual Education in Louisiana, reports that the State of Louisiana's Department of Education, together with CODOFIL (the Council for the Development of French in Louisiana, a state agency created by the legislature in 1968 to serve the needs of French speakers in Louisiana) have applied to the U.S. Department of Education for a three-year grant to pilot-test the French-specific ACTFL guidelines so that these guidelines can be used effectively to evaluate both the curriculum and student achievement.

Dyess pointed out that Louisiana is unique in having a state-funded elementary program (Grades 1–8) for second-language students of French, Spanish, Hungarian, and Italian. This program was established by the Second Language Specialists. Another aspect of the grant would be to investigate the possibility of developing software to be used in computer instruction.

Frances Hinofotis, Department of English (ESL Section) at UCLA, received her initial training in the area of oral proficiency testing at UCLA in September 1980 in a workshop conducted by Ray Clifford and Pardee Lowe. Hinofotis' area of expertise is in testing English as a second language, and the "English Language Supplement" which she is developing with the Defense Language Institute to complement the government's handbook on oral testing (5) is an effort to standardize a procedure to train testers to test for English proficiency. In addition, Hinofotis is part of a team of researchers in the Department of English at UCLA who are presently engaged in a research project to assess the functional language proficiency of prospective foreign TAs. Using the ILR oral interview procedure as a criterion, this group of specialists is gathering data to compare the Test of Spoken English with the ILR procedure. Hinofotis reports that Kathleen Bailey, Director of MA in TESOL Programs at the Monterey Institute for International Studies, in a recent study on nonnative-speaking teaching assistants at UCLA (Bailey, 1) found that for the most part, instructors who scored below the Advanced Level (ILR 2) were perceived by their students as being ineffective teachers. Interestingly, Bailey's study also reports that instructors who scored in the Advanced range (ILR 2/2+) were often perceived as effective teachers when *all* factors in the evaluation were taken into account. This suggests that factors other than simple oral proficiency contribute to a nonnative's success at "getting the job done," and that in certain areas at certain levels of instruction the traditional threshold requirement of Superior (ILR 3) may be unnecessarily high. This work of Hinofotis and her colleagues is a first step in the use of an oral proficiency test in the selection of foreign TAs.

In addition to serving as guidelines for *oral* communication, the ILR level definitions have played a major role in assessing communicative skills of those who work with the deaf. In 1981, Catherine Moses, Assistant Professor of Social Work at Gallaudet College, a liberal arts college for the deaf in Washington, D.C., along with Will Madsen, a colleague in the Department of Sign Communication, underwent training in the administration of the oral proficiency interview. The training was supported by Gallaudet College with a view to an eventual revision of the somewhat unreliable diagnostic test that is currently used to measure proficiency in signing. This test must be passed by a faculty member wishing to teach at Gallaudet.

Moses points out that the adaptation process, which is still being refined, is complicated by variations within the visual modes of signing based on *only* spoken and/or written American Sign Language, a language separate and distinct from English that is used by many deaf people in the United States and Canada. She also indicated that the definition of Level 5, the ENS level, may be a problem, as most deaf people are educated later in life. She proposes that this level be called simply "native proficiency." Moses and Madsen have already developed training materials which include videotapes of interviews that they have conducted, but they express a need for more formal training as well as familiarization with the ACTFL refinement of the ILR rating system.

William Newell of the National Technical Institute for the Deaf at the Rochester Institute of Technology in Rochester, N.Y., echoes Moses' comments about the difficulties encountered in adapting the oral proficiency interview scale to signing, due to the various dialects of sign language. In his position as Chairperson of Communication Training, Newell is directly responsible for providing communication training for those who work with the NTID students.

Newell's familiarity with the oral proficiency interview comes both from an initial involvement with the OPI as developed by the Defense Language Institute and a later initiation to the ACTFL guidelines at a workshop held in Princeton in September 1982. The NTID scale for signing, as developed by Newell and his colleagues, is based largely on the ACTFL model, with a further refinement at the upper end of the scale (Levels 4, 5). Concurring with Moses, Newell pointed out that the ENS level is difficult to identify in native signers. To account for this, the ACTFL/ETS levels have been renamed in the NTID terminology as Novice, Survival, Intermediate, Advanced, and Superior, with a plus at each level. The Superior rating corresponds to a 5 on the ILR scale. The Sign Language Proficiency Interview levels emphasize the functional ability to communicate rather than knowledge of grammar, and this allows for a variety of sign languages and dialects to be measured by scale. A Superior Plus rating on this scale would be given to persons able to use all aspects of signing fluently and accurately to discuss a variety of topics, and whose signing is accepted in all respects by highly skilled and knowledgeable native signers.

At NTID the translated and revised ACTFL guidelines are used on a voluntary basis for those faculty who want to support their tenure/ promotion documents with an objective evaluation of their signing skills.

Perhaps the largest proficiency project in action is the one just starting in Texas. Under a grant from the Department of Education, ACTFL will conduct a three-year program that will lead to incorporating proficiency standards into foreign-language teacher certification throughout the state. In January of 1984 and again in 1985, college and university professors will be trained as interviewers and raters. Beginning in April of 1984 and continuing through 1985, graduating foreign-language majors throughout the state will take an oral proficiency test. By 1986, standards and procedures will have been established, and thereafter, certification as a foreign-language teacher in Texas will depend in part on meeting the proficiency criteria. The work of coordinating the State Board of Education, the fifty-two teacher-training institutions, and the public school systems will be handled by an Academic Coordinating Committee chaired by Joan Manley of the University of Texas at El Paso, a participant at both the Houston and Miami workshops. It is hoped that this project will serve as a pilot program that other states can adapt to their own instructional needs.

Impact: The Houston Experience

As stated in the preceding section, a significant step toward the training of college-level foreign-language teachers in oral proficiency interviewing and rating was taken jointly by ACTFL and ETS through the Oral Proficiency Interview Workshop held in Houston (February 1982). This intensive workshop, funded under Title VI of the Higher Education Act, brought together a total of thirty faculty members of Spanish and French, representing private and state colleges and universities from a wide geographical distribution in the United States. Of particular importance to this chapter is the workshop's followup questionnaire developed by Judith Liskin-Gasparro of ETS to obtain a sample of the participants' impressions of the impact of their training on the profession. The questionnaire asked ten questions on a variety of topics, ranging from changes in the classroom and testing practices to research endeavors motivated by the newly acquired training. It addressed four major areas of potential impact: (1) teaching and testing methodology and criteria for textbook evaluation and selection, (2) language departments' curricular and programmatic changes, (3) potential applications of the oral interview inside and outside the university, and (4) research on oral proficiency and related projects.

Teaching and testing methodology and textbook evaluation

Participants in the Houston workshop were asked about the extent to which their training has had an impact on their teaching philosophy and techniques, on their current testing instruments, and on their criteria for textbook selection. A majority of the respondents agreed that their training has served to strengthen and clarify their ideas on teaching and learning a foreign language, especially in the area of stressing oral communication in the classroom. The experience also helped them conceptualize in more precise terms what previously they had been doing intuitively and, perhaps, unsystematically. Many respondents said that they were now in clear possession of a procedure designed to measure their students' oral competence accurately in terms of *functional ability.* As a result, the oral interview and the role-playing "survival situations" adapted from the ILR and ACTFL/ETS models are becoming increasingly common in college and university classrooms across the nation.

In addition, respondents were unanimous on the impact of the workshop on their course planning at all levels, including upper-level language and literature courses. The ILR concept of the functional trisection (see Chapter 1) with its discrete, graduated levels of competence within the totality of language production, was found to be a useful tool in leading students through a series of steps, each of which required mastery of particular communicative functions and linguistic structures. Thus, program goals are clear from the beginning and materials are selected which reflect the graduated movement toward these goals, all of which define a coherent whole of language acquisition and performance. In addition, the interview procedure and the rating system provided the participants with some useful insights into how their students progress from one level to another in language learning.

Many participants felt that, in spite of some recent developments in teaching materials, most foreign-language textbooks still fail to provide for the development of real communicative competence. No matter how innovative the format of the texts may be, ultimately they tend to underestimate the students' ability and do little to encourage creativity in the functional use of the target language. In spite of any given textbook's claims, many respondents expressed their frustration over the time-consuming task of providing supplementary materials with a functional orientation. While it is clear that no single textbook can or should substitute for the instructor's creativity and imagination, there is a unanimous feeling that in the future textbooks must focus on developing oral-aural skills and, more important, must account in a precise and systematic way for the different levels of proficiency which students are expected to attain.

In conclusion, the workshop's participants generally felt that present textbooks are too ambitious in terms of the grammatical materials they present and fail to recognize the actual progression students follow in assimilating functional linguistic concepts. These foreign-language teachers would welcome—at all levels—textbooks designed from a proficiency-based perspective, with graduated language-specific goals that lead to functional competence in the language.

In line with the above, the testing instruments at various institutions of higher education are beginning to change. Given such obvious variables as size and complexity of language programs, as well as faculties' diverse philosophies on the most appropriate testing mechanisms for their departments, many participants were expecting neither swift nor global changes. However, while the majority of respondents claimed that their language programs still depend primarily on achievement tests or discrete-point exams for evaluation purposes, the use of strictly oral, proficiency-based exams is quickly becoming an integral element in their programs. In first- and second-year language courses, the oral interview, adapted to fit course content, is already a standard part of many testing programs. In some institutions, students who enroll in any basic language courses are required to have an OPI as part of their final grade. Other participants report that the language laboratory oral-aural test is giving way to an adapted version of the oral interview. George Cabell-Castellet at Oregon State University reports that oral testing has been greatly emphasized at his institution since his return from Houston. His department has acquired a room which is used exclusively for oral testing and interviews and which includes all sorts of props to provide for re-creating "survival situations."

A majority of the respondents agreed that the necessity for having tests administered and graded by a large number of their colleagues, as well as the need to measure literacy skills, has made retention of discrete-point testing a practical and necessary element in their program. However, a high percentage of language teachers who have received training in oral proficiency are taking a more holistic approach in their evaluation instruments and are currently using the oral proficiency interview as an integrated part of their grading.

Curricular and programmatic changes

Upon returning from Houston, participants in the workshop shared their initial reactions with their colleagues in a variety of ways, ranging from formal familiarization workshops and departmental seminars or panel discussions to short oral or written briefings at departmental meetings. While colleagues' responses have been uniformly positive, or at least receptive when not openly enthusiastic, many have reacted with skepticism at the possibility of training others to be reliable interviewers and raters in just a few days. Doubts also emerged about time constraints with regard to the practicality and efficiency of implementation of the oral interview as a procedure for testing. In addition, questions generally arose with respect to the control and verification of standards across the country.

The Miami Trainers' Workshop, in April of 1983, addressed these concerns by setting up and testing established procedures and guidelines for the training of future oral proficiency interviewers. Apprentice trainers conducted two one-day familiarization workshops for Dade County foreign-language teachers covering the history, concepts, and elaboration of the oral proficiency interview; elicitation skills; and rating techniques. Post-Miami workshops have been and will continue to be informed by the guidelines and by a networking system established in Miami. Additional steps toward standardization have been taken by ACTFL and ETS through the dissemination of the ACTFL Provisional Proficiency Guidelines.

In light of the above, many language departments reportedly are beginning to revise their curricula along the lines of a proficiency orientation based on the ACTFL guidelines. Some departments are moving faster than others, but the picture emerging from the responses to the questionnaire clearly shows that foreign-language educators across the country are meeting to restructure course sequences in a manner more closely reflecting the stages of linguistic proficiency enunciated in the guidelines. Also, the recent increase in "courses for the professions" among the traditional language and literature offerings has made clear the need for some sort of oral proficiency exit exam. It is in this light that the ACTFL guidelines and the oral interview are rapidly gaining converts.

A substantial number of the Houston workshop participants has recognized a new awareness that present curricula do not typically address the needs of students searching for functional linguistic ability. As was the case with methodology and course goals, the Houston workshop has initiated or increased serious discussions about curricular revision in many language departments across the country. While concrete revisions seem to be taking place in those courses having a clear practical orientation— i.e., intermediate and advanced conversation courses and "courses for the professions"—foreign-language teachers at the postsecondary level are recognizing the need to reorient every aspect of their programs toward precise and well-defined goals. The ACTFL Provisional Proficiency Guidelines, designed to provide a graduated sequence of learning goals in all modalities of language acquisition (speaking, listening, reading, writing, and culture), are increasingly being used as a criterion-referenced basis for curriculum planning and classroom teaching.

Potential applications of the oral interview

Respondents to the questionnaire have identified a variety of ongoing and potential applications inside and outside academia. The preceding pages have already reported on the use of the oral interview as an effective teaching and evaluation tool. In addition to these applications, some respondents report that their institutions have begun to use or refine the oral interview and rating techniques to screen incoming graduate teaching assistants. Also, familiarization and intensive workshops have been widely offered as orientation and training devices. Other departments are contemplating offering a proficiency certificate based on the oral interview for students who plan to seek employment in areas where foreign-language skills are desirable. The oral interview is also used as a placement test for incoming freshmen and transfer students. Maria Paz-Haro, a participant in the Houston workshop and Director of the Spanish Language Program at Stanford University, reports that a fifteen-minute oral interview has been added to the program's current placement test. A student must score at the Intermediate Level (ILR Level 1) or higher to fulfill the three-quarter foreign-language requirement. Finally, at the University of Florida, as of Spring semester 1984, Spanish majors will be required to score at the Advanced/Advanced Plus levels (ILR Level 2/2+) in an oral interview as part of their graduation requirements.

The oral interview has also served as a pedagogical and evaluative tool in training other faculty members with a professional interest in and/or affiliation with internationally oriented university programs and research centers. At the University of Florida, Carol Murphy has been involved in training faculty members in the university's Institute of Food and Agricultural Services, in preparation for the FSI exam which is required of faculty members involved in federally funded international programs. Finally, several respondents to the questionnaire report that they have shared duties in the area of oral proficiency testing of graduating seniors in the College of Education at their institutions, especially in the programs of Bilingual Education.

Outside the university environment, participants in the Houston workshop have reported on their new and increasing role in the area of bilingual teacher certification requirements in their respective states. While not all of the respondents are officially certified raters and interviewers, many have assisted ETS trainers in training state education officials and teachers in interviewing and rating. As a result of their participation, these faculty members are being asked to collaborate at the state level in establishing quality control procedures for other testers of candidates for bilingual teacher credentials. In addition, many of these faculty members are increasingly participating in the articulation of language proficiency levels for bilingual teacher certification with Boards of Education in the different states.

Other potential uses of the oral interview, as reported, include administering oral interviews and ratings for employees of export and import businesses, as well as in other commercial enterprises with an international orientation.

Research on oral proficiency and related projects

Since the Houston workshop included a substantial number of faculty members whose fields of research lie outside the area of foreign-language pedagogy, it is not surprising to find that the amount of research stimulated by the Houston experience is still in the embryonic stage among the respondents to the questionnaire. However, from their responses we have been able to determine that individual efforts have already begun, especially in areas such as participation in national foreign-language conferences, grant writing, and language textbook reviews and production. Further, it is clear that the impact of their newly acquired training has been very strong, and many participants spoke with enthusiasm on their scholarly commitment to the area of oral proficiency and, specifically, to its possible adaptation to their classroom and their present testing instruments.

References, Proficiency Projects in Action

1. Bailey, Kathleen M. "Teaching in a Second Language: The Communicative Competence of Non-native Speaking Teaching Assistants." Ph.D. dissertation, UCLA. 1982.
2. Freed, Barbara. "Application of FSI Oral Proficiency Testing at the University Level," in Judith E. Liskin-Gasparro and James R. Frith, eds., *Measuring Spoken Language Proficiency.* Washington, DC: Georgetown University Press, 1983.
3. _____. "Establishing Proficiency-Based Language Requirements." *ADFL Bulletin* 13, ii (1981):6–12.
4. Higgs, Theodore V., and Ray Clifford. "The Push Toward Communication," pp. 57–79 in Theodore V. Higgs, ed., *Curriculum, Competence, and the Foreign Language Teacher.* The ACTFL Foreign Language Education Series, vol. 13. Lincolnwood, IL: National Textbook Co., 1982.
5. Lowe, Pardee. *ILR Handbook on Oral Interview Testing,* Field Test Version. Washington, DC: DLI/LS Joint Oral Interview Project, July 1982.
6. Muyskens, Judith A.; Alice C. Omaggio; Claudene Chalmers; Claudette Imberton; and Philippe Almeras. *Rendez-Vous: An Invitation to French.* New York: Random House, 1982.
7. Omaggio, Alice C. *Testing Language Skills in Context.* Language in Education: Theory and Practice. Washington, DC: Center for Applied Linguistics, forthcoming.
8. _____. *Kaleidoscope: Grammar in Context.* New York: Random House, forthcoming.
9. Reschke, Claus. "Measuring Foreign Language Oral Proficiency." *Glottodidactica* 10 (March 1978):101–12.
10. _____. "Oral Proficiency Testing in High School and College: Why and How?" *Proceedings: Pacific Northwest Council on Foreign Languages,* Part II, 29 (February 1979):83–87.
11. _____. "Adaptation of the FSI Interview Scale for Secondary Schools and Colleges," pp. 75–88 in John L. D. Clark, ed., *Direct Testing of Speaking Proficiency: Theory and Application.* Princeton, NJ: Educational Testing Service, 1978.

12. Rochester, Myrna J.; Judith A. Muyskens; Alice C. Omaggio; and Claudene Chalmers. *Bonjour, ça va?* New York: Random House, 1983.
13. Young, Howard. "On Using Foreign Service Tests and Standards on Campuses," pp. 64–69 in James R. Frith, ed., *Measuring Spoken Language Proficiency.* Washington, DC: Georgetown University Press, 1980.

Appendix A:
The ACTFL Provisional Proficiency Guidelines

Provisional Generic Descriptions—Speaking

Novice—Low   Unable to function in the spoken language. Oral production is limited to occasional isolated words. Essentially no communicative ability.

Novice—Mid   Able to operate only in a very limited capacity within very predictable areas of need. Vocabulary limited to that necessary to express simple elementary needs and basic courtesy formulae. Syntax is fragmented, inflections and word endings frequently omitted, confused or distorted and the majority of utterances consist of isolated words or short formulae. Utterances rarely consist of more than two or three words and are marked by frequent long pauses and repetition of an interlocutor's words. Pronunciation is frequently unintelligible and is strongly influenced by first language. Can be understood only with difficulty, even by persons such as teachers who are used to speaking with nonnative speakers or in interactions where the context strongly supports the utterance.

Novice—High   Able to satisfy immediate needs using learned utterances. Can ask questions or make statements with reasonable accuracy only where this involves short memorized utterances or formulae. There is no real autonomy of expression, although there may be some emerging signs of spontaneity and flexibility. There is a slight increase in utterance length but frequent long pauses and repetition of interlocutor's words still occur. Most utterances are telegraphic and word endings are often omitted, confused, or distorted. Vocabulary is limited to areas of immediate survival needs. Can differentiate most phonemes when produced in isolation but when they are combined in words or groups of words, errors are frequent and, even with repetition, may severely inhibit communication even with persons used to dealing with such learners. Little development in stress and intonation is evident.

Intermediate—Low   Able to satisfy basic survival needs and minimum courtesy requirements. In areas of immediate need or on very familiar topics, can ask and answer simple questions, initiate and respond to simple statements, and maintain very simple face-to-face conversations. When asked to do so, is able to formulate some questions with limited constructions and much inaccuracy. Almost every utterance contains fractured syntax and other grammatical errors. Vocabulary inadequate to express anything but the most elementary needs. Strong interference from native language occurs in articulation, stress, and intonation. Misunderstandings frequently arise from limited vocabulary and grammar and erroneous phonology but, with repetition, can generally be understood by native speakers in regular contact with foreigners attempting to speak their language. Little precision in information conveyed owing to tentative state of grammatical development and little or no use of modifiers.

Intermediate—Mid   Able to satisfy some survival needs and some limited social demands. Is able to formulate some questions when asked to do so. Vocabulary permits discussion of topics beyond basic survival needs such as personal history and leisure-time activities. Some evidence of grammatical accuracy in basic constructions, for example, subject-verb agreement, noun-adjective agreement, some notion of inflection.

219

Intermediate—High   Able to satisfy most survival needs and limited social demands. Shows some spontaneity in language production but fluency is very uneven. Can initiate and sustain a general conversation but has little understanding of the social conventions of conversation. Developing flexibility in a range of circumstances beyond immediate survival needs. Limited vocabulary range necessitates much hesitation and circumlocution. The commoner tense forms occur but errors are frequent in formation and selection. Can use most question forms. While some word order is established, errors still occur in more complex patterns. Cannot sustain coherent structures in longer utterances or unfamiliar situations. Ability to describe and give precise information is limited. Aware of basic cohesive features such as pronouns and verb inflections, but many are unreliable, especially if less immediate in reference. Extended discourse is largely a series of short, discrete utterances. Articulation is comprehensible to native speakers used to dealing with foreigners, and can combine most phonemes with reasonable comprehensibility, but still has difficulty in producing certain sounds, in certain positions, or in certain combinations, and speech will usually be labored. Still has to repeat utterances frequently to be understood by the general public. Able to produce some narration in either past or future.

Advanced   Able to satisfy routine social demands and limited work requirements. Can handle with confidence but not with facility most social situations including introductions and casual conversations about current events, as well as work, family, and autobiographical information; can handle limited work requirements, needing help in handling any complications or difficulties. Has a speaking vocabulary sufficient to respond simply with some circumlocutions; accent, though often quite faulty, is intelligible; can usually handle elementary constructions quite accurately but does not have thorough or confident control of the grammar.

Advanced Plus   Able to satisfy most work requirements and show some ability to communicate on concrete topics relating to particular interests and special fields of competence. Generally strong in either grammar or vocabulary, but not in both. Weaknesses or unevenness in one of the foregoing or in pronunciation result in occasional miscommunication. Areas of weakness range from simple constructions such as plurals, articles, prepositions, and negatives to more complex structures such as tense usage, passive constructions, word order, and relative clauses. Normally controls general vocabulary with some groping for everyday vocabulary still evident. Often shows remarkable fluency and ease of speech, but under tension or pressure language may break down.

Superior   Able to speak the language with sufficient structural accuracy and vocabulary to participate effectively in most formal and informal conversations on practical, social, and professional topics. Can discuss particular interests and special fields of competence with reasonable ease. Vocabulary is broad enough that speaker rarely has to grope for a word; accent may be obviously foreign; control of grammar good; errors virtually never interfere with understanding and rarely disturb the native speaker.

Provisional Generic Descriptions—Listening

Novice—Low   No practical understanding of the spoken language. Understanding limited to occasional isolated words, such as cognates, borrowed words, and high-frequency social conventions. Essentially no ability to comprehend even short utterances.

Novice—Mid   Sufficient comprehension to understand some memorized words within predictable areas of need. Vocabulary for comprehension limited to simple elementary needs and basic courtesy formulae. Utterances understood rarely exceed more than two or three words at a time and ability to understand is characterized by long pauses for assimilation and by repeated requests on the listener's part for repetition and/or a slower rate of speech. Confuses words that sound similar.

Novice—High   Sufficient comprehension to understand a number of memorized utterances in areas of immediate need. Comprehends slightly longer utterances in situations where the context aids understanding, such as at the table, in a restaurant/store, in a train/bus. Phrases recognized have for the most part been memorized. Comprehends vocabulary common to daily needs. Comprehends simple questions/statements about family members, age, address, weather, time, daily activities, and interests. Misunderstandings arise from failure to perceive critical sounds or endings. Understands even standard speech with difficulty but gets some main ideas. Often requires repetition and/or a slowed rate of speed for comprehension, even when listening to persons such as teachers who are used to speaking with nonnatives.

Intermediate—Low   Sufficient comprehension to understand utterances about basic survival needs, minimum courtesy, and travel requirements. In areas of immediate need or on very familiar topics, can understand nonmemorized material, such as simple questions and answers, statements, and face-to-face conversations in the standard language. Comprehension areas include basic needs: meals, lodging, transportation, time, simple instructions (e.g., route directions), and routine commands (e.g., from customs officials, police). Understands main ideas. Misunderstandings frequently arise from lack of vocabulary or faulty processing of syntactic information often caused by strong interference from the native language or by the imperfect and partial acquisition of the target grammar.

Intermediate—Mid   Sufficient comprehension to understand simple conversations about some survival needs and some limited social conventions. Vocabulary permits understanding of topics beyond basic survival needs such as personal history and leisure-time activities. Evidence of understanding basic constructions, for example, subject-verb agreement, noun-adjective agreement; evidence that some inflection is understood.

Intermediate—High   Sufficient comprehension to understand short conversations about most survival needs and limited social conventions. Increasingly able to understand topics beyond immediate survival needs. Shows spontaneity in understanding, but speed and consistency of understanding uneven. Limited vocabulary range necessitates repetition for understanding. Understands commoner tense forms and some word order patterns, including most question forms, but miscommunication still occurs with more complex patterns. Can get the gist of conversations, but cannot sustain comprehension in longer utterances or in unfamiliar situations. Understanding of descriptions and detailed information is limited. Aware of basic cohesive features such as pronouns and verb inflections, but many are unreliably understood, especially if other material intervenes. Understanding is largely limited to a series of short, discrete utterances. Still has to ask for utterances to be repeated. Some ability to understand the facts.

Advanced   Sufficient comprehension to understand conversations about routine social conventions and limited school or work requirements. Able to understand face-to-face speech in the standard language, delivered at a normal rate with some repetition and rewording by a native speaker not used to dealing with foreigners. Understands everyday topics, common personal and family news, well-known current events, and routine matters involving school or work; descriptions and narration about current, past and future events; and essential points of discussion or speech at an elementary level on topics in special fields of interest.

Advanced Plus   Sufficient comprehension to understand most routine social conventions, conversations on school or work requirements, and discussions on concrete topics related to particular interests and special fields of competence. Often shows remarkable ability and ease of understanding, but comprehension may break down under tension or pressure, including unfavorable listening conditions. Candidate may display weakness or deficiency due to inadequate vocabulary base or less than secure knowledge of grammar and syntax. Normally understands general vocabulary with some hesitant understanding of everyday vocabulary still evident. Can sometimes detect emotional overtones. Some ability to understand between the lines, i.e., to make inferences.

Superior   Sufficient comprehension to understand the essentials of all speech in standard dialects, including technical discussions within a special field. Has sufficient understanding of face-to-face speech, delivered with normal clarity and speed in standard language on general topics and areas of special interest; understands hypothesizing and supported opinions. Has broad enough vocabulary that rarely has to ask for paraphrasing or explanation. Can follow accurately the essentials of conversations between educated native speakers, reasonably clear telephone calls, radio broadcasts, standard news items, oral reports, some oral technical reports, and public addresses on nontechnical subjects. May not understand native speakers if they speak very quickly or use some slang or unfamiliar dialect. Can often detect emotional overtones. Can understand "between the lines" (i.e., make inferences).

Provisional Generic Descriptions—Reading

Novice—Low   No functional ability in reading the foreign language.

Novice—Mid   Sufficient understanding of the written language to interpret highly contextualized words or cognates within predictable areas. Vocabulary for comprehension limited to simple elementary needs such as names, addresses, dates, street signs, building names, short informative signs (e.g., no smoking, entrance/exit), and formulaic vocabulary requesting same. Material understood rarely exceeds a single phrase and comprehension requires successive rereading and checking.

Novice—High   Sufficient comprehension of the written language to interpret set expressions in areas of immediate need. Can recognize all the letters in the printed version of an alphabetic system and high-frequency elements of a syllabary or a character system. Where vocabulary has been mastered, can read for instruction and directional purposes standardized messages, phrases, or expressions such as some items on menus, schedules, timetables, maps, and signs indicating hours of operation, social codes, and traffic regulations. This material is read only for essential information. Detail is overlooked or misunderstood.

Intermediate—Low   Sufficient comprehension to understand in printed form the simplest connected material, either authentic or specially prepared, dealing with basic survival and social needs. Able to understand both mastered material and recombinations of the mastered elements that achieve meanings at the same level. Understands main ideas in material whose structures and syntax parallel the native language. Can read messages, greetings, statements of social amenities or other simple language containing only the highest frequency grammatical patterns and vocabulary items including cognates (if appropriate). Misunderstandings arise when syntax diverges from that of the native language or when grammatical cues are overlooked.

Intermediate—Mid   Sufficient comprehension to understand in printed form simple discourse for informative or social purposes. In response to perceived needs, can read for information material such as announcements of public events, popular advertising, notes containing biographical information or narration of events, and straightforward newspaper headlines and story titles. Can guess at unfamiliar vocabulary if highly contextualized. Relies primarily on adverbs as time indicators. Has some difficulty with the cohesive factors in discourse, such as matching pronouns with referents. May have to read material several times before understanding.

Intermediate—High   Sufficient comprehension to understand a simple paragraph for personal communication, information, or recreational purposes. Can read with understanding social notes, letters, and invitations; can locate and derive main ideas of the introductory/ summary paragraphs from high interest or familiar news or other informational sources; can read for pleasure specially prepared, or some uncomplicated authentic prose, such as fictional narratives or cultural information. Shows spontaneity in reading by ability to guess at meaning from context. Understands common time indicators and can interpret some cohesive factors such as objective pronouns and simple clause connectors. Begins to relate sentences in the discourse to advance meaning but cannot sustain understanding of longer discourse on unfamiliar topics. Misinterpretation still occurs with more complex patterns.

Advanced   Sufficient comprehension to read simple authentic printed material or edited textual material within a familiar context. Can read uncomplicated but authentic prose on familiar subjects containing description and narration such as news items describing frequently occurring events, simple biographic information, social notices, and standard business letters. Can read edited texts such as prose fiction and contemporary culture. The prose is predominantly in familiar sentence patterns. Can follow essential points of written discussion at level of main ideas and some supporting ones with topics in a field of interest or where background exists. Some misunderstandings. Able to read the facts but cannot draw inferences.

Advanced Plus   Sufficient comprehension to understand most factual information in non-technical prose as well as some discussions on concrete topics related to special interests. Able to read for information and description, to follow sequence of events, and to react to that information. Is able to separate main ideas from lesser ones, and uses that division to advance understanding. Can locate and interpret main ideas and details in material written for the general public. Will begin to guess sensibly at new words by using linguistic context and prior knowledge. May react personally to material but does not yet detect subjective attitudes, values, or judgments in the writing.

Superior   Able to read standard newspaper items addressed to the general reader, routine correspondence reports and technical material in a field of interest at a normal rate of speed (at least 220 wpm). Readers can gain new knowledge from material on unfamiliar topics in areas of a general nature. Can interpret hypotheses, supported opinions, and conjectures. Can also read short stories, novels, and other recreational literature accessible to the general public. Reading ability is not subject-matter dependent. Has broad enough general vocabulary that successful guessing resolves problems with complex structures and low-frequency idioms. Misreading is rare. Almost always produces correct interpretation. Able to read between the lines. May be unable to appreciate nuance or stylistics.

Provisional Generic Descriptions—Writing

Novice—Low   No functional ability in writing the foreign language.

Novice—Mid   No practical communicative writing skills. Able to copy isolated words or short phrases. Able to transcribe previously studied words or phrases.

Novice—High   Able to write simple fixed expressions and limited memorized material. Can supply information when requested on forms such as hotel registrations and travel documents. Can write names, numbers, dates, one's own nationality, addresses, and other simple biographic information, as well as learned vocabulary, short phrases, and simple lists. Can write all the symbols in an alphabetic or syllabic system or 50 of the most common characters. Can write simple memorized material with frequent misspellings and inaccuracies.

Intermediate—Low   Has sufficient control of the writing system to meet limited practical needs. Can write short messages, such as simple questions or notes, postcards, phone messages, and the like within the scope of limited language experience. Can take simple notes on material dealing with very familiar topics, although memory span is extremely limited. Can create statements or questions within the scope of limited language experience. Material produced consists of recombinations of learned vocabulary and structures into simple sentences. Vocabulary is inadequate to express anything but elementary needs. Writing tends to be a loosely organized collection of sentence fragments on a very familiar topic. Makes continual errors in spelling, grammar, and punctuation, but writing can be read and understood by a native speaker used to dealing with foreigners. Able to produce appropriately some fundamental sociolinguistic distinctions in formal and familiar style, such as appropriate subject pronouns, titles of address, and basic social formulae.

Intermediate—Mid   Sufficient control of writing system to meet some survival needs and some limited social demands. Able to compose short paragraphs or take simple notes on very familiar topics grounded in personal experience. Can discuss likes and dislikes, daily routine, everyday events, and the like. Can express past time, using content words and time expressions, or with sporadically accurate verbs. Evidence of good control of basic constructions and inflections such as subject-verb agreement, noun-adjective agreement, and straightforward syntactic constructions in present or future time, though errors occasionally occur. May make frequent errors, however, when venturing beyond current level of linguistic competence. When resorting to a dictionary, often is unable to identify appropriate vocabulary, or uses dictionary entry in uninflected form.

Intermediate—High   Sufficient control of writing system to meet most survival needs and limited social demands. Can take notes in some detail on familiar topics, and respond to personal questions using elementary vocabulary and common structures. Can write simple letters, brief synopses and paraphrases, summaries of biographical data and work experience, and short compositions on familiar topics. Can create sentences and short paragraphs relating to most survival needs (food, lodging, transportation, immediate surroundings, and situations) and limited social demands. Can relate personal history, discuss topics such as daily life, preferences, and other familiar material. Can express fairly accurately present and future time. Can produce some past verb forms, but not always accurately or with correct usage. Shows good control of elementary vocabulary and some control of basic syntactic patterns but major errors still occur when expressing more complex thoughts. Dictionary usage may still yield incorrect vocabulary of forms, although can use a dictionary to advantage to express simple ideas. Generally cannot use basic cohesive elements of discourse to advantage such as relative constructions, subject pronouns, connectors, etc. Writing, though faulty, is comprehensible to native speakers used to dealing with foreigners.

Advanced   Able to write routine correspondence and simple discourse of at least several paragraphs on familiar topics. Can write simple social correspondence, take notes, and write cohesive summaries, résumés, and short narratives and descriptions on factual topics. Able to write about everyday topics using both description and narration. Has sufficient writing vocabulary to express himself/herself simply with some circumlocution. Can write about a very limited number of current events or daily situations and express personal preferences and observations in some detail, using basic structures. Still makes common errors in spelling and punctuation, but shows some control of the most common formats and punctuation conventions. Good control of the morphology of the language (in inflected languages) and of the most frequently used syntactic structures. Elementary constructions are usually handled quite accurately, and writing is understandable to a native speaker not used to reading the writing of foreigners. Uses a limited number of cohesive devices such as pronouns and repeated words with good accuracy. Able to join sentences in limited discourse, but has difficulty and makes frequent errors in producing complex sentences. Paragraphs are reasonably unified and coherent.

Advanced Plus   Shows ability to write about most common topics with some precision and in some detail. Can write fairly detailed résumés and summaries and take quite accurate notes. Can write most social and informal business correspondence. Can describe and narrate personal experiences and explain simply points of view in prose discourse. Can write about concrete topics relating to particular interests and special fields of competence. Normally controls general vocabulary with some circumlocution. Often shows remarkable fluency and ease of expression, but under time constraints and pressure, language may be inaccurate and/or incomprehensible. Generally strong in either grammar or vocabulary, but not in both. Weaknesses and unevenness in one of the foregoing or in spelling result in occasional miscommunication. Areas of weakness range from simple constructions such as plurals, articles, prepositions, and negatives to more complex structures such as tense usage, passive constructions, word order, and relative clauses. Some misuse of vocabulary still evident. Shows a limited ability to use circumlocution. Uses dictionary to advantage to supply unknown words. Writing is understandable to native speakers not used to reading material written by nonnatives, though the style is still obviously foreign.

Superior   Able to use the written language effectively in most formal and informal exchanges on practical, social, and professional topics. Can write most types of correspondence, such as memos and social and business letters, short research papers, and statements of position in areas of special interest or in special fields. Can express hypotheses, conjectures, and present arguments or points of view accurately and effectively. Can write about areas of special interest and handle topics in special fields, in addition to most common topics. Good control of a full range of structures, spelling, and a wide general vocabulary allow the writer to convey his/her message accurately, though style may be foreign. Can use complex and compound sentence structures to express ideas clearly and coherently. Uses dictionary with a high degree of accuracy to supply specialized vocabulary. Errors, though sometimes made when using more complex structures, are occasional, and rarely disturb the native speaker. Sporadic errors when using basic structures. Although sensitive to differences in formal and informal style, still cannot tailor writing precisely and accurately to a variety of audiences or styles.

Provisional Generic Descriptions—Culture

Novice   Limited interaction. Behaves with considerateness. Is resourceful in nonverbal communication, but is unreliable in interpretation of nonverbal cues. Is limited in language, as indicated under the listening and speaking skills. Lacks generally the knowledge of culture patterns requisite for survival situations.

Intermediate   Survival competence. Can deal with familiar survival situations and interact with a culture bearer accustomed to foreigners. Uses behavior acquired for the purpose of greeting and leave-taking, expressing wants, asking directions, buying food, using transportation, tipping. Comprehends the response. Makes errors as the result of misunderstanding; miscommunicates, and misapplies assumptions about the culture.

Advanced   Limited social competence. Handles routine social situations successfully with a culture bearer accustomed to foreigners. Shows comprehension of common rules of etiquette, taboos, and sensitivities, though home culture predominates. Can make polite requests, accept and refuse invitations, offer and receive gifts, apologize, make introductions, telephone, purchase and bargain, do routine banking. Can discuss a few aspects of the home and the foreign country, such as general current events and policies, as well as a field of personal interest. Does not offend the culture bearer, but some important misunderstandings and miscommunications occur in interaction with one unaccustomed to foreigners. Is not competent to take part in a formal meeting or in a group situation where several persons are speaking informally at the same time.

Superior   Working social and professional competence. Can participate in almost all social situations and those within one vocation. Handles unfamiliar types of situations with ease and sensitivity, including some involving common taboos, or other emotionally charged subjects. Comprehends most nonverbal responses. Laughs at some culture-related humor. In productive skills, neither culture predominates; nevertheless, makes appropriate use of cultural references and expressions. Generally distinguishes between a formal and informal register. Discusses abstract ideas relating the foreign to the native culture. Is generally limited, however, in handling abstractions. Minor inaccuracies occur in perception of meaning and in the expression of the intended representation but do not result in serious misunderstanding, even by a culture bearer unaccustomed to foreigners.

Near-Native Competence   Full social and professional competence. Fits behavior to audience, and the culture of the target language dominates almost entirely. Has internalized the concept that culture is relative and is always on the lookout to do the appropriate thing. Can counsel, persuade, negotiate, represent a point of view, interpret for dignitaries, describe and compare features of the two cultures. In such comparisons, can discuss geography, history, institutions, customs and behavior patterns, current events, and national policies. Perceives almost all unverbalized responses, and recognizes almost all allusions, including historical and literary commonplaces. Laughs at most culture-related humor. Controls a formal and informal register of behavior. Is inferior to the culture bearer only in background information related to the culture such as childhood experiences, detailed regional geography, and past events of significance.

Native Competence   Examinee is indistinguishable from a person brought up and educated in the culture.

ACTFL would like to thank the following educators who worked so diligently to create these guidelines:

Sabine Atwell	Gail Guntermann	Nina Levinson	June K. Phillips*
Jeannette D. Bragger	Charles R. Hancock	Judith E. Liskin-Gasparro*	Micheline Ponder
Raymonde Brown	Juana A. Hernández	Helene Z. Loew	Claus Reschke
Kathryn Buck	Theodore V. Higgs	Pardee Lowe, Jr.*	Jean-Charles Seigneuret
James Child	Nancy A. Humbach	Frankie McCullough	Dagmar Waters
Ray T. Clifford	Joseph Labat	Howard L. Nostrand	Eugene Weber
Barbara F. Freed	Dale L. Lange*	Alice C. Omaggio*	

*Language Coordinator

Appendix B:
Interagency Language Roundtable Level Definitions

Elementary Proficiency (S-1)   *Able to satisfy routine travel needs and minimum courtesy requirements.* Can ask and answer questions on very familiar topics; within the scope of very limited language experience, can understand simple questions and statements, allowing for slowed speech, repetition or paraphrase; speaking vocabulary inadequate to express anything but the most elementary needs; errors in pronunciation and grammar are frequent, but can be understood by a native speaker used to dealing with foreigners attempting to speak the language; while topics which are "very familiar" and elementary needs vary considerably from individual to individual, any person at the S-1 level should be able to order a simple meal, ask for shelter or lodging, ask and give simple directions, make purchases, and tell time.

Limited Working Proficiency (S-2)   *Able to satisfy routine social demands and limited work requirements.* Can handle with confidence but not with facility most social situations including introductions and casual conversations about current events, as well as work, family, and autobiographical information; can handle limited work requirements, needing help in handling any complications or difficulties; can get the gist of most conversations on nontechnical subjects (i.e., topics which require no specialized knowledge), and has a speaking vocabulary sufficient to respond simply with some circumlocutions; accent, though often quite faulty, is intelligible; can usually handle elementary constructions quite accurately but does not have thorough or confident control of the grammar.

Professional Working Proficiency (S-3)   *Able to speak the language with sufficient structural accuracy and vocabulary to participate effectively in most formal and informal conversations on practical, social, and professional topics.* Can discuss particular interests and special fields of competence with reasonable ease; comprehension is quite complete for a normal rate of speech; general vocabulary is broad enough that he or she rarely has to grope for a word; accent may be obviously foreign; control of grammar good; errors virtually never interfere with understanding and rarely disturb the native speaker.

Full Professional Proficiency (S-4)   *Able to use the language fluently and accurately on all levels normally pertinent to professional needs.* Can understand and participate in any conversation within the range of own personal and professional experience with a high degree of fluency and precision of vocabulary; would rarely be taken for a native speaker, but can respond appropriately even in unfamiliar situations; errors of pronunciation and grammar quite rare and unpatterned; can handle informal interpreting from and into the language.

Native or Bilingual Proficiency (S-5)   *Speaking proficiency equivalent to that of an educated native speaker.* Has complete fluency in the language such that speech on all levels is fully accepted by ENS in all of its features, including breadth of vocabulary and idiom, colloquialisms, and pertinent cultural references.

Index to
Persons Cited

A

Aaronson, Doris R. 9
Action, William 115, 138
Aitken, Kenneth 135
Allen, Edward D. 128, 135
Almeras, Philippe 82, 216
Altman, Howard B. 168, 173, 174
Anderson, Dixon 206
Arendt, Jermaine 175
Ariew, Robert 191, 198
Armengol, Armando 208
Arthur, Bradford 115, 138
Ascham, Roger 14
Atwell, Sabine 224
Azevedo, Milton M. 138

B

Bailey, Kathleen M. 209, 216
Bailey, Leona G. 180, 198
Baker, Reid E. 177
Banathy, Bela H. 160, 173
Barnes-Felfeli, Paul 170, 177
Barrows, Thomas S. 168, 173
Belasco, Simon 145, 177
Bell, Terrell H. 117
Berd, Luz 206
Berger, Pamela 195, 199
Bernhardt, Elizabeth B. 170, 173
Birckbichler, Diane W. 59, 61,
    67, 69, 70, 81
Birkmaier, Emma Marie 41
Bishop, G. Reginald, Jr. 153, 173
Bloch, Bernard 18
Bloom, Benjamin S. 155, 173
Bloomfield, Leonard 18
Bonham, George W. 168, 173
Bonin, Thérèse 67, 81
Born, Warren C. 168, 173
Bowen, J. Donald 130, 135
Boylan, Patricia C. 62, 81, 82, 83
Bragaw, Donald H. 156, 159, 173
Bragger, Jeannette D. 224
Briere, Eugene J. 137
Brod, Richard I. 29–30, 40

Brooks, Nelson 20, 40, 140,
    150, 161, 168, 173
Brown, Bruce B. 117, 137
Brown, Raymonde 224
Brown, Richard W. 22, 40
Brumfit, Christopher J. 161, 173
Buck, Kathryn 224
Burn, Barbara B. 30, 40
Burt, Marina K. 79, 81

C

Cabell-Castellet, George 213
Canale, Michael 44, 81
Candlin, C. 62, 81
Carroll, Brenden J. 135
Carroll, John B. 2, 9, 18,
    25, 40, 114, 115, 129,
    135, 182, 196,198
Carter, James Earl 30
Carton, Aaron S. 129, 135
Carver, Ronald 130, 135
Chalmers, Claudene 82, 83, 216
Chastain, Kenneth 78, 81
Child, James 224
Christensen, Clay B. 62, 81
Chung, Ulric 73
Clark, John L. D. 40, 41,
    124, 135, 193–94, 216
Cleveland, Harlan 170, 173
Clifford, Ray T. 4, 5, 7, 9, 35,
    41, 45, 46, 47, 49, 50, 54,
    78, 81, 114, 130, 135, 183,
    184, 185, 186, 187, 188, 199
    205, 208, 209, 216, 224
Cohen, Andrew D. 170, 173
Collins, H. Thomas 140, 168, 174
Conner, Maurice W. 176
Conrad, Christine 129, 137
Cooper, Thomas C. 59, 81
Corbin, Donald 81
Coulombe, Roger 66, 81
Crawford, Linda M. 147, 174
Crawford-Lange, Linda M. 139,

146, 160, 163, 167, 174
Culver, Anke   71, 81

D

Davis, F. B.   124, 136
Day, J. L.   83
Debyser, Francis   70, 81
Delisle, Helga   78, 81
Dobson, Julia M.   114, 136
Dodge, James W.   155, 168, 173
Dorwick, Thalia   82
Dulay, Heidi   79, 81
Dyen, Isidore   18
Dyess, H. B.   208–09

E

Ensz, Kathleen Y.   78, 81
Erwin, Gerard   181, 198

F

Farhady, Hossein   115, 136
Ferrán, Francisco R.   82
Finnochiaro, M.   81
Fitzpatrick, R.   116, 136
Flynn, Mary B.   190, 191, 198
Frappier-Mazur, Lucienne   204
Freed, Barbara F.   24, 40,
   187, 189, 192, 193, 198,
   204, 216, 224
Freire, Paulo   139, 146,
   147, 163, 174
Fries, Charles C.   114, 136
Frith, James R.   23, 24,
   40, 42, 216

G

Galloway, Vicky B.   78, 81
Gardner, Robert C.   157, 174
Garfinkel, Alan   117, 136,
   175, 199
Gaudiani, Claire   196, 198
Geno, Thomas E.   173
Germain, Claude   114, 136
Goodman, Kenneth S.   125, 136
Gradman, Harry   121, 136
Graham, James   203
Grandin, John   207
Grittner, Frank M.   21, 33, 34,
   41, 180, 182, 189, 198
Groot, Peter J. M.   136
Guilford, J. P.   69, 81
Guiora, Alexander Z.   115,
   138, 157, 174
Guntermann, Gail   74–75,
   76–77, 78, 81, 156, 174,
   187, 191, 192, 198–99, 224

H

Hagiwara, Michio P.   181, 199
Hamilton, Stanley   175
Hancock, Charles R.   180,
   199, 224
Hanvey, Robert G.   166, 174
Harbour, Leslie J.   65, 81
Harlow, Linda L.   35, 41,
   114, 136
Hauptman, Philip C.   124, 136
Heaton, J. B.   136
Heflin, William H.   138
Hendon, Ursula S.   163, 174
Henning, Grant H.   123, 129, 136
Hernández, Juana A.   224
Herron, Carol A.   14, 41,
   181, 199
Higgs, Theodore V.   1, 4, 5,
   7, 9, 35, 41, 45–46, 47,
   49–50, 54, 78, 81, 111, 136,
   183, 184, 185, 186, 187, 188,
   195, 198, 199, 205, 208, 216, 224
Hinofotis, Frances B.   129,
   136, 137, 208, 209
Hiple, David   196
Hockett, Charles F.   2,
   9, 18
Hodge, Carlton T.   18
Honhart, Michael   207
Hosley, Deborah 115, 124,
   136
Hudson, Thom   124, 136
Humbach, Nancy A.   224
Hyman-Opler, Ruth   138
Hymes, Dell   114, 136

I

Imberton, Claudette   82, 216

J

Jakobovits, Leon A.   114, 136
Jarvis, Donald K.   163, 174
Jarvis, Gilbert A.   56, 61,
   62, 81, 176, 200
Jenks, Frederick L.   156, 174
Jennings, Lee B.   128, 136
Jespersen, Otto   51, 52, 81
Jiménez, Reynaldo   201
Johnson, David W.   154, 174
Johnson, Francis   203
Johnson, Keith   136, 161,
   173, 174
Johnson, Roger T.   54, 174
Joiner, Elizabeth G.   62, 82,

83, 182, 192, 199
Jonas, Sister Ruth A., S.C.   174
Jones, Randall L.   42, 113,
    114, 116, 117, 128, 132, 134,
    136, 137, 198
Jorstad, Helen L.   71, 82,
    143, 144, 146, 156, 174, 183,
    195, 196, 199

K
Kelly, Louis G.   15, 41,
    160, 175
Kettering, Judith   62, 82
Knop, Constance K.   181, 194–95,
    199
Knorre, Marty   57, 82, 83
Komensky, Jan Amos   14
Kraft, Wolfgang, S.   145, 175
Krashen, Stephen D.   3, 4, 6,
    7, 9, 46, 47, 48, 49, 50, 54,
    62, 71, 79, 82, 118, 137, 162,
    171, 175
Krathwohl, David R.   155, 175

L
Labat, Joseph   224
Ladu, Tora T.   155, 175
Lafayette, Robert C.   163, 168,
    173, 175
Laitenberger, Heidi   70, 81, 82
Lambert, Wallace E.   157, 174
Lamy, A.   82
Lange, Dale L.   21, 41, 139,
    143–44, 146, 160, 167, 168,
    171, 173, 174, 175, 176, 177,
    184, 198, 199, 200, 205, 224
Larson, Jerry W   113, 124, 137
Lett, John   62, 66, 82, 83
Levinson, Nina   224
Levno, Arley W.   145, 175
Linder, Cathy   137, 168, 174,
    175, 176, 177, 198, 199, 200
Liskin-Gasparro, Judith E.
    1, 41, 196, 208, 211, 216, 224
Littlewood, William T.   54, 62, 82
Livingston, Samuel A.   22, 41
Locke, John   14
Loew, Helene Z.   156, 159, 173, 224
Lohnes, Walter F. W.   145, 175
Lowe, Pardee, Jr.   75, 82, 208,
    209, 216, 224
Ludwig, Jeannette   78, 82
Lusetti, Walter   82

M
MacAllister, Archibald   181, 199
Mackey, James   167, 175
Madsen, Harold S.   117, 137
Madsen, Will   209–10
Magidson, Edgar   167, 175
Malandain, Jean-Louis   145, 176
Mallinson, Vernon   14, 41
Manley, Joan   211
McCullough, Frankie   224
McDade, Michael   111
McLaughlin, Barry   47–48,
    49, 54, 82
Mead, Robert G.   155, 175
Meredith, Keith   115, 124, 136
Myers, Pamela J.   175
Morain, Genelle   163, 168, 175
Moreau, Paul Henri   145, 176
Morello, Joseph G.   207
Morrison, E. J.   116, 136
Moses, Catherine   209–10
Moskowitz, Gertrude   181, 182,
    191, 192, 199
Moulton, William G.   18
Murphy, Carol J.   201, 215
Muyskens, Judith A.   53, 58,
    59, 82, 83, 179, 181, 190,
    195, 198, 199, 216
N
Nerenz, Anne G.   181, 199
Neuner, Gerd   145, 176
Newell, William   210
Newmark, Leonard   76, 82
Nickel, Gerhard   137
Nord, James R.   118, 137,
    162, 178
Nostrand, Howard L.   142–43,
    144, 147, 156, 163, 176, 224
Nusbaum, Marlene   77, 82
O
O'Brien, Maureen Concannon   135
Ollendorf, H. G.   15, 31, 41
Oller, John W., Jr.   114, 115,
    122, 129, 130, 135, 136, 137,
    169, 176
Omaggio, Alice C.   12, 37,
    41, 43, 51, 59, 60, 62, 63,
    73, 81, 82, 83, 111, 184, 186,
    189, 190, 194, 197, 199, 200,
    204, 208, 216, 224
Oudot, Simone   145, 176
Ozete, Oscar   130, 137

P

Paquette, F. André   21, 41, 114, 137
Pardo, Aristóbulo   82, 83
Paul, Regina H.   179, 200
Paulston, Christina B.   62, 82
Paz-Haro, Maria   214–15
Perkins, Kyle   136
Pfister, Guenter G.   145, 175
Phillips, June K.   74, 75, 76, 81, 137, 174, 187, 188, 191, 198, 199, 200, 224
Piazza, Linda Gaylord   78, 82
Plötz, K.   15, 31, 41
Ponder, Micheline   224
Ponterio, Marie   73, 77, 82
Ponterio, Robert   80, 82
Porter, D.   129, 137
Postovsky, Valerian A.   118, 137–38
Posvar, Wesley W.   168, 176

R

Rallo, John A.   71, 82
Ramos, Myrna Bergman   174
Rassius, John A.   52, 83
Ratke, Wolfgang   14
Ratliff, William R.   62, 82, 83
Reboullet, André   145, 176
Redden, James E.   137
Reibel, David A.   76, 82
Renjilian-Burgy, Joy   73, 83
Reschke, Claus   207–08, 216, 224
Rieber, Robert W.   9
Riley, Pamela M.   125, 138
Rivers, Wilga M.   16, 17, 18, 41, 70, 83, 118, 126, 138, 168, 176
Robinson, Gail L. Nemetz   168, 176
Rochester, Myrna J.   83, 216
Rybski, Marsha   145

S

Sandoval, Manuel G.   145, 176
Savignon, Sandra   66, 161, 176
Scebold, C. Edward   208
Schmidt, Elizabeth   70, 83
Schulz, Renate A.   71, 83, 181, 200
Schumann, John H.   3, 9
Sebeok, Thomas   18
Seelye, H. Ned   71, 83,

140, 143, 144, 145, 156, 157, 163, 176, 177
Seigneuret, Jean-Charles   224
Selekman, Howard R.   62, 82
Seliger, Herbert W.   49, 54, 83, 120, 138
Sewell, Penelope M.   128, 138
Sexton, Malcolm   72, 83
Shinall, Stanley   77, 83
Shor, Ira   160, 170
Silva, Anthony   73, 83
Simon, Paul   30
Slager, William R.   51, 55, 57, 83
Smith, Frank   125, 138
Smith, Philip D., Jr.   39, 41
Sollenberger, Howard E.   19, 41
Sonka, Amy L.   128, 138
Sorenson, John L.   163, 177
Spolsky, Bernard   42, 114, 121, 135, 136, 137, 198
Stanislawczk, Irene   62, 83
Steiner, Florence   145, 177
Stephens, Dor. S.   162, 177
Stern, H. H.   114, 116, 168, 176
Stevick, Earl W.   47, 78, 79, 83, 85, 192, 200
Strasheim, Lorraine A.   163, 168, 175, 176
Streiff, Virginia   137
Strothmann, F. W.   145, 175
Swaffar, Janet King   162, 177
Swain, Merrill   44, 81

T

Taylor, H. Darrel   163, 176
Taylor, William   129
Thompson, Richard T.   17, 18, 41
Thorndike, R. L.   136
Titone, Renzo   13, 14, 15, 16, 17, 41
Tollinger, Suzanne   114, 137
Trivelli, Remo   207

U

Undank, Jack   155, 173
Upshur, John A.   115, 125, 128, 138

V

Valdman, Albert   32, 41, 145, 168, 177
Valette, Jean-Paul   145, 177
Valette, Rebecca M.   21, 41, 83, 129, 138, 145, 177
van Ek, Jan A.   161, 177

Verdier, Liliane 77, 82
Verdol, Jacques 145, 176
W
Wallerstein, Nina 160, 177
Walz, Joel C. 79, 83
Wardhaugh, Ronald 125, 138
Warriner, Helen P. 31, 42
Warriner-Burke, Helen P.
  168, 177
Waters, Dagmar 224
Weber, Eugene 224
Weiss, Edda 145, 177
Wesche, M. 51, 83
Westphal, Patricia 82, 83
Whiteson, Valerie 120, 138
Whitely, M. Stanley 82
Widdowson, Harry G. 138,
  161, 177
Wilds, Caludia P. 19,

42, 129, 135
Wilkins, David A. 76,
  83, 114, 138, 160, 177
Winfield, Fairlee E. 170, 177
Wing, Barbara H. 180,
  200, 205
Winitz, Harris 118, 137,
  138, 162, 176, 177
Woodford, Protase 27
Wooster, Judith 156, 159, 173
Y
Yavener, Symond 62, 83
Young, Howard T. 24, 42,
  203, 216
Yousef, Fathi S. 157, 177
Z
Zais, Robert S. 167,
  168, 177
Zelson, Sidney 62, 69, 83

Index to Topics
and Institutions Cited

A

Acquisition heuristics 48
Acquisition versus learning 3, 49–50
ACTFL guidelines 11–12, 21, 22, 29,
35, 37, 44–45, 55, 184, 217–26
ACTFL rating scale 25–28
compared with government scale 28
Activity types (see also "Exercise
formats") 59–69
Adapting materials 190–91
American Council of Learned
Societies 17–18, 19–20, 28
Association of Departments of
Foreign Languages (ADFL) 203
Audiolingual method 2, 17–18, 19–21
Authentic language use 71–73

B

Behaviorism 2–3
Bilingual education 22–23
Bridges 91–102
segments of 93–102
Brigham Young University 206

C

Carnegie Corporation 16
Central College 203
Central Intelligence Agency
Language School 208
The Church of Jesus Christ of
Latter-Day Saints 23, 206
Classroom instruction, value of 47
Classroom procedures 50–80
Cloze tests 129–30
Cognitive psychology 3, 47–51
Cognitive strategies 47–51
Coleman Report 16
Committee of Eleven 143
Committee of Twelve (NEA) 16
Common Yardstick Project 27–28, 31
Comprehensible input 37, 47
Contextualized practice 51–59, 186
Contrasting two cultures 148
Controlled processing 48–49
Cultural materials 79–80

Cultural syllabuses 168
Culture as an educational objective
154–59
Culture as content 139–72
Culture as information 141–42
Culture in the curriculum 160–63
Culture study as process 142–46
Culture-learning strategies 163–66
Curricular emphases 87–90

D

Defense Language Institute
19, 208, 209, 210
Direct method 14, 15, 16

E

Eclectic method 4, 8
Educational Testing Service 22–23,
27–28, 196, 203, 208, 211
Error correction 49–50, 77–79,
186–87, 192
Exercise formats (see also
"Activity types") 59–69
Experiment in International Living
23–24
Extended Standard Theory 3
Exxon Foundation 39

F

FAST Courses 106–11
Fossilization 49
Foreign Service Institute 19, 22,
23–24, 85–87
FSI Testing Kit Workshops 23–24, 27,
201, 203
Functional trisection 4–5, 35–36
Functional/notional syllabuses 5, 8,
31–35, 73–77
Functions 73–77

G

Gallaudet College 209
George Williams College 206
Georgetown University 203
Global education 166–68
Goals of instruction 17, 45, 87

Goethe Institute   208
Grammar-translation method   2, 15

I

Illinois Foreign Language Teachers'
    Association   39
Impact of proficiency testing   211–16
Information processing
    Automatic processes   48–49
    Controlled processes   48–49
Input hypothesis   47
Inservice teacher training   195–97
Interdependence of language
    modalities   113–14

L

Language acquisition   2–3, 46–50
Learning environments   4, 79, 191–93
Learning objectives   12
Learning styles   3–4
Learning theory   2–4, 46–50
Learning versus acquisition   3, 46–50
Lesson planning   189, 191
Linguistic theory   2, 3
Listening tasks   119–20
Louisiana Department of Education   208

M

Matrix dialogues   103
Methods courses   184–95
Minnesota Department of Education   143
MLA-ACLS Language Task Forces
    Project   28–30, 31
Modern Language Association   21, 28–29
Monitor Model   46–49
Monterey Institute for International
    Studies   209

N

National Defense Education Act   20–21
National Education Association   16
National Endowment for the
    Humanities   28
Natural Order hypothesis   46
New Brunswick (Canada) Education
    Department   22

O

Oregon State University   213
Output hypothesis   46–47

P

Peace Corps   19, 22
Pomona College   203
Preservice teacher education   180–95
President's Commission   11–12, 13, 30–31
Princeton University   203
Proficiency testing, rationale for   116–17

Proficiency versus achievement
    testing   115–16

Q

Question triads   104–06

R

Reading tasks   126
Relative contribution model   5–7, 8
Rochester Institute of
    Technology   210
Rockefeller Foundation   28

S

San Diego State University   208
Standard Theory   3
Stanford University   215
Structural linguistics   2–3, 16
Structuralism   2–3, 16
Student competencies   44–46
Student teaching   194–95

T

Task universals (see "Functions")
    73–77
Teacher competencies   21, 40, 182–84
Teacher training   16, 39, 179–98
Teaching styles   4
Testing cultural proficiency   150,
    154, 169–70
Testing listening   118–23
Testing reading   123–32
Testing writing   132–34
Two-track curriculum   45–46

U

Unitary factor hypothesis   114–15
University of California at
    Los Angeles   208, 209
University of Florida   215
University of Houston   207
University of Illinois   204, 208
University of Michigan   19
University of Minnesota   205
University of New Hampshire   205
University of Pennsylvania   204
University of Rhode Island   204
University of Southern
    California   203
University of Texas at
    El Paso   208, 211
U.S. Department of Education   11,
    196, 201, 202, 207, 209, 210
U.S. Office of Education   27

W

Writing tasks   133–34